The Revolutions of 1848

REVOLUTIONS IN THE MODERN WORLD

General Editor: JACK P. GREENE, *John Hopkins University*

The Revolutions of 1848

Peter N. Stearns

Professor of History, Rutgers University

Weidenfeld and Nicolson
London

© 1974 by Peter N. Stearns

First published in Great Britain by
Weidenfeld and Nicolson
11 St John's Hill London SW11

ISBN 0 297 76813 1

Printed in Great Britain by
REDWOOD BURN LIMITED
Trowbridge & Esher

Contents

Maps

Introduction

THE REVOLUTIONARY OUTBURST of 1848 was unprecedented in Europe. Two centuries before to the very year, revolts had developed in southern Italy, Spain, and Muscovy, while Leveller agitation crested in Britain and the Fronde rebellion shook France. These revolts had some common features with those of 1848, including a severe famine in the two preceding years, but they were not the result of direct revolutionary contagion and for the most part their impact was muted. Revolutionary change had spread widely in Western and Central Europe after the French Revolution of 1789, but, except in France, this was due mainly to the conquests of French armies, not to a series of rebellions. More recently still, 1830 had proved a foretaste of the revolutionary current. Revolt in France was followed by outbreaks in Belgium, Poland, and central Italy, while agitation mounted in Germany and Britain. But only in 1848 did revolution assume virtually continental proportions. Russia and Spain were exempt, of the larger countries. Serious revolutions broke out in France, Italy, German, Austria, Bohemia, and Hungary, while there were stirrings of some significance in Switzerland, Denmark, Rumania, Poland, and Ireland. Britain, although apparently immune to formal revolution, saw the last wave of Chartist agitation, And for the most part these various risings were interconnected, linked by economic causation, ideology, and by the fascination of revolution itself. Knowledge that a regime elsewhere had been shaken seemed a valid reason to try the same thing in one's own backyard.

This was a special moment, for the revolutionary current has never been so strong in Europe since that time. Indeed this kind of contagion has few parallels anywhere in world history. There have been some peak revolutionary years since World War II in the developing nations—1958 in parts of the Near East and Asia, for example. These offer some interesting analogies with 1848 in Europe, where most of the countries involved in revolution were undergoing the stress of mounting industrialization and commercialization and where nationalism was spreading to many new areas. Clearly, a special combination of factors is required for revolution to flow so easily across state boundaries, without being imported by force of arms.

Of course each separate revolution in 1848 had its own character. The "stirrings" must be distinguished from the real revolts. Nationalist intellectuals and professional people had a week of agitation in Ireland, but they could not rouse the masses and could not contend with clever British repression. The effort does not loom large in the history of Irish protest. The Rumanian revolt also failed to catch fire, for here the masses were not roused by nationalism and found no other issues. But the attempt by agitators drawn from the small middle class and elements of the aristocracy fed further discontent and helped prepare the formation of the Rumanian nation a decade later. Chartist protest in Britain completely failed to make a revolution. In this case large segments of the lower classes did stir, but they lacked any cooperation from above; and they were divided among themselves and few of them were consciously revolutionary.

In France the revolution was above all an effort to complete the work of the radical phase of the great French Revolution to create a new, more open political regime. The most articulate revolutionary leaders sought a democratic republic that would guarantee key liberties to all citizens and that would enact some humanitarian reforms without destroying the social order. In this sense the revolution was far less fundamental than its predecessor, which had to overturn an older social structure in addition to battling for political change. The legal basis of the old regime was already gone, with the establishment of substantial equality under the laws and the abolition of the legal privileges of church and aristocracy. The revolution of 1830 still had anti-aristocratic overtones, and despite its mildness did succeed in chasing the more obdurate aristocrats and churchmen from power. 1848 had no such obvious targets. It sought to juggle the holders of power, not to overturn the basic structure. It is therefore much less important in French history than the revolution of 1789, much less important in European history than many of the risings it induced elsewhere in 1848–1849.

Yet France was the most advanced country in which revolution did occur in those years, not only politically but also economically and socially. Industrialization was more extensive than in Central Europe. The major social classes were better defined and were involved, willy-nilly, in more new ways of doing things. It is not surprising, then, that beneath the surface of the revolution an array of movements and ideas took shape that had quite a modern ring. Some of these came to the fore during the revolution itself. The June Days of 1848, which so cruelly ended the political thrust of the revolution, were in part the repetition of traditional battles between the urban poor and the established order, but they had elements of more modern class warfare as well. Other protest currents, such as feminism, did not play a major role in the revolution itself, but were given a significant boost. In France more than elsewhere, we might say that the revolution of 1848 put items on the agenda for the next great surge of protest, in which we are to a great extent still engaged.

At the other extreme was Hungary, where the revolution was really a new round of conflict between the local aristocracy and the Habsburg government. The Magyar aristocracy was unusually large and included many people who were quite poor; it harbored some social tensions that set class against class in other countries. But at least locally it was a ruling class, fighting to retain or revive its privileges. It used a rhetoric that resembled that of revolutions elsewhere. Liberalism and nationalism, sincerely advocated by leaders such as Lajos Kossuth, were useful additions to the arsenal of the aristocrats. The revolution itself proved how they could be disfigured in the interests of an older order. The revolution was profoundly important in Hungarian history. It set the tone for further strivings for a Hungarian state and for bitter ethnic and class tensions within that state, once achieved. But it differed most from the risings that developed elsewhere in the same years. This was an area barely touched by new social and economic currents, an agrarian country in which new ideas inevitably found a distinctive, and often limited, reception.

The revolutions in Central Europe proper, in Austria and

particularly in the German states, were the most important of the lot. They challenged the existing diplomatic structure, in the name of nationalism. They sought a new political structure as well, and along with this, at least implicitly, a new social order. For these areas had had no great revolution like the French. The old regime still predominated. It had introduced some reforms, at least in the German states, which is one reason the revolutionaries lacked the zeal of their French counterparts a half century before. But this was the Germans' chance to make a new society, and they failed. They caused important changes, directly or indirectly. For some key groups, such as the peasants in many areas, a real revolution did occur at least in law. But the revolutions left enough of the old order intact to insure that only further revolution could create a liberal society. Yet they so disillusioned most revolutionaries that they made renewed revolt most improbable. Some historians have traced the whole of German history, through Hitler at least, to the failures of 1848. Others have found these failures themselves inevitable, because of fatal flaws in the German political character. Even for those who take a less deterministic view, it is clear that analysis of the causes and results of the German and Austrian revolutions is fundamental to an understanding of the modern history of Central Europe.

The Italian revolution, though similar to the German in many ways, has something of its own style. Part of the difference is subjective, because of the later histories of the two countries. The revolution was profoundly important in Italian history. Even more than in Germany it encouraged forces of nationalism that would triumph within a generation. As in Germany, liberalism failed in the revolutions; when it revived it was far more circumspect, even corruptible, than before. But none of this seems to matter as much in Italy, because Italy played a less villainous or at least less importantly villainous a role in European history thereafter. Hence historians have bemoaned the fate of the Italian revolutions less loudly, and outside of Italy they have analyzed it less extensively. Yet it is also true that while liberals were actively engaged in the Italian revolution, liberalism was less prominent than in Germany and Austria. Local risings, in

Rome and in Venice, attacked the old regime directly. Indeed the Roman revolutionaries sought to go farther than any revolutionary regime of the period, seeking social as well as political change: but except in Rome and briefly in Sicily, the Italian revolutions did not take place in the most backward areas of Italy, where the regimes surpassed that of the Habsburg empire in their devotion to an unenlightened traditionalism leavened by police repression. And most of the revolutionaries did not focus on internal political change. They wanted it and they assumed it would come, but there was a more obvious enemy in the foreign —Austrian—domination that blanketed most of northern Italy. Much of the Italian revolution was thus a war of liberation, not a revolution at all. Though no less significant to subsequent national history, it was less complex than the German risings and it left the country's political future more open-ended. Italian liberalism undeniably changed as a result of the revolution, but it still seemed the wave of the future. Hence Piedmont, the ultimate leader of unification, began to assume a more liberal guise in the 1850s, while Prussia was on the whole confirmed in its conservatism even as it created a new Germany.

So much for the national nutshells. It is obvious that any generalization about the revolutions of 1848 must be seriously qualified for each key area. Each revolution must be assessed in its own context, each had a distinctive impact. The revolutions spread from one point to another. They interacted to a limited extent. Even within the Habsburg empire where they theoretically faced a common foe in the existing regime, the major centers of revolution had little to do with each other. The drama of each revolution unfolded separately. Each had its own heroes, its own crises. Each therefore demands its own narrative. Almost all the existing histories of the revolution, and there are a number of good ones, understandably proceed on a case-by-case basis, with at most a few general remarks.[1]

Yet the revolutions had more in common than their date. If no generalization covers the whole situation, there is significance

1. See, for example, Priscilla Robertson, *The Revolutions of 1848; A Social History* (Princeton, 1952) and William L. Langer, *The Revolutions of 1848* (New York, 1971).

to "the revolutions" that transcends each particular situation. Else why write a history of the revolutions, instead of a single one that strikes the fancy, much less read one?

The collective impact of the revolutions shattered the diplomatic framework of Europe that had been created by the Congress of Vienna. The results were delayed, to be sure, surfacing clearly only after 1856 with the Crimean War settlement and the split among the conservative powers. But even before that it was obvious the revolution had opened new horizons to existing states. The King of Prussia began to think about a federated Germany with himself at its head. Piedmont began to prepare for aggrandizement, though defeated during the revolution itself. France elected a president vowed to remake the European map. This was not the main reason for his election, but there was little question that the revolutionary forces in France were tired of the nation's passive attitude and eager for a policy that would at once liberate other areas from conservative regimes and add to France's glory—the classic formula of revolutionary French nationalism. Nationalists elsewhere, seeking to create new states, failed in their immediate efforts but learned from their failure. Even as they worked for their own nation alone, they contributed to a general and fundamental reordering of European diplomacy.

Yet, if this is the most obvious common element of the revolutions, it is not the most important one. Almost everywhere the revolutions flowed from similar forces, both social and ideological. Almost everywhere they foundered on common problems, including severe tensions among the social groups that made them and important contradictions within their ideological base.

The failure of the revolutions must be assessed with care. None failed completely. All unleashed or encouraged forces that would win still greater victories, though without revolution and with important limitations, within a generation. Yet nowhere save perhaps in Switzerland were the revolutions really successful in achieving their professed goals. Hence, to the multiplicity of revolutions must be added their quick defeat. This makes it difficult to analyze them in terms of any model of revolution. We can analyze characteristics derived from knowledge of great revolutions, like the Russian or the French, to assess these revolts and help explain their collapse; in this sense they may help test existing models. But they went through few of the classic stages of a successful revolution. It can plausibly be argued, in fact, that they were not really revolutions at all, in that in most instances they did not provide an alternate political and military structure and in many the revolutionary leaders did not even want to do so. Why, then, bother with them?

In the first place, the revolutions ended an era. With the revolutions the age of romanticism drew to a close. Heirs of the romantic tradition continued their work—they continue it still. But romanticism's dominance in the realm of ideas was over, and so was the confidence of romantics themselves that they could remake the world in their image. More basically the revolutions signaled a change in the relationship between intellectuals and society. It seemed natural for intellectuals to assume leadership of the revolutions, although in fact they had never wielded such broad powers before. They had, after all, spearheaded most of the political movements that fed the revolutions. Their role was assuredly not exhausted by the revolutions, but never again, in Western and Central Europe, could they assume command. Changes in their own outlook and in the nature of political organization, both of which the revolutions furthered, reduced their prestige.

Above all, the revolutions of 1848 ended the age of revolutions that had begun in the eighteenth century. None of the countries involved in the 1848 risings, except Hungary, has ever again experienced revolution save as the aftermath of defeat in war, and even in Hungary's case the 1956 rising was indirectly the product of loss in war. The revolutions of 1848 played a major role in this dramatic change. Because of them, established governments learned better how to maintain order. They improved their ability both to repress and to conciliate. Key groups that had supported revolutions for almost a century, such as many peasants and artisans, either won their major demands or lost their nerve as a result of their failure. More basic processes were at work, to be sure. Artisans were losing ground in an industrializing society. Improvements in the regularity of food supplies after midcentury removed one of the classic grievances of the lower classes. Nevertheless the revolutions stand as the last major traditional protest by the masses in Western and Central Europe and the last major effort directly to block the spread of industrialization itself. Along with the decline of revolution in the most economically advanced sections of Europe came a more general change in the nature and purpose of protest. The dimensions of this change began to emerge in the later stages of the revolutions themselves.

All of which is to say that revolutions were not only an end but a beginning. Many of the positive goals of the articulate revolutionaries pointed the way to a new age. Nationalism, liberalism, socialism—most of the basic political forces that are with us today were changed and enhanced by the revolutions. Nationalism was undoubtedly the biggest gainer. A minor, sputtering movement before the revolutions, it won new currency despite the formal failure of the nationalist goals. But all the new political movements earned new attention and their proponents learned new, often more effective means of organization. The transition from utopian socialism to Marxism, for example, was immeasurably furthered by the lessons of the revolutions.

The results of 1848 encouraged the articulation of a modern class structure. The middle classes were placed on the side of the established order, because of the gains they won but even more because of the new fears they acquired. New lower-class groups, notably many factory workers, were drawn into protest during the course of the revolutions and the lower classes generally began to veer away from traditional demands as they developed a more modern political sense. These changes were only beginning. We must not expect to see, at the revolutions' end, a militant factory proletariat facing a terrorized bourgeoisie. The revolutions did, nevertheless, tend to further a new kind of social polarization.

In what they ended and in what they began, the principal revolutions of 1848 served as a transition from an old society to a new one. They captured the growing pains of areas on the verge of industrialization. In this, as much as in their specific achievements and failures, lies their fascination. In this lies also their contribution to an understanding of other societies, even in the

present day, which are in a similar situation. Most of the participants in the revolutions sought to protest change, to return to
older ways. They lost, even as conservative governments seemed
to win the day. The revolutions opened the way to further change
as they forced governments to adopt new methods to stay in
power and as they helped reshape the mentality of large groups
within the society at large. The revolutions, the result of a pre-
carious balance between old and new, tipped the scales.

PART I CAUSES OF THE REVOLUTIONS

BECAUSE THEY OCCURRED during a time of rapid social transformation, because they embodied elements of the old and and the new, the revolutions of 1848 defy easy explanation. Not all historians have been daunted by this fact. One eminent scholar dubbed the revolutions in Central Europe a "revolution of the intellectuals," conveniently ignoring the fact that virtually no intellectual appeared on the barricades.[1] Recent students of protest, while not pretending to study the revolutions as a whole, have focused exclusively on their lower-class component.[2] And of course many studies deal with purely national causes, finding few if any unifying features from one revolution to the next.

All of these approaches have some validity. The specific causes of each revolution were many and varied, and can only be dealt with one by one. But there is a general pattern of causation that applies to most of the major revolutions, with Hungary being the most stubborn exception. Overall the articulate leaders of revolution, the ones who appeared in the provisional governments, were drawn from the middle classes; they included a sizable component of intellectuals. To understand the revolutions, we must therefore deal with the major ideological currents in-

1. Lewis Namier *1848: The Revolution of the Intellectuals* (New York, 1964).
2. George Rudé, *The Crowd in History* (New York, 1964), 164–178; Charles Tilly, "The Changing Place of Collective Violence," in Melvin Richter, ed., *Essays in Theory and History* (Cambridge, Mass., 1970), 139–164.

volved and also the social position of these key groups. There was something of a crisis of the middle classes during the 1840s, and without it the revolutions probably could not have occurred.

Yet the lower-class ingredient cannot be neglected. The revolutions of 1848 were vital to the history of the lower classes, influencing their development for decades to come. At the same time, while middle-class leaders often set the stage for revolution, and then seized on its fruits, lower-class elements, particularly urban craftsmen, most directly created the fact of revolution itself. They provided the muscle. Only occasionally did other groups, such as university and secondary school students, risk outright physical disorder.

A combination of forces is obviously common in major revolutionary outbreaks. The group that provides the violence is seldom ready to assume political leadership. But in 1848 the various revolutionary components were unusually distinct. Class divisions between street fighters and others, for example, were much more significant than in France during the Revolution of 1789. It was true that, in 1789, the major social groups were activated by different sets of causes.[3] But they had more common enemies, in the aristocracy and the church, than was the case in 1848, and they had no reason quickly to recognize their mutual differences. In 1848 the major revolutionary groups have to be separated to understand their motives and functions, for they were almost immediately aware of the divisions among them. The class structure was firmer than in 1789, while the wide knowledge of the meaning of revolution, provided by the many uprisings between 1789 and 1848, encouraged a conscious defense of class interest. The middle classes, even when backing revolution, feared attack from below, while the lower classes quite properly worried lest the gains of revolution be turned against them once again.

No discussion of revolutionary causation can deal with the attacking forces alone. The 1848 outbreaks resulted from weakness and confusion in the governing elite, as well as the push from below. The weakness was in part superficial or at least remediable. In the final analysis, failure of the revolutions prob-

3. Georges Lefebvre, *The Coming of the French Revolution* (Princeton, 1947).

ably owes more to the resiliency of the elite than to divisions among the revolutionaries. But in France and Germany the governing elite was seriously troubled, while elsewhere the old regime showed even more ominous signs of decrepitude.

ONE *The Lower Classes and the Countryside*

THE HORRORS OF working-class life during the early industrial revolution have been recounted by many observers. Britain, where industrialization was most advanced, provides the most familiar examples, but there were many analogies on the continent as mechanization spread after 1820. Textile workers in France and Germany labored thirteen to fourteen hours a day. Child labor was extensively involved, to the detriment of health and family life. Budgets were minimal, even with several members of the family at work. Approximately 70 percent of all working-class income had to be spent on food, leaving little margin for rent and clothing and none for expenditures on nonsubsistence items. Workers crowded into small apartments with little heat or furniture; many were clad in rags, and walked several miles to work each day barefoot. And even the normal, appalling material conditions were insecure. An illness or an accident, both common in the dirty, crowded factories, could leave a family destitute. Economic crises were frequent. Poor harvests drove up grain and bread prices and at the same time induced a slump in manufacturing. Many workers were dismissed, and pay fell for those who retained jobs. Small wonder that death rates increased notably in recession years, in manufacturing cities such as Lille or Barmen.[4]

4. Arthur Dunham, *The Industrial Revolution in France 1815–1848* (New York, 1955), 186–197; André Lasserre, *La Situation des ouvriers de l'industrie textile dans la région lilloise sous la monarchie de juillet* (Lausanne, 1952), 105–151; Jürgen Kuczynski, *The Rise of the Working Class* (New York, 1967), 137 ff.

The psychological pressure of factory labor could be even harder to bear. Many employers made little effort to be civil; some small factory owners even feared their workers as social competitors. In a few cases foremen imposed beatings on recalcitrant workers, while more commonly they exerted every effort to impose a rigorous work discipline. Factory gates were locked fifteen minutes after the work bell rang, and a tardy worker lost at least a half day's pay. Increasingly rigorous shop rules forbade singing, swearing, dirtiness, smoking, drunkenness, wandering around, and these were enforced by fines that could wipe out a day's meager earnings. Workers could be searched when they left the factory, "without there being any need to give him the reason." [5] Every year saw new attempts to increase the orderliness of the industrial process and "to demand the blindest submission on the part of the worker." [6] In the cities, workers torn from the countryside were surrounded by strangers and faced with situations for which their traditional values left them unprepared. Religion, for example, that age-old comfort to the poor, now made little sense. Big-city churches were not centered in working-class districts, their priests were conservative and often unsympathetic, and the whole setting was intimidating, recalling little of the friendly ritual of rural religion. So many factory workers lost, if not their belief, at least their habit of religious practice; yet it was difficult to find a satisfactory substitute. The whole society could seem hostile. Government officials, often even more than employers, viewed workers as a potential source of disorder above all, and tried to repress the slightest outcry. Social legislation was virtually nonexistent. France passed a limitation on child labor in 1841, but it was badly enforced. A similar law in Prussia, dating from 1839, had a bit more effect; and most continental countries enforced a few minimal safety provisions in mining and metallurgy. But for the most part, if a worker encountered the state at all, it was during a police action against disorder.

Here, surely, is an awesome backdrop to the revolutions of 1848. Many historians have expanded on the hardships and ten-

5. Departmental archives of the Haut-Rhin (France) 1M123-1, shop rules from the Bueck textile company.
6. Departmental archives of the Nord (France) M60-9, report of July 1842.

sions of early factory industry as the major explanation for lower-class unrest.[7] Yet the approach is almost completely misleading. The horrors existed, without question, though we will see that a bit of qualification is needed. But factory workers did not play a significant role in the outbreak of revolution. In some important cases the revolutions, once started, roused them to action, but even this was a minor theme in the ensuing agitation. Ironic as it may seem, then, given our knowledge of later labor unrest, we could virtually omit factory workers from a discussion of the revolutions of 1848 without major distortion. The industrial revolution cannot be dismissed, but its role was much more subtle.

There were, in fact, relatively few factory workers on the continent in 1848. Mechanization had conquered cotton and wool spinning, but weaving was still largely a manual operation. Metallurgy was being rapidly transformed, but in France a full half of the metallurgical product still issued from small, traditional charcoal-burning forges. Mining was expanding greatly, but from a very small base. There were approximately 400,000 factory and mine workers in France at the outbreak of the revolution—at most a tenth of all manufacturing workers. Some estimates put the corresponding percentage in Prussia a bit higher, but in no case did factory industries employ more than a small minority of the urban lower classes. Furthermore, most factory workers were distant from the chief political centers. Paris had boasted a factory population in the late eighteenth century, before mechanization, but most of this had since disappeared, the victim of rising rents and wages. Metallurgical and mining operations clustered around the sources of coal, textiles around water power. Berlin, Paris, and Vienna had barely been touched by the new industry, in terms of the composition of the lower classes. The notion, still surprisingly common, that factory workers and factory-caused grievances played a major role in the revolutions of 1848 exaggerates the extent of industrialization on the continent and ignores its actual location.

Students of the crowds in Paris during 1848 would make one

exception to this general statement: most have noted the presence of railroad workers on the barricades.[8] Correctly stating that this was a new group, they go on to suggest that these workers offer at least a foretaste of the recasting of lower-class protest. But, even here, no more than a foretaste is claimed, for traditional craftsmen played a much larger role. And many of the "new" workers had been trained as metal craftsmen. The unskilled and semiskilled factory workers simply do not figure in the major outbursts.

Indeed, factory workers in France and Germany had been relatively quiet during the preceding years—to find them leading the crowds in 1848 would be truly surprising. Their strike rate was low.[9] They showed few signs of sweeping demands or of political consciousness. In some cases their calmness was the result of satisfaction. Wages for male factory workers were high compared to those of traditional urban artisans, in Prussia and in many cases in France. In both countries the factory labor force was harder to recruit than it had been in Britain, with the result that wages and other benefits gave many workers a relatively superior position. More generally, factory workers were simply too new to their situation to have a clear basis for framing grievances. They took out their discontent in individual ways—by stealing from their employers, by taking time off or changing jobs, by drinking. These acts limited their ability to protest collectively; many potential strikes ended after a day, when workers, meeting in a tavern, drowned their sorrows in drink, and thus their ability to plan further action. Confused and often illiterate, most factory workers had no contact with the new doctrines that suggested remedies to their plight. Socialists who toured factory districts in France found some interest among manufacturers, but little among workers themselves.[10] Many factory workers, wedded to a

8. Rudé, *Crowd in History*, 1177; Tilly, "Changing Place of Collective Violence," 159.

9. Peter N. Stearns, "Patterns of Industrial Strike Activity during the July Monarchy," *American Historical Review* (1965), 371–394; Theodore S. Hamerow, *Restoration, Revolution, Reaction: Economics and Politics in Germany, 1815–1871* (Princeton, 1958).

10. Marie-Madelaine Kahan-Rabecq, "La Propagande fouriériste en Alsace," *L'Alsace française* (1938), 1–6, 29–31.

local dialect, could not even understand the speeches an outsider might try to make. Occasionally of course they did rise, almost invariably as a result of intense economic crisis when their wages fell and food prices rose. There were several such outbursts in French factory cities in 1847. But they were brief and focused on very limited goals; most commonly the workers attacked bakers, whom they held responsible for rising prices.

Except for these brief, though horribly intense, years of recession, continental factory workers did not suffer the same degree of hardship as their British counterparts did during the 1830s and 1840s. And they were much less numerous and much more traditional in their expectations. It is not surprising that they were still much quieter.

One other important lower-class group in the cities falls largely into the nonrevolutionary category: the very poor, whose numbers had been swelling in centers such as Paris and Vienna, were rarely found on the barricades. Crowded into filthy housing, dependent on occasional jobs as manual laborers—carters or dockers or ditchdiggers—the situation of the poorest element in the big cities had certainly been deteriorating in the two decades before 1848. Their growth in numbers was not matched by an expansion of jobs. Occasional public works projects—Paris built new city walls in the 1830s—gave temporary solace but they served also to draw new workers in. When unemployment returned it was all the harder to relieve. Not surprisingly slums expanded and their character became steadily more foul. More and more of the urban poor turned to begging or to crime.[11] Yet these people were not in a position to protest. They lacked any ability to formulate collective goals. They lacked the time and the resources to risk any dangerous action. Many were too enfeebled by inadequate diets and disease. Hence the familiar, perhaps smug, point that the very poor do not revolt applies to the revolutions of 1848 almost everywhere. It means that we cannot move easily from description of the worst Paris slums—of the sort so dramatically provided by the novels of Eugène Sue during the 1840s—to an understanding of what moved the actual revolution-

---

11. Louis Chevalier, *Laboring Classes and Dangerous Classes in Paris during the First Half of the Nineteenth Century* (New York, 1973), *passim*.

aries to their uprising. Again, the actual causation of the revolutions is more subtle.

But the very poor, unlike the factory workers, were well located; they strongly influenced the character of the leading political centers. Some would be drawn into key stages of the revolution, and their very presence influenced other groups. Middle-class sentiment in Paris became more rigid toward the lower classes, well before the revolutions broke out, as criminality and squalor increased. It became easier to think of the lower classes generally as real or potential criminals. Elements of the lower classes, who lived near the poor, were inevitably affected as they saw conditions worsen. They had a legacy of sympathy for the poor in general, and they could easily fear a similar fate for themselves or their children.

As is now obvious, the key urban protest group came from the ranks of artisans. In Paris the revolutionary crowds consisted of many crafts that had been prominent in earlier agitation, from the riots of 1789–93 through abortive risings during the 1830s and early 1840s, plus some interesting newcomers. Traditional leaders of street fighting included construction workers and butchers, while metalworkers were newer to the ranks.[12] Weavers played a major role in the Berlin revolution, which began in a weaving district. Artisans of various sorts spearheaded the rising in Vienna. And apart from these major centers, craftsmen were prominent in revolutionary agitation in cities like Marseilles and Lyons, while artisan congresses during the German revolution drew support from a wide range of cities.[13]

Unfortunately we do not know as much about artisans in this period as we should. Historians interested in this kind of subject have devoted most of their attention to factory industry or to describing the political activities in which artisans were involved. Hence we lack precise information about pay scales or job condi-

12. Rudé, *Crowd in History*, 193–213; Albert Soboul, *Les Sans-culottes parisiens en l'an II* (Paris, 1958), *passim*.
13. Hamerow, *Restoration*, 38–55; Paul Noyes, *Organization and Revolution: Working-Class Associations in the German Revolution of 1848–1849* (Princeton, 1966); William Sewell, "La Classe ouvrière de Marseille sous la Seconde République: structure sociale et comportement politique," *Mouvement social* (1971), 27–66.

tions. It is obvious, also, that conditions varied even among those artisan groups that contributed substantially to the revolution. We do not yet know precisely why some groups without a major tradition of protest joined the fray in Paris. Some artisans were directly threatened by industrialization while others actually benefited by it, at least in the short run, yet both might be involved in the revolutions. But despite gaps in our knowledge, some of which are beginning to be filled, the basic grievances of artisans are not hard to fathom.

Urban artisans were involved in an increasingly commercial economy, which violated many of their traditions. Contrary to a common impression, few of them were directly displaced by early industrialization. The situation was worst in textiles. Urban artisans had always specialized in the fancier cloths, which were hardest to mechanize, and in other highly skilled processes that were too complicated for rural manufacture. But by the 1830s some urban weavers faced machine competition, and other specialists, such as cloth shearers, were either thrown out of work or forced into a factory setting. This prompted some Luddism—destruction of new machinery—in France and Germany.[14] Still more artisans, such as the metalworkers, were affected by new methods and some ambiguous new temptations because of the advent of industrialization. Their metals came increasingly from factories, refined by coal rather than charcoal; this caused complaints about shoddy materials. Metalworkers were also in great demand in the new metallurgical factories and machine-building shops. They could earn good money in these places, but at a real cost to their sense of independence. Hence a growing concern among metalworkers who stuck to the old ways that they might be losing ground to their bolder fellows, while the latter could easily regret the choice they had made. Still more generally, artisans, even if remote from factory industry, feared for their future. They were aware of the threat, and many hoped to combat it before it became acute.

More immediately, artisans faced major changes in their relationships in their own workshop. Traditionally, artisans enjoyed a kind of equality; they were not divided into employers and em-

14. Frank Manuel, "The Luddite Movement in France," *Journal of Modern History* (1938), 180–211.

ployees. Journeymen lacked the property their masters had, but with time and saving they could hope to become masters in their own right, and while waiting they shared their master's society. Typically they ate with the master's family and often they were housed there. This situation had broken down often enough in the past. It was not new for masters and journeymen to find their interests in conflict, but a major protest seldom resulted, for the ideal of comradeship was powerful and attractive. Many groups of journeymen most prone to agitation, such as construction workers, were precisely those who were furthest from the ideal. During the first half of the nineteenth century, more and more masters, in a variety of trades, began to behave like small employers. Freed from traditional restrictions, aware of the opportunities for profit created by urban growth and rising wealth, artisanal employers began to take on more workers and tried to speed up the work process. In some cases they tried to slight traditional training, in favor of increasing production. Many stopped working alongside their journeymen, spending their time instead on purely business matters. Relationships became more formal. Above all, masters closed their own ranks. While the number of artisans increased rapidly, the number of masters remained stationary. Fewer and fewer journeymen could plan to rise in the traditional manner. Some, to be sure, sought other kinds of mobility. Many became teachers, or pastors, or priests, or noncommissioned officers. But the hunger for advancement was far greater than the market allowed. It left many journeymen frustrated, while others, though angry at their new inferiority, never tried to better themselves at all. In a final twist on the pattern, some artisans remained close to their masters but both were caught up in a commercial process beyond their control. Silk weavers in Lyons continued to live and work with their masters, but both were dominated by large merchants who kept the masters' profits and, through this, workers' wages low.[15] In one way or another, artisans were subjected to a system alien to their tradition and often directly damaging to their social status and earnings.

15. Fernand Rudé, *Le Mouvement ouvrier à Lyon de 1827 à 1832* (Paris, 1944), *passim;* Robert Bezucha, "Aspects du conflit des classes à Lyon, 1831–1834," *Mouvement social* (1971), 5–26.

At the same time competition among artisans increased greatly. Massive population growth in the countryside drove more and more people to the cities, including many who had received artisanal training in small towns. Blacksmiths, for example, naturally sought entry to the metal crafts in the large cities. Competition was another thing alien to the tradition of the urban artisans, for their impulse had always been to limit their numbers. But in many areas—France, northern Italy, the states of west Germany—guild regulations, which had previously restricted entry, were now illegal, and even where guild regulations remained they could easily be overwhelmed by the sheer numbers flocking to the city. Of course job opportunities increased as well. Growing cities required more tailors and bakers, jewelers and masons. But the new competition increased hardships in slack years, and above all it increased fear. The times were out of whack.

In some cases newcomers to the city felt the greatest frustration. Marseilles artisans most active in political agitation were disproportionately born in other areas. Trained in various skills, they found that Marseilles artisans managed to reserve the most prestigious crafts for themselves (therefore finding little need to join the ranks of agitators). Elsewhere the division was less clear. Studies of Parisian crowds indicate rough correspondence between the number of Parisian-born participants and the number of Parisian-born artisans.[16]

It is not possible to claim that rising competition and falling status led to a decline in the artisanal standard of living. Many urban artisans had a margin above subsistence in normal times; heavy participation in savings banks was one sign of this—but living standards may have tended downward. With crowding, the conditions of traditional artisanal quarters undoubtedly deteriorated, even when the real incomes did not. And many artisans were aware that other urban groups, notably the business classes, were improving their lot while their own conditions stagnated at best.

State and city governments, finally, were becoming more hostile. The abolition of guilds signaled the conversion of the gov-

16. René Gossez, *Les Ouvriers de Paris* (Paris, 1966), *passim;* Sewell, "Classe ouvrière de Marseille," 27 ff.

ernments of Western Europe to a free labor market. No longer could artisans defend traditional methods of work against innovation. The same governments installed rigorous prohibitions against alternate groupings that might defend artisanal interests in other ways. Unionization was outlawed, and although some artisans got around this, the barriers were formidable, which brought those artisans who were interested in organizing in direct conflict with the state.[17] Vigorous repression of artisanal groups and collective bargaining efforts in Lyons in the early 1830s was only one of many clashes throughout Western and Central Europe. In Prussia, guilds were preserved until the 1840s, though frequently threatened, but then deprived of most of their privileges in 1845. This caused great dismay. Because guilds were such a recent memory, many German artisans were still appealing for their full restoration in 1848, whereas artisans in France and in the western German states sought newer kinds of organizations instead.[18] This was a vital difference, with important political overtones. But the impulse to seek organizational protection against the vagaries of a hostile economy was widespread.

The various pressures on artisanal life produced abundant unrest in the decades before 1848. Though beleaguered, artisans were sufficiently stable and sure enough of their values to protest frequently; this was what differentiated them from others in the urban lower classes. In Germany strikes and riots centered disproportionately in the older cities, where artisans retained their greatest strength.[19] French artisans struck with considerable frequency, and were prominent in all urban riots. Everywhere artisans developed organizations that could be relevant to social conflict. Mutual aid societies spread widely, and these were tolerated by the major governments because they provided insurance funds against illness and burial expenses. Yet aid societies gave artisans new experience in cooperation and helped develop leaders among them, and were in fact the forerunners of a formal trade union movement. Some turned, surreptitiously, into what

17. Jean Pierre Aguet, *Les Grèves sous la monarchie de juillet* (Geneva, 1954), 282–287.
18. Noyes, *Organization and Revolution, passim.*
19. Richard Tilly, "Popular Disorders in Nineteenth-Century Germany," *Journal of Social History* (1970), 1–40.

the French called resistance societies, capable of mounting strikes and on occasion engaging in collective bargaining. In no sense were urban artisans in perpetual ferment, for many were able to make gains as individuals, but the potential for a deep-seated protest against the changing social order was obvious well before 1848.

Some artisans, finally, had developed outright political demands. It should be apparent that artisans were not motivated by narrow economic causation; their concerns involved a desire for independence and a certain kind of equality as well as a search for greater material security. On the other hand we must guard against assuming that artisans easily translated even these broad interests into politics. French artisans in the larger cities, particularly in Paris, had considerable experience in political gains. Parisian artisans interviewed after the 1830 Revolution were articulate in their demands for greater power for parliament and for more religious freedom and liberty of the press. But while many had demanded a republic they yielded fairly readily to Lafayette's symbolic and foolish embrace of a new monarch, Louis Philippe. When the new regime proved repressive, republican sentiment spread. Lyons silkweavers, put down in their demonstrations for economic gains in 1831, raised republican demands when they renewed their agitation in 1833. Small numbers of Parisian artisans participated in abortive political revolts thereafter, and smaller numbers still joined republican clubs. So there was active political awareness among artisans in France, though its extent should not be exaggerated. Radical underground newspapers furthered this sentiment, though the leading papers directed toward artisans, notably *L'Atelier*, were quite cautious politically.[20]

Outside of France, where artisans lacked a tradition of political revolt and where the press was tightly censored, political awareness was undoubtedly limited. Few German or Italian artisans were militantly republican or even nationalist at the outbreak of revolution. On the other hand the general artisanal tradition included an awareness of government and an expecta-

20. Quentin-Bauchart, *La Crise sociale*, 128 ff.; Edouard Dolléans and Gérard Dehove, *Histoire du travail en France* (Paris, 1953), 184-253.

tion that the state would assist its subjects in certain respects. Artisans were accustomed to appealing for state aid to alleviate high bread prices or the enforcement of guild regulations. They could easily translate their new concerns into demands for new assistance.[21] Hence though the artisanal revolution, particularly outside of France, was not the product of political frustrations in the modern sense—despite the general absence of political rights —it could easily take a political turn and it inevitably challenged the existing states.

Artisanal socialism is as slippery a topic as political awareness, though it is slightly different. And this is another subject to which we must return in discussing the course of the revolutions themselves. There was undeniable affinity between the leading kinds of socialism advocated before 1848, which are collectively termed "utopian," and artisanal values. We must leave aside Saint-Simonianism here, for it was barely socialist—it has been mislabeled for convenience, being in fact a doctrine of technocracy—and played no direct role in the revolution of 1848. Certainly the Saint-Simonian doctrines of rapid economic growth directed by technical experts would find faint echo among artisans, who feared growth and scientific management alike. But other utopian offerings, stressing small productive units and voluntarism, reflected an idealized artisanal past. Shortly before 1848 individual artisans began producing their own socialist theory. Pierre Joseph Proudhon, a largely self-educated typesetter, wrote vigorous attacks against capitalism, beginning with *What Is Property?* in 1840. The German tailor Wilhelm Weitling, strongly influenced by French Christian socialism, published similar denunciations of private property. Weitling and other German craftsmen who were won to socialism were forced into exile. Many fled to Switzerland, where socialism had won some indigenous support, while others went to Paris where they formed their own organization, the League of the Just, and often joined French secret societies as well. It is clear, however, that socialism had no wide influence over German artisans at this point. Far

21. Charles Tilly, "Collective Violence in European Perspective," in Hugh Davis Graham and Ted Gurr, eds., *Violence in America* (New York, 1969), 41–44.

more middle-class intellectuals than actual workers were converted. The same holds true for Italy. In almost all cases rigorous censorship restricted the circulation of socialist writings.

Only in Paris did socialist writings win any broad audience before 1848, and even here the impact is hard to measure. Catholic socialism, urging fundamental economic reforms in the name of religion, won support among a number of literate artisans. The newspaper *L'Atelier,* whose motto was "He who will not work, shall not eat," was a product of this movement. Several of the secret societies in which artisans were involved preached socialism as well as political revolution, without religious overtones.[22] Louis Blanc, who published the *Organization of Labor* in 1840, was probably the most widely known socialist theorist among the artisans. He advocated political democracy as the basis for worker control of the state; the state would then support workers' production associations which would in turn do away with exploitative private enterprise. His theory was hardly profound, but he was a good publicist and his work had a catchy title. We cannot tell how many artisans were won to theories of this sort, but it is clear that some individuals were devoted to the socialist cause and that there was fairly widespread knowledge of its existence.

During the revolution, a Parisian mechanic urged the new government to issue new bank notes, to build warships for piracy against the English, and to complete all canal and railway construction. Hardly a socialist program, but the same mechanic stated that his ideal was the "organization of labor, building yards, and national workshops everywhere, even in the forests, today or tomorrow if possible." Even when wed to no strict theory, artisans, particularly in Paris, could show their awareness of new ideas.

Artisans, then, had a variety of deep-seated grievances against the social order being formed around them. They had a tradition of vigorous protest. They had ongoing organizations and leadership. Some, particularly in France, were open also to political and social ideologies. Many traveled extensively, for the

22. D. G. Charlton, *Secular Religions in France 1815–1870* (London, 1963), 65–95.

artisanal tour, particularly for a few years after completion of apprenticeship, remained a well-established institution; so if artisans in one place showed definite awareness of new ideas it is probable that there was some knowledge of them elsewhere.[23] These new influences, added to the deep-seated sense of justice that the artisanal tradition provided, made for a potent revolutionary mix.

THE COUNTRYSIDE

There were two general pressures on the rural populations of Western and Central Europe during the decades before 1848. The first and most devastating was massive population growth. This growth had begun during the preceding century, but in many countries its rate increased after 1800 and everywhere its cumulative impact became more severe. Germany's growth rate reached 1.25 percent per year. Austria's population expanded almost as rapidly. Italy and France lagged somewhat—Italy because her major demographic burst was still to come and France because earlier expansion now trailed off. But even in these areas the population grew considerably. It was relieved somewhat by migration to the cities—the migration that so disturbed the artisanal world—but urbanization did not yet account for the whole growth; nor was there much emigration abroad. So the countryside was burdened with rising numbers of people. Pressure on the land and the whole rural economy was the inevitable result. The peasantry, uneducated and lacking capital, found it difficult to respond with new techniques. There was some improvement in methods, some specialization in market crops, but not enough to prevent growing rural poverty. Furthermore, efforts at accommodation disturbed many peasants. Production for the market put peasants at the mercy of outside buyers; commercial motives were even more alien to peasants than to artisans.[24]

23. Emile Coornaert, *Les Compagnonnages* (Paris, 1966); 52–105; Eric Hobsbawm, "The Tramping Artisan," in *Labouring Men* (New York, 1967) 41–74; Agricole Perdiguier, *Mémoires d'un compagnon* (Paris, 1943).
24. B. H. Slicher van Bath, *The Agrarian History of Western Europe, 500–1840* (London, 1963), 221 ff.; Charles Tilly, *The Vendée; A Sociological Analysis of the Counterrevolution of 1793* (New York, 1967), 114–145.

One means of dealing with population pressure, the spread of manufacturing work in the countryside, had been widely adopted, for it had offered wages to people who could not find work in agriculture, but it was now being brutally called into question. Throughout Western and Central Europe, domestic manufacturing had spread rapidly during the eighteenth and early nineteenth centuries. Millions of rural inhabitants worked full time or part time as spinners, weavers, makers of metal utensils, and so on. By the 1840s these jobs became more and more difficult to maintain. Spinners had been thrown out of work entirely, through the mechanization of the industry. Weavers now faced the competition of machines, as industrialization spread on the continent and English imports captured a large share of the market. Other rural workers were similarly affected. Even where machines were not widely introduced, the growing productivity of urban artisans and the development of improved transportation and marketing techniques made significant inroads on the rural crafts. Rising competition meant growing periods of unemployment for rural manufacturing workers. Wages fell. Hours of work increased, when work was available at all, as workers tried to compensate for their low wage rates. Urban merchants, who controlled the production process because they supplied raw materials and marketed finished goods, became more arbitrary in their behavior, for they too were hard pressed and the system invited exploitation of the workers. After all, the workers had invested their own capital in equipment and they were, besides, emotionally reluctant to leave their traditional surroundings, so they hung on. The death of rural manufacturing was agonizing and prolonged. Its victims tried repeatedly to protest, despite the difficulty of organizing scattered producers. A number of strikes developed among French weavers in the 1830s and 1840s. In the mid-1840s, weavers in Silesia rose up against the machines that were destroying their livelihood. Against the pressure of a rising population, the dramatic decline of rural manufacturing created ominous tensions.

Very generally, then, the peasants of Western and Central Europe were being disturbed and in some cases grievously harmed by a rapidly changing economy. Unwilling to initiate changes themselves, peasants found it difficult to resist because population growth undermined their own traditional economy. They had more to do with money and merchants than ever before. From their own ranks emerged new commercial types: the farmer intent on buying up the land of his weaker neighbors and expropriating common lands for his own use; the miller who took advantage of a fluctuating grain market. Peasants had much to fear from the extension of capitalism into the countryside, and they found some obvious targets for their resentment. The state was one. Most governments increased the level of rural taxation during the first half of the nineteenth century. State expenses were rising, and the growing commercialization of agriculture seemed to open a source of new funds. But the smaller peasants found it difficult to pay the new taxes. Small wonder that the rate of rural protest was high and that tax riots became increasingly common.

Within this general framework, however, the situation of the peasantry differed markedly from one area to the next, and so did their involvement in the revolutions of 1848. There was significant rural unrest in France before and during the revolution, but the peasants did not really revolt. Their later agitation was significant and played an important part in the course of the revolution, but their grievances were not nearly so general or so sweeping as they had been in 1789. French peasants were not burdened with manorial dues or a predominance of large landholdings. They had won a part of their revolution already, so their reactions in 1848 were somewhat muted.

Rural unrest in Italy, particularly in Sicily, played a more definite role in the onset of revolution. Landlords in southern Italy and in the Po valley had been taking over growing numbers of small holdings, reducing the peasantry to a day laborer status. This naturally added to the general pressures within the rural world, producing a rising tide of brigandage and collective protest. Only in northwestern Italy, where the peasant situation resembled that of France, was there relative calm.[25]

25. Antonio Lucarelli, *Il Brigantaggio politico del mezzogiorno d'Italia dopo la seconda restaurazione borbonica* (Bari, 1942); Eric Hobsbawm, *Primitive Rebels, studies in archaic forms of social movement in the nineteenth and twentieth centuries* (New York, 1957), 57–73, 93–107.

Peasants in the Habsburg empire were still locked within a feudal system, owing work services and tax payments to the landlords; few owned much land outright.[26] And the landlords had been tampering with this system to their own advantage. Hungarian landlords, trying to profit from growing grain markets in the cities of Western Europe, increased the annual work service demanded of their peasantry. They also took over the common pastures, on which the traditional village economy had depended heavily. The situation was less severe in Austria and Bohemia, but here too peasants had many bitter complaints about their landlords' encroachments.

The situation of German peasants varied considerably. Those in western Germany were largely small holders and had been freed from manorial obligations.[27] This freedom was a mixed blessing, however, for it deprived them of some of the protection landlords had offered in bad times. As freemen, peasants were naturally expected to pay greater taxes to the state; many of them owed cash redemption payments to their former landlords as well. So they were forced, ill-prepared, into a market economy in order to gain a money income; and it was in western and southwestern Germany that the population pressure was most intense. In Prussia and other east German states, a modified manorialism remained, and here too landlords tried to manipulate it to their increasing advantage. Prussia had emancipated the serfs in 1807, but at a great price. Those peasants who won abolition of feudal dues had to turn over a third to a half of their land to their former masters; common lands were also enclosed, with peasants receiving only about 14 percent of the total, mostly wasteland. Large numbers of small holdings were completely absorbed in the large estates, for now that it was legal to buy and sell land many peasants yielded to pressures to sell. Many thus became agricultural laborers. Others remained within the manorial system, but were increasingly hard pressed.

26. Jerome Blum, *Noble Landowners and Agriculture in Austria, 1818–1848* (Baltimore, 1948), *passim;* György Spira, "La Dernière génération des serfs de Hongrie," *Annales* (1968), 353–367.
27. Werner Conze, ed., *Quellen zur Geschichte der deutschen Bauernbefreiung* (Göttingen, 1957); Hamerow, *Restoration,* 38–55.

Hence, despite great variety, peasants in the major centers of the 1848 revolution, except in France, were locked into a situation that was in many ways worse than that of the old regime. They were certainly more at their landlords' mercy than French peasants had been in 1789. Could they respond to the challenge of revolution? 1848 was to provide a crucial test.

THE ECONOMIC CRISIS

For all elements of the lower classes, rural and urban, the years 1846 and 1847 brought devastating hardship. These were the worst years of the nineteenth century in terms of sheer human suffering. A sudden shortage of food was both the cause of the general crisis and its worst feature. Beginning in the autumn of 1845, potatoes were attacked by a strange new fungus. They turned black and mushy and were largely inedible. The crop of 1846 was virtually nonexistent, that of 1847 only somewhat better, and the crop of 1848 very poor once again. The lower classes in many areas of Europe depended heavily on the potato as the basis of their diet. Suffering was greatest in Ireland, whose population had soared because of the potato supply alone. Hundreds of thousands died of starvation and hunger-induced diseases. But the lower classes in the Low Countries, northern France, and Germany relied on the potato too, and its failure produced great misery. Almost as serious was a poor grain harvest in 1846 and again in 1847.[28]

The food crisis affected many rural areas. Peasants lost income when their harvests were below normal. Agricultural laborers were thrown out of work. In areas of the most severe crop failures, including potato-growing regions particularly, even landowning peasants lacked food. The situation was worsened when governments requisitioned grain to feed the starving cities. This was standard practice in such situations, as governments feared urban discontent above all, but the requisitions could inflame the peasants and undeniably threatened some of them with starvation.

28. See Cecil Woodham-Smith, *The Great Hunger* (New York, 1963), and Sigmund Fleischmann, *Die Agrarkrise von 1845–1855* (Heidelberg, 1902).

In the cities the food shortage was translated into a dizzying price rise. The price of bread rose by 50 percent between 1845 and 1847 in Paris, while that of potatoes nearly doubled.[29] Governments did distribute some food. The German states imported grain and opened soup kitchens. Private charities and business firms provided food also, out of philanthropy and also a desire to prevent disorder, but hunger was widespread all the same.

A business depression added immensely to the problem. With food prices up, many people were unable to purchase normal quantities of manufactured goods. So production fell, and with it employment and wages. In some French factory centers over a third of the labor force was out of work, and the situation among artisans may have been even worse. German and French governments set up public works to alleviate the situation, but they could only make a small dent in the problem. An official in Nuremberg described the suffering among respectable artisans: "If we should enter the home of a craftsman, we would see at once the bitterest want, so anxiously concealed and kept secret. The lack of orders or of markets and low prices frequently bring the most industrious man into such distress that he and his family must suffer more than a public beggar." [30] Unemployment and low pay obviously exacerbated the food crisis, for prices and incomes were moving in diametrically opposite directions. And the countryside was affected too. Domestic manufacturing slumped badly. Many urban workers returned to the country in search of food or jobs, which added to the existing problems.

Death rates rose markedly in both countryside and city. Mortality rates in Paris, 24.4 per 1000 in 1842, soared to 29.3 per 1000 in 1847. Charity resources were inadequate to meet the crisis. Workers were unable to pay rents or buy clothes; many had to pawn their tools. Thousands wandered through the countryside or from city to city, hoping desperately to find some way out of their misery. Many peasants survived only by eating

29. Ernst Labrousse, *Aspects de la crise et de la dépression de l'économie française 1846–1851* (Paris, 1956), *passim*; Jeanne Singer-Kérel, *Le Coût de la vie à Paris de 1840 à 1859* (Paris, 1961), 454, 462 ff.
30. Edward Shorter, "Middle-Class Anxiety in the German Revolution of 1848," *Journal of Social History* (1969), 199.

roots, grasses, and carrion. In France, many came into the larger cities—probably those thrown out of rural manufacturing work above all—hoping to obtain charity relief. Crime increased everywhere.

Beginning in 1846 the economic crisis began to produce serious unrest. There were food riots and tax riots in a number of rural areas of France. Grain transports were frequently attacked. Major food riots broke out in 1847 in Berlin and other German cities. Workers set up barricades and eventually troops had to be called out to restore order. Viennese workers also attacked and plundered the foodshops. Serious rioting occurred in a number of French cities.

By the winter of 1847–48 the situation had improved very slightly. The potato shortage was unabated, but the grain harvest of the preceding autumn was back to normal. Unemployment declined somewhat. Yet there is no doubt that the revolutions that began in February were triggered by the two years of desperate misery. The slight improvement in conditions merely gave the lower classes a bit more resource and energy—it was difficult to mount more than a short, if intense, riot when the bulk of the population was weak from hunger. This was one reason that revolutionary agitation could not catch on among the lower classes in Ireland in 1848: misery was still too severe. On the continent, 1848 thus followed the pattern of 1789 and 1830, in occurring during an economic upturn following a severe crisis.

Yet the fact that revolution broke out after the worst misery was past raises two other points. First, lower-class rebellion, though provoked by desperate suffering, had larger goals. The rioting of 1846–47 was confined to immediate problems: the demands raised in 1848 went much further. This is why the deep malaise of important lower-class groups commands as much attention as the crisis that provoked its expression. Second, though, the lower classes did not make the revolutions alone and perhaps would not have been able to. Where other groups did not stir, there was no revolution. Suffering in Belgium was as severe as that in Germany; it too provoked riots.[31] But the middle classes,

31. G. Jacquemyns, *Histoire de la crise économique des Flandres, 1845–1850* (Brussels, 1929), Books II and III.

victors in the revolution of 1830, were contented; they provided no pretext for general rebellion. The same situation prevailed even more clearly in Britain. Here, misery caused a number of riots. It also sparked the last major Chartist demonstrations, in which workers of all sorts signed petitions demanding political rights and then gathered to support their demands. But the middle classes were satisfied. They had won their right to vote through the Reform Bill of 1832 and had gained much favorable economic legislation since that time. So they did not stir, and there was no revolution. In contrast, in France it was the middle class that provided the spur which turned urban rioting into revolution, and this sparked similar combinations in Central Europe.

TWO   *The Middle Classes and Revolution*

O F ALL THE straightforward approaches toward understanding the revolutions of 1848, the simplest is that which
sees them as a bid by the rising middle classes to take
political control, from which they were effectively excluded.[32]
The approach has much to commend it. There is no question
that the middle class was rising. Early industrialization and the
extension of a market economy increased its numbers and wealth.
All levels of the class were involved in these changes. The rich
bourgeoisie of Paris underwent a dramatic change in personnel
between 1820 and 1848, and its average wealth rose considerably.
The middle ranks of the class swelled with the expansion of
professional groups—such as the lawyers who benefited from
heightened commercial activities—and aspiring industrialists and
businessmen. At the lowest levels shopkeepers proliferated, as
there were more goods to distribute and cities to serve.[33] This
middle-class growth was as characteristic of Austria as of France;
only Eastern Europe, where the commercialization of the economy had yet to penetrate, was immune.

There is no question, either, that this rising middle class was
excluded from political power. France and a few of the states in
southwestern Germany had parliaments based on limited suffrage. But most of the middle class lacked the vote. Property
qualifications in France restricted the suffrage to less than 250,000

32. Charles Morazé, *The Triumph of the Middle Classes* (Cleveland, 1966),
191 ff.
33. Adeline Daumard, *La Bourgeoisie parisienne de 1815 à 1848* (Paris, 1963).

people. Government rigging of elections during the 1840s meant that even many voters were not freely represented. But the number of people excluded outright attracted growing criticism. At most, a quarter of adult middle-class males were enfranchised, for landed property was favored in the system of voting qualifications so that many well-to-do urban residents could not vote; most of the new industrialists did not qualify. The same was true of most intellectuals and a variety of professional people. In most of the German states, including Prussia, and in the Habsburg empire and Italy, there was even less outlet for middle-class political interests. Prussian city governments had considerable autonomy and the middle class could often participate at this level. Provincial diets included representation of the "third estate," which embraced the middle class along with many other groups, but they had few powers, met infrequently, and their representatives voted by estate, not by head, which further obscured their representativeness. In effect, the middle class in Southern and Central Europe had no rights of political participation.

Nor did they have equal access to the bureaucracy. The Habsburg bureaucracy, notoriously inefficient, included many nonaristocrats at the lower levels, who served as chief paperpushers, but the aristocracy dominated the positions of power. The same was true of most of the Italian states. In Prussia reforms earlier in the century had removed any aristocratic monopoly. But it required a great deal of money to enter the bureaucracy and even those new entrants who could afford the necessary education and apprenticeship were discouraged in many ways. The upper bureaucracy, whether titled or not, existed as a class apart, so the system could not serve the political interests of the middle class.[34] To a somewhat lesser extent the same was true of France. Some aristocrats had withdrawn from state service after the revolution of 1830, but the aristocracy still played a considerable role, as did nonnoble landowners.[35] New middle-class ele-

34. John Gillis, *The Prussian Bureaucracy in Crisis, 1840–1860* (Stanford, 1971), 49–88.
35. Nicholas Richardson, *The French Prefectoral Corps 1814–1830* (Cambridge, 1966); René Rémond, *The Right Wing in France from 1815 to*

ments could not yet easily afford the kind of education that would qualify them for the bureaucracy. And in France the centralization of political power deprived the middle class of significant political activities on the local level. They did win the mayoral elections in most of the growing cities, but the mayors' powers were so limited that the sense of participation was stunted.

So lack of political power there was. The contrast with Britain and Belgium, where virtually the entire middle class could vote, is obvious, while in Eastern Europe the middle class had too little substance to constitute a threat. So in a very general way the formula: rising middle class / absence of corresponding political voice, is a valid means of approaching the revolutions. Yet to move from this to an understanding of how the middle classes were actually involved is no easy matter.

In the first place we should not assume, too blithely, that the middle classes lamented their exclusion from politics. Numerically, a sizable percentage of the middle class—probably a clear majority—was still made up, not of new business and professional types, but of traditional merchants and teachers, local judges and clerks. They lived not in the rapidly growing industrial and commercial centers, but in the small towns that had dotted preindustrial Western and Central Europe. These people had never sought political representation. They believed in a social hierarchy in which they constituted a local elite but deferred in larger matters to the aristocracy. They were concerned about their slipping position in society at large, at an extreme fearing that the whole middle class would be eroded. A German cleric expressed a common view in claiming that "machines divide people into two classes, rich and poor, the masters and the oppressed, and sentence the latter to eternal poverty by removing them from the middle class. The curse of thousands rests upon them." [36] But these people would not easily look to new political systems to settle their grievances, and certainly they

---

de Gaulle (Philadelphia, 1966); 52–86; Patrick Higonnet and Trevor Higonnet, "Class, Corruption and Politics in the French Chamber of Deputies, 1846–1848," *French Historical Studies* (1967), 204–224.
36. Shorter, "Middle-Class Anxiety," p. 266.

could not join the rising middle class in seeking power—for the rising middle class, the people that were introducing machines and other innovations, were in fact their main enemies. If the old middle class looked to politics at all, it was to appeal to traditional authorities, above all to the established monarchs, to turn back the clock and restore the old order.

Even if we concentrate on the new middle class, political interest was often limited. Officials in Roubaix, a fast-rising industrial city in northern France, complained that manufacturers could not be induced to take an interest in civic affairs, devoting their entire energy to their own enterprises. Generally the political consciousness of businessmen remained on a low level. In France individual businessmen could be found at virtually every spot on the political spectrum. There were ardent republicans and partisans of the Bourbon monarchy that had fallen in 1830, as well as active supporters of the July Monarchy that had replaced it. But most businessmen displayed what might be called a friendly apathy to political issues in the 1830s and 1840s. The regime did little to harm their interests. Occasionally threats to lower tariffs on industrial products roused concern; and there was some feeling—quite correctly—that the government was not promoting industrial development as vigorously as it might. Lack of political representation was not, however, keenly felt. Successful businessmen could count on winning the vote; some were in fact elected to parliament. But the issue does not seem to have been of paramount importance in a period when most of the dynamic businessmen were just getting started in industry or commerce.

The economic crisis of 1846–47 undoubtedly shook this complacent attitude. Many companies failed, while profits plummeted everywhere. Businessmen cast about for villains, and it was easy to criticize government inaction. Businessmen urged subsidies, relief programs, encouragements to export. Even now they did not call the regime into question, but their commitment to it, never very active, was lessened. Hence, while they were not found in the ranks of the revolutionaries—in contrast to the direct encouragement that some had offered in the revolution of 1830—they did not immediately oppose the rising either.

The situation was somewhat different in Central Europe, for here businessmen faced positive barriers to their activities that required some political attention. The Prussian state enforced guild restrictions on technical innovation. Though it offered some encouragement to individual industries, setting up model factories and the like, its overall investment policies favored agricultural over business interests.[37] The Prussian tariff policy, spread to the whole of Germany through the *Zollverein,* which united the German states in a customs union, was intelligently conceived and designed to encourage all sorts of economic activity, but it offered little protection to infant industry. Support for transportation, particularly railroads, was more active than in France, but more for military than economic reasons. Governments in the Habsburg empire and in Italy were more backward still. Inefficient financial systems consumed much of the limited capital available for state expenses. Transportation improved only slowly.

Businessmen in these areas thus developed some natural political concerns, quite apart from any general desire to match middle-class wealth with political power. Chambers of commerce urged governments to pay more attention to the business interest, which meant some kind of political reform. These groups often discussed political and economic theories. Economic publications in Italy, which were one of the only outlets that could escape the censorship, played a major role in keeping liberal doctrines alive after the failure of the revolutions of 1830. It was not surprising, then, that individual businessmen and business organizations were ready to try to use the revolutions of 1848 to their own advantage.

Italian and German businessmen had one other obvious interest: a concern about the political divisions in their countries. A multiplicity of small states meant real or potential tariff barriers, lack of transportation coordination—painfully evident in the different rail gauges adopted in the various German states— and impediments to the movement of capital and labor. These problems were more severe in Italy than in Germany, where the

37. Richard Tilly, *Financial Institutions and Industrialization in the Rhineland* (Madison, 1966), 30–45, 134–138.

Zollverein facilitated trade, but they attracted wide attention in both countries. The Italian journals dealing with economic affairs kept alive an interest in proposals for federation. Few businessmen were rabidly nationalist, but nationalist arguments had potential attraction for them.[38]

Generally, however, the political interests of businessmen even in Central Europe were rather muted. Most of them wanted reform, but not at the price of disorder which would inevitably damage the economic climate. Few found the policies of existing regimes insupportable. Hence businessmen, though fundamental to the rising importance of the middle class, were not deeply wedded to the political goals of the 1848 revolutions, even though most were probably initially sympathetic.

The most highly politicized segment of the middle class consisted of professional people—lawyers, doctors, journalists, teachers. The professionals often seemed to be arguing for the interest of the middle class as a whole—at least the dynamic, innovative segment of the class. It can be contended that the concentration of professional people in political activity constituted an effective division of labor within the middle class. The businessmen made money, while the professional people translated this economic success into political demands. This argument is probably correct in broad outline and in the long run. But it needs careful handling if it is to be applied to the revolutions of 1848.[39] Most businessmen did not feel explicitly represented by the professional people. Most were not only much less politically aware but also naturally more moderate than many of the professional people in politics. Many had long distrusted professional people as being too theoretical, lacking in the good common sense that making money both required and demonstrated. For their part, professional people often resented businessmen. And they were responding to their own set of impulses in their participation in the revolutions of 1848. Their political goals reflected some values

38. Kent R. Greenfield, *Economics and Liberalism in the Risorgimento, 1815–1848* (Baltimore, 1965).

39. Lenore O'Boyle, "The Middle Class in Western Europe," *American Historical Review* (1966), 827–845; Alfred Cobban, "The 'Middle Class' in France, 1816–1848," *French Historical Studies* (1967), 42–51.

that were widely held in the new middle class but they were not explicitly tailored to the business interest.

The interest of professional people in politics is hardly surprising. The professions required considerable education—at least through secondary school, often through the universities. Businessmen, in contrast, rarely completed secondary school, preferring training in the firm itself. Hence professional people were unusually open to ideas. Lawyers naturally had contact with agencies of the state. Many, perhaps most, law students intended to enter the state bureaucracy. Most journalists hoped to write about political affairs, even if the censorship sometimes diverted them to other areas. Most teachers, outside the ranks of the clergy, were employed by the state on the continent. Many doctors dealt with government bureaus, and often had contacts with poor patients that gave them unusual insights into social problems. Professional people thus could easily come to believe that they had a special political competence and could resent their exclusion from the centers of power.

Their own experience tended to enhance this political sense and turn them against the state. Their student days exposed them to a variety of restrictions. This was particularly true in Central Europe. German and Austrian universities were infiltrated by secret police, who kept files on students which could be used later if they tried to enter the civil service. No student political association was permitted. Professors were judged by their orthodoxy. Leading figures, like the historian Georg Gervinus, were expelled from the system for political publications. All of this set up a vicious cycle. Student groups, often nonpolitical in their inception, could easily be driven underground, and radicalized, by police repression, while the groups themselves frightened the authorities into further rigor. The leaders of the German *Burschenschaften,* a nationalist student group, at first disdained politics; in 1817 they proclaimed, "Yours is not to discuss what should or should not happen in the State." But their nationalism was political nonetheless; the authorities tried to repress the movement, and so it turned increasingly hostile to the existing regimes.

The atmosphere of repression continued to affect the more

articulate professionals. University teachers were obviously hemmed in, and naturally became more interested in political change as their outlets for expression were eliminated. Journalists chafed under the censorship, and this problem affected France under the July Monarchy only to a somewhat lesser extent than in Central Europe. Gustav Freytag described the atmosphere in Germany during the 1830s and 1840s: "Every word an author wrote on any question of the day was attended with a feeling of humiliation. . . . The effort to give publicity to a judgment of his own constituted a continuous feud between craftiness and unreasonable authority." Many books and newspapers were seized, many authors brought to trial. Small wonder that professors and journalists sought means to spread doctrines of reform by word of mouth or through anonymous publications.

The professions faced a still more general problem by the 1840s: there were more people seeking jobs than there were jobs.[40] This was the first incidence of what was to become a recurrent problem in Europe. Eagerness to attain the prestige and security of professional status attracted many middle-class elements. The relevant schools expanded to handle the influx. Enrollment in the French *lycées,* which prepared for the universities, doubled during the first half of the nineteenth century. Fees were lowered in the German universities in 1807, prompting a steady increase in university attendance. But the jobs did not keep pace.

The overproduction of lawyers was particularly acute. In Prussia most people entered law school with the intention of entering the state bureaucracy. During the 1830s and 1840s state posts stagnated, while despite official warnings the numbers of law students rose. The number of law students in Prussian universities increased by almost a third in the decade after 1841. To meet this pressure the state toughened the civil service examination, by testing for detailed knowledge in contrast to the theoretical training offered by the universities. Twenty-five percent failed outright. Those who passed then had to endure a long apprenticeship in the bureaucracy. They received no pay during

40. Lenore O'Boyle, "The Problem of an Excess of Educated Men in Western Europe, 1800–1850," *Journal of Modern History* (1970), 471–495.

this period but were forbidden to take a second job. In 1848 there were 4000 apprentices in the system. Betwen 1836 and 1848 the judicial branch offered but twenty permanent positions a year, while ten apprentices died annually while waiting. And during the apprenticeship, candidates were compelled to maintain a rather expensive front, purchasing expensive clothes, while their political behavior and morality continued to be monitored by the police. Even in junior posts, men were cut off from senior bureaucrats, given no voice in policies, and encouraged to curry their supervisors' favor by toadying.

And these, of course, were the lucky ones. Large numbers could not enter the bureaucracy at all, and while opportunities for private law practices were increasing they remained inadequate. Many trained professionals, or people forced to drop out of school because of lack of funds, had to seek work they considered below their station. A number became journalists, which meant that many journalists were disgruntled and that the number of journalists vastly exceeded the regular employment available. This pattern characterized most of the continental countries and explains much of the political intensity with which professional people set the stage for the revolutions of 1848 and then seized their direction.

Most professional people were not explicitly revolutionary. There were some, to be sure, and it was true that most declared revolutionaries were drawn from the professional classes. Auguste Blanqui was the son of a French university professor and the brother of a leading economist, but he devoted his life to the cause of revolution.[41] He helped organize the Society of the Seasons at the end of the 1830s, a rigorously secret organization divided into cells and run on a hierarchical basis. His revolutionary preaching and his organizational ideas inspired a number of contemporaries and influenced later, more successful practitioners such as Lenin. Blanqui and other agitators attempted a number of risings prior to 1848 that may have shaken the political order somewhat. They were active also in 1848. But the explicit revolutionaries were not representative of most profes-

41. See Samuel Bernstein, *Auguste Blanqui and the Art of Insurrection* (London, 1971).

sional people and their effectiveness was often quite limited. The pre-1848 efforts of Blanqui, or of Giuseppe Mazzini in Italy— trained as a lawyer—were easily put down, demonstrating that intent alone could not start a revolution. Even during 1848 many of the revolutionaries found scant room to maneuver. We must attend to their activities during the course of the uprisings, but we need not consider them as a major factor in causing the outbreaks.

The more general disgruntlement of professional people, on the other hand, played a direct role. Professional people flocked to the banquets in France that demanded an expanded suffrage; these in turn provided the immediate spur to revolution. These professional people had not advocated revolution but they were not averse to using it. Similar groups surged to the fore in the Central European risings. The Frankfurt assembly, called by German nationalists, was dominated by lawyers, professors, and civil servants—the latter constituting 20 percent of the total. So was the Prussian parliament elected in a system of near-universal manhood suffrage in 1849; 42 percent of the deputies were bureaucrats. In a real sense, then, the political revolutions of 1848, riding on the back of lower-class agitation, were revolutions of professional people, not of the whole middle class. Too much insistence on this distinction can seem otiose, but it is essential to recognize that the middle class was profoundly divided in its level of political interest and in its commitment to significant change.

THREE *The Ideological Build-up and the Weakness of the Elite*

THE REVOLUTIONS OF 1848 were preceded by growing advocacy of a variety of political theories, all designed to alter the existing order. The outpouring of ideas was a vital element in causing the revolutions and in influencing their course. They combined with political and economic grievances to spur professional people and to a lesser extent other elements of the middle and lower classes.

There were three main strands in the ideologies of protest, with socialism a significant lesser theme. One was liberalism. Liberals sought a genuinely representative government, based on limited suffrage—only those with property and education should vote. They wanted protection for freedoms of thought, speech, publication, and assembly. They wanted efficient government, run by men chosen for their talents, not their birth or status. They wanted full equality under the laws. They favored economic development, and intended to eradicate legal restrictions on economic change. These goals inevitably brought them into conflict with the existing order, even in France where the regime had been created under the auspices of a moderate liberalism. But despite its far-reaching purposes, liberalism was decidedly ambiguous as a revolutionary doctrine. While seeking freedom it also defended rights of property, which revolutions could so easily challenge. More than this, liberals believed in human reason and the possibility of progress through education. As men became more enlightened, the social and political structure would inevitably improve. This reliance on evolutionary methods, on persuasion, was heightened by what liberals saw as the results of the revolution of 1789 in France: launched with all good intentions, the revolution had led to bloody chaos and then to dictatorship, to the antithesis of liberal values. Liberals would participate in revolutions once begun, but they remained nervous about revolutionary methods.[42]

Shading off from liberalism, and much more prominent in the revolutionary ideological currents of the 1840s, was political radicalism. Radicals did not produce a terribly distinctive or organized set of doctrines. In a sense they operated in a liberal tradition, and they certainly wanted the same things the liberals wanted. But they were fairly clearly marked off from the liberals because they wanted more besides. Most of them were democrats, and all wanted a wide suffrage. Most of them, particularly in France and Italy, wanted a republic. They were not socialists but they were concerned about economic injustice and talked of the need for social reform to protect the working classes.[43]

Nationalism was the other main current in the political ideologies of the day.[44] Nationalists sought to promote the national culture, defined primarily in terms of language and historical heritage, and to equate political structure with this culture. In Germany and Italy, this meant some form of unification of existing subnational states; in Italy, it involved driving out Austria, which governed Lombardy and Venetia and influenced the states of the central part of the peninsula. In the other Habsburg lands nationalists could argue for breaking up the empire in favor of independent national states, but in fact only some of the Hungarian nationalists went so far. Most Slavic nationalists, particularly the Czechs, who were most articulate at this point, sought some system of national autonomy within the empire. But against even this moderate approach was the impulse of German nation-

---

42. Guido de Ruggiero, *A History of European Liberalism* (Boston, 1959), 158–248.
43. Georges Weill, *Histoire du parti républicain en France (1814–1870)* (Paris, 1928), 138–187.
44. See Hans Kohn, *The Idea of Nationalism: A Study of Its Origins and Background* (New York, 1961); Boyd Shafer, *Nationalism: Myth and Reality* (New York, 1955); Theodor Schieder, ed., *Sozialstruktur und Organisation europäischer Nationalbewegungen* (Munich, 1971).

alists in Austria to preserve the empire with the German interest proponderant. Obviously, even in theory, nationalists easily ran afoul of each other. But most nationalists believed, in principle, that each nation should have its place in the sun. They purported not to vaunt their own nation at the expense of others. Each united, independent nation would allow its people to make their maximum contribution to the general good of humanity. Nationalism thus meant general progress. It was also compatible with liberal or radical political goals within the state. With national independence would come parliaments and individual rights and, according to the radical nationalists, democracy and social reform as well.

For most nationalists, national and liberal or radical goals were part of the same package. They saw no contradictions. And yet there were some conflicts in theory that deserve attention. First, the nationalist obviously believed in the importance of a unity above the individual. The liberal looked to the individual first of all. Mazzini, the most articulate of the nationalist theorists, made this distinction explicit when he wrote of the primacy of individual duties to the nation.[45] The nation would grant liberty as well, but at its pleasure and with the good of the whole—and not merely the sum of the individual parts—in mind. There was further the related question of which was to come first, liberal or national goals. To the nationalist there was no doubt: national independence or unity had priority, for without this liberal gains were impossible and/or meaningless. That this raised potential problems when political choices had to be made was not recognized, for it was assumed that all goals could be achieved. But if choices were necessary, nationalist writers like Mazzini had already signaled what would be preferred.

Underlying all the political ideologies, including also much of socialism, was the enthusiasm of romanticism, now in its final glow. Romanticism almost defies definition. It was not necessarily political at all, and certainly lent itself to almost any political current.[46] But most romantics by the 1840s were radical and

45. Gaetano Salvemini, *Mazzini* (Stanford, 1957).
46. Arthur O. Lovejoy, "On the Discrimination of Romanticisms," in Arthur O. Lovejoy, ed., *Essays in the History of Ideas* (Baltimore, 1948), 232–253; George L. Mosse, *The Culture of Western Europe* (Chicago, 1961), 13–41.

nationalist in addition to being interested in new forms of artistic expression. This lent a great enthusiasm to the ideas being advocated. These romantics believed in the power of the human spirit and in the forces of history. They admired action and great deeds. They scorned dull, calculating regimes. In these ways romanticism was a great fillip for revolutionary action. Yet romanticism encouraged also a certain vagueness about method and detail. Carl Schurz described how German students in the 1840s were captivated by the romantic poets who praised the fatherland, using images of Teutonic knights in armor. But he added: "By what means the dreams of liberty and unity were to become accomplished—whether as [Georg] Herwegh advised in one of his poems, which we all knew by heart, we were to tear the iron crucifixes out of the ground and forge them into swords, we were not at all clear in our thoughts." [47] Historians partisan to romanticism quite properly advise us not to confuse the movement with words like "unrealistic" or "impractical".[48] Yet it is impossible to avoid the impression that students and others, including revolutionary leaders such as the romantic poet Lamartine, derived from the romantic spirit a tendency to leap from the desire to the act without much planning in between. On the other hand, without this they might not have been drawn into the excitement of the revolution at all.

The ideological build-up was most overt in France, during the 1840s, for some freedom of expression was possible here. Nationalism played only an indirect role, since France was a unified, independent country. But French nationalism was an active force, inherited from the great revolution. It saw France leading the peoples of Europe to freedom. It wanted glory for France, glory by the example of a revolutionary France but glory also by French arms expelling the oppressors from Europe. The July Monarchy, though created by the 1830 revolution, fell far short of these goals. Lamartine claimed "France is bored" as the government pursued a very tame foreign policy, seeking to content French dreams of glory by completing the contruction of the Napoleonic Arch of Triumph and bringing Napoleon's body back for burial in Paris and, for those whose dreams went even further back, by

47. Carl Schurz, *Reminiscences* (New York, 1887), 73.
48. Jacques Barzun, *Classic, Romantic, and Modern* (Boston, 1961), *passim*.

refurbishing Louis XIV's palace at Versailles. How widely nationalist or patriotic discontent spread in France, how many Frenchmen were bored, is not easy to determine. Radical and socialist
commentary was more explicit in criticizing the regime's internal
failings during the 1840s. But the various strands easily intertwined.

The most obvious sign of intellectual ferment in France in fact
appealed directly to France's revolutionary-nationalist tradition.
A spate of histories of the great revolution appeared in the 1840s,
most of them focused on the more radical phases. Robespierre's
writings were edited. Louis Blanc and other socialists wrote sympathetic histories, recalling the socialist agitation of Babeuf and
the meaning of the revolution to the common people. Jules
Michelet, a distinguished scholar and an immensely popular
teacher at the Collège de France who was dismissed just before
the 1848 outbreak, wrote a glowing tribute to the revolution as
the expression of the peoples' spirit. For him the revolution was
a stirring epic of liberty and democracy. Lamartine, who turned
republican in 1843 and was disgusted with the July Monarchy,
made his massive *History of the Girondists* more directly propa-
gandistic, claiming that "France is revolutionary or it is nothing.
The Revolution of 1789 is her political religion." Within three
months of publication 25,000 copies of his eight volumes had
been sold. Even Adolphe Thiers, at one time a minister under
Louis Philippe but now out of favor, came up with a history of
Napoleon's regime, stressing his glorious deeds on the battlefield.

It was also in the 1840s that the new wave of socialist writers,
such as Proudhon and Louis Blanc, began publishing widely. In
1840 Blanc wrote his *History of Ten Years,* a bitter condemnation
of the July Monarchy's failure to live up to its stated principles.

Books and pamphlets poured from the pens of romantics,
radicals, and socialists, directly or indirectly attacking the existing
order. A number of new newspapers also took up the cry, despite
the limitations by censorship. Of central importance was *La
Réforme,* founded in 1843 by Blanc, the scientist François Arago,
and Alexandre Ledru-Rollin, a wealthy Parisian lawyer. This
paper, which quickly received wide attention not only in France
but abroad, advocated universal suffrage and a republic, which
would in turn allow the lower classes to transform society through

political action. It called for some specific social reforms, toward guaranteeing employment and protecting workers on the job, but its main thrust was directed at a complete revamping of the political structure.

Vienna was a center of cultural activity during the two decades prior to 1848, yet its writers and poets suffered from the preliminary censorship required of all publications. Not surprisingly, they found ways to make their views known. The poet Franz Grillparzer wrote essays criticizing Metternich. Anastasius Grün (the pseudonym of Count Anton Alexander von Auersberg, a liberal aristocrat) published his *Rambles of a Viennese Poet* in 1831, nostalgically recalling the enlightened, reforming period of Joseph II. Discontent mounted in the 1840s as the country showed no signs of reform and lagged behind the economic development of Germany and Western Europe. Many critical writings were published in Leipzig or Hamburg and then smuggled in. Baron Victor von Andrian-Werburg, in *Austria and Her Future*, castigated the policy of repression and declared the empire "a lifeless mummy." Published anonymously by a government official, the book knowledgeably attacked the financial inefficiency of the state, urging a system of provincial estates crowned by an imperial diet to introduce reforms. Like many German liberals, Andrian admired the British constitution and sought to adapt it to the situation in the empire. Also in the 1840s a number of groups formed to advocate similar ideas. A writers' association petitioned for the abolition of censorship in 1845. The Juridical-Political Reading Society, designed to enable university and government personnel to keep up with foreign political writings, formed in 1841. It included lawyers, professors, military officers as well as civil officials and it naturally paid particular attention to French and British publications, which presented not only doctrines but also information on reform efforts in each country. This group, despite its lack of any political program, helped circulate new ideas and prepared the sort of people who would take charge of the revolution of 1848. Meanwhile, the circulation of clandestine publications aroused a wider audience and, in some, deeper passions.[49]

Liberal writings spread also in Hungary. Publications by

49. See R. John Rath, *The Viennese Revolution of 1848* (Austin, 1957).

Count István Széchenyi, a huge landowner, urged liberal reforms in the interest of preventing a peasant uprising. His views also gained prominence among the nobles who met in county assemblies and the national diet which helped represent the great nobles and the massive gentry against the Viennese government. In the 1840s leadership in the diet was taken over by Lajos Kossuth, a brilliant writer and orator who was a vigorous liberal and nationalist. Imprisoned for seditious activity, Kossuth learned English and read widely in English, French, and American political materials. After his sentence he became editor of the *Budapest Gazette,* which urged liberal and democratic reforms. Translation of a number of studies of the United States, including Tocqueville's *Democracy in America,* fanned the growing political radicalism. At the same time Kossuth's nationalism became more extreme, for he urged complete independence for Hungary. Other intellectuals, siding with Kossuth against the more moderate Széchenyi, also wrote about Hungary's peasant problem, advocating dramatic reforms.

Liberal and nationalist ideas spread elsewhere in Eastern Europe. A secret liberal society formed in Rumania in 1843, while nationalist publications spread. Rumanian students in Paris organized a group in 1845; inspired by their belief in democracy and nationalism, some participated in the French revolution in 1848, and many tried to duplicate the event in Rumania later in the year. Nationalism spread more widely among Czech intellectuals. A major Czech cultural revival began around 1825. Poets and historians praised their country's past and urged cooperation among Slavic peoples. The poet Jan Kollár predicted that within a century "flood-like, Slavic life will inundate everything, expanding its influence everywhere." The historian František Palacký, the secretary of the National Academy in Prague, gave Czech nationalism a political turn. His *History of the Czech People,* the first three volumes of which appeared between 1836 and 1848, recalled Czech independence and urged a new defense of historic rights. Under Palacký's sponsorship, Karel Havlíček, who became editor of the *Prague Gazette* in 1846, urged Czech equality with Germans in the Habsburg monarchy. He founded the Czech Repeal Club in 1847 to press for legal reform toward the federal reorganization of the empire on national lines. Nationalist plays and pamphlets, plus civic clubs created to further projects such as a national theater, proliferated. As in Hungary, nationalism had clearly fired the imagination of Czech intellectuals and many in the upper classes. Nationalist writings and organizations also developed among the Slovaks and among the South Slavs, the Slovenes, and particularly the Croats.[50]

Intellectual ferment in Italy had peaked in the 1830s, when Mazzini formed the radical, nationalist Young Italy movement to fight for independence from Austria. But Mazzini was then exiled to London and, while he continued to write, his influence dwindled and the Young Italy movement virtually disappeared. Liberal writings in the 1840s were more moderate. Vincenzo Gioberti published *Concerning the Moral and Civil Primacy of the Italians* in 1843. He stressed Italy's glorious past, attacking French culture and claiming Italian preeminence in virtually all fields of endeavor. Gioberti was not one to stint on the nationalist principle. But instead of a centralized Italy he urged a federation under the leadership of the pope. Other nationalist publications shortly before 1848 discussed peaceful means of getting the Austrians out of the peninsula. Nationalism undoubtedly spread widely; there were riots against Austrian troops in Ferrara in 1847, and popular pressure built up for further action. In 1847 liberals were also encouraged by a visit from the British reformer Richard Cobden, who urged peaceful change. But, in Italy, there was no particular concentration of intellectual activity right before the revolution, although a growing political excitement after 1846 to some extent substituted. Yet most intellectuals were agreed on the need for change, and throughout the decade they corresponded actively among themselves and met periodically, particularly at national scholarly conferences that began in 1839.[51]

In Germany, where nationalism was more shallowly rooted because of the absence of foreign ocupation, the 1840s did see a

50. See Robert Kann, *The Multinational Empire: Nationalism and National Reform in the Hapsburg Monarchy, 1848–1918* (2 vols., New York, 1951).
51. Greenfield, *Economics and Liberalism;* G. F. H. Berkeley, *Italy in the Making* (Cambridge, 1932–40), II, *passim.*

great increase in political discussion. In the states of southwestern Germany, Baden and Württemberg, liberals could criticize the governments in parliament. They also published elaborate political tracts, such as the *Political Encyclopedia* edited by Karl von Rotteck and Karl Theodor Welcker, urging liberal doctrines. In 1847 two radical members of the Baden parliament, Friedrich Hecker and Gustav Struve, called a meeting near Frankfurt which advocated a democratically elected federal parliament, freedom of the press and education, free public education, and a variety of social reforms including a progressive income tax. More moderate liberals met later in the year to urge more limited reforms. Such activities were impossible in Prussia itself. But in 1842 liberal industrialists, many of whom had been educated in France and England, founded the *Rhenish Gazette,* which advocated progressive economic and political doctrines. This was suppressed, however, in 1843 and most political commentary came from outside the country or through underground publications. Heinrich Heine, writing from Paris, attacked German complacency and urged his countrymen to take action on their grievances, and many other poets and pamphleteers worked in Paris. Karl Marx's *Communist Manifesto,* published early in 1848, was a more detailed program issued in exile. More influential were unauthorized publications within Prussia itself, which included even a clandestine press directed toward the working class. Nationalist songs and poems circulated widely among students. And word of mouth kept nationalist and liberal doctrines alive. Student groups, ostensibly social in nature, were fervently nationalist. Carl Schurz describes the mood: " 'God, Liberty, Fatherland' had still remained the common watchword; we still wore the prohibited black-red-gold ribbon under our coats." Scholarly conferences on a national level, which began first in 1822, also encouraged the nationalist spirit. Scientists, philologists, doctors all had their groups, which could easily take up political topics. Even more obviously political was the Conference of University Teachers of German Law, German History, and German Language, which first met in 1846.

Throughout Western and Central Europe, the new ideas circulated widely despite the barriers erected against them. By importing books from abroad, publishing secretly, or conveying ideas through veiled references, the message got across. Newspapers in most countries expressed discontent. Discussion groups and even formal organizations were hard to stop. Censorship was a barrier, and dissidents were arrested and jailed. But the movement was not halted. The ideas spread mainly among professional people, beyond the ranks of intellectuals themselves. There is little evidence of popular interest in nationalism, except for the anti-Austrian sentiment in Italy which was more xenophobic than positively nationalistic. The limitations of interest in radicalism and socialism have already been discussed. But the various protest ideologies reached enough people to provide a challenge to existing regimes and a deeply felt motivation to revolt. Moreover the institutions set up to spread ideas not only educated but also trained people to organize. They prepared leaders. The editorial board of *La Réforme* easily entered the revolutionary government. Discussion groups such as the Reading Society in Vienna acquainted potential leaders with each other. Precisely because some careful planning was required to circulate ideas, given official opposition, the effort provided some practical political experience.

Almost none of the main ideologies was explicitly revolutionary, however; most radicals and nationalists talked about pressure and bargains on the eve of 1848. The historian Gervinus urged the Conference of University Teachers to seek "change without violence, through legalism and the power of the spirit." Italian liberals looked to King Charles Albert of Piedmont to lead in driving the Austrians out of Italy, though the king was no liberal. They were cheered also by the election of the liberal Pius IX as pope in 1846. Czech nationalists wanted peaceful reform. Dissidents throughout Central Europe were profoundly impressed by the success of Daniel O'Connell's peaceful agitation for Catholic emanicpation in Ireland and the more recent triumph, through propaganda and petitions, of the Anti-Corn Law League in Britain. Nor were radicals of *La Réforme* revolutionary; they too sought a peaceful victory. There was little theoretical basis for revolutionary effort in any of the main isms, including utopian socialism. Quite obviously this did not prevent revolutions, but it did condition the efforts of intellectuals as they sought to master a situation which they had only indirectly called into being.

THE REVOLUTIONARY CAST OF CHARACTERS

The significance of ideology in the revolutions is obvious even in a preliminary and partial look at the people who became revolutionary leaders. They shared important elements in terms of social background, as more came from the middle classes than from any other group. Above all, however, almost all of them had a distinctive ideological motivation that pushed them toward the top, once the revolutions had begun.

Three men are particularly representative of liberal leadership, though they only begin a long list of liberals who became involved. Ludolf Camphausen (1803–1890) was a banker from Cologne, from a well-established upper-class family. He had long been active in political and social questions. He was unusual among German businessmen in favoring free trade and a vigorous competitive system, though he wanted government to help those who were harmed by excessive competition for profits. Camphausen was drawn to the problems of the lower classes by the riots in Silesia during the mid-1840s, though he had few remedies to propose. In a speech in 1847 he blamed the distress of the poor on population growth and industrialization, but his remedy was freer international competition which would benefit the public by reducing inefficiencies. He assumed that this competition would prevent the spread of factories in Germany— liberalism for him was a means of preserving the social status quo. He also urged, in 1847, that the government distribute money to the poor, to encourage their social stability. Camphausen thus combined liberalism with a sense of *noblesse oblige,* the obligation of the upper classes to help the lower. His reputation for liberalism plus his obvious devotion to the existing social structure made him an ideal appointment to the Prussian cabinet that King Frederick William granted during the first days of the March revolution. Just as predictably, Camphausen could not control the forces that had produced the revolution and he resigned within a few months.

Camillo di Cavour (1810–1861) was a liberal of a different sort, who saw political reform as an instrument of economic progress. The younger son of a Piedmontese noble family, he too was a man of great wealth, which he steadily increased; Cavour imbibed his liberalism through extensive travels in France and England. The French Revolution of 1830 showed him that liberty and monarchy were compatible, while England taught him the benefits of free trade and industrialization. Between 1835 and 1848 Cavour led in the introduction of scientific farming in Piedmont, and was also active in banking, the chemical industry, and the development of steamboats. He further organized the first railroad in Piedmont. With his liberal views and his great influence, he easily became a leading adviser to the king during the revolution. It was he who persuaded Charles Albert to grant political reforms. He also encouraged Piedmont's participation in the nationalist struggle, for while he was no ardent Italian nationalist he did see greater unity as part of the progressive cause. Cavour's great days were yet to come, of course. His liberalism, more progressive than that of Camphausen, had a longer future. Cavour was made chief minister in 1851, and began the process which did lead to Italian unity a decade later.

Odilon Barrot (1791–1873) was yet another kind of liberal. Born in a provincial town in France, he never considered a business career. He was trained as a lawyer and early entered government service, serving as a bureaucrat in the early days of the July Monarchy. Barrot's liberalism was a matter of impulse, not of doctrine or principle. Indeed an acquaintance noted that "in the realm of ideas he was always a day late; he used to think profoundly about nothing." But he was popular with crowds, for he had a fine voice and gestured impressively, and he had a vigorous sense of self-interest. Excluded from the government in the 1840s, he led opposition forces in parliament and by 1847 was calling for a liberal reform of the suffrage. It was Barrot who organized the banquet campaigns that in turn triggered the revolution. As a liberal, Barrot had no voice in the revolutionary government but when a more moderate mood prevailed, after June 1848, he regained some importance as a parliamentary leader, battling the radicals who insisted on democracy and always seeking the appropriate position for himself.

Liberals undoubtedly had a larger constituency among the politically articulate segments of the middle class than radicals did, but during the effervescence of the revolution the radical leaders were more numerous and more important. In France, Alphonse de Lamartine (1790–1869) stood somewhat between the two groups. It was Lamartine who assumed the leadership of the revolution in France, having been in opposition to the July Monarchy as a rather isolated member of parliament during the 1840s. Lamartine was a poet of great renown, specializing in the kind of elegiac melancholy that characterized many romantic writers. Lamartine started his career as a political conservative, but moved steadily left during the 1830s. Yet even by 1848 he had not decided whether or not democracy was desirable. He wanted reform but he was vague on the details, and he shunned any challenge to the existing order. He wrote winningly of the sorrows and beauty of the life led by the common people, but he had little concrete notion of serving them. Hence as head of the government, Lamartine tried mainly to hold the line against social change, aided initially by his ability to appeal to the crowds. But his popularity steadily declined, as more genuine radicals blamed him for the failures of the revolution while conservatives attacked him for inept leadership. Always the intellectual seeking to prove himself in action, Lamartine tried for the presidency of the republic that the revolution had established, and failed. Bitter, he spent much of the rest of his life in exile and died in poverty.

Gustav Struve (1805–1870) was a much more thoroughgoing radical—indeed he wanted the *von* omitted from his name as a sign of his devotion to equality. He was a journalist and a long-standing advocate of republicanism. Like many republican leaders in Germany, Struve was obstinate, even fanatical—not for him a policy of compromise. He was driven by political passion. He took no care for his appearance, leaving his beard uncombed. Struve drank no wine, ate no meat, and bathed in cold water. When he married he sought an unpassionate woman, and though there is no clear record of his success in this regard he chose a wife who served him well in politics. When Struve led the several radical risings in Baden during the revolution of 1848 she helped supply his armies and organized a nursing corps. But Struve himself was less well organized. He knew his political goals; he knew that the established system and its leaders had to be toppled. But he did not know how to carry out the effort. He believed stories fed him by political spies. He left incriminating papers about, which in one case led to the arrest of a close associate. As a military leader he once ordered troops armed only with scythes to attack a regular military force. And when his rebellion failed he could not understand why.

Adolf Fischhof (1818–1893), one of the chief radical leaders in Vienna, was far more effective. Fischhof, a Jew, was an assistant physician in obstetrics at the Vienna General Hospital when the revolution broke out. Here clearly was the kind of younger professional person who could easily be pulled into a revolutionary movement. Fischhof's hospital cared for up to 3000 patients a day, but it had only thirty-six doctors on the staff. A young physician could easily sympathize with the plight of the poor, and his own position was hardly enviable, for he earned less than forty cents a day. Fischhof had been raised in Hungary, and entered medicine mainly because Jews were barred from other professions. But he read widely in politics, and became a political philosopher of some importance. In 1848 he was only three years out of medical school, but came to prominence by urging the crowds gathered in the early days of the revolution to press for political reforms.

Like the radicals, with whom they shared many ideas, nationalist leaders varied widely in their practical organizing abilities. Giuseppe Mazzini (1805–1872) was above all a theorist, although he had earlier, in the 1830s, contributed to revolutionary practice by urging that revolutionary nationalists organize in small, secret cells. Mazzini was born in Genoa and educated to be a lawyer, but his early opposition to Austrian domination in northern Italy and his advocacy of Italian rebirth and unity forced him into exile to avoid arrest. It was mainly in England that he developed his theories of nationalism. But he had the makings of a popular leader as well, as he demonstrated when he returned to Italy in 1848–49. His appearance was striking and he had an infectious enthusiasm. But he was driven by his ideology, and after a brief attempt at pragmatism in Milan, when he tried to urge compromise and moderation, he gave full vent to his desire for revolutionary purity. He was, as a result, an inspirational leader during the 1849 revolt in Rome, but he could not win the populace to his goal of a final glorious struggle once it became obvious that defeat was inevitable. Mazzini returned to exile, where he played a significant role among radicals in England.

Lajos Kossuth (1802–1894), the leader of the Hungarian revolution, lacked Mazzini's broad philosophy, but his dedication to the Hungarian nation was as intense as Mazzini's to Italy. Kossuth came from a poor noble family. He was a Slovak, but he saw that Magyar nationalism was the only real cultural force in Hungary and it was for this that he worked. Like so many radical leaders, Kossuth was a magnificent orator with a magnetic personality. He was also a good organizer, as his work in the revolution was to demonstrate. He had edited two newspapers at various times before the revolution, one of them the first paper established in Hungary; his journalism had brought him a jail sentence. He had also served as delegate to the Hungarian diet, and it was from this position that he sparked the revolt against Habsburg domination. Like Mazzini, Kossuth saw national freedom as more than an end in itself, advocating social justice; but he was willing to compromise social reform for the nationalist cause in the short run.

Finally, though their role was less significant, there were socialist leaders. Louis Blanc (1811–1882) was the most renowned proponent of socialism in France, and his views propelled him into the thick of the revolutionary struggle even though he had not advocated violence to achieve his goals. Blanc was the son of a French official, but like many people of modest professional background he had great difficulty establishing himself in life. Eventually he won a position as tutor to the sons of a rising manufacturer, which roused his interest in the situation of the workers. He soon moved into journalism, and began writing denunciations of the existing political regime which won wide notice. But his chief target was capitalist competition, which left the poor deprived and the rich always fearful of attack. Blanc was more than a crusader against injustice; he had a personal ax to grind: Blanc was extremely short, only a bit taller than a dwarf, and even contemporaries, without any complex psychological interpretations, saw that his war on capitalism involved more than ideas. Blanc, although initially popular with the Parisian crowds because of his writings—the crowds carried the small man into the meeting of the first revolutionary government and required that he be included—was not at home with crowd action. He proved easily intimidated and at several key points failed to provide the leadership that the Parisians sought. And like other radical leaders—Mazzini and Kossuth most obviously—Blanc had a pronounced authoritarian streak. It was he who should organize democracy, his own way. This streak may be essential in a successful revolutionary leader; when it is combined with uncertainty about tactics, as with Blanc, it proves disastrous.

Stefan Born (1824–98), who came to be a leader of working-class forces in Berlin, had a more enduring impact on socialism than did Louis Blanc. Born was a printer, extremely interested in education and ideas. While an apprentice he had listened to lectures at the University of Berlin during lunch hours. Like many young artisans he traveled about for a year, in 1847, going to Belgium, France, and Switzerland. This brought him into contact with more advanced ideas. It was in Paris that he met Karl Marx and Friedrich Engels, who were to support him during the revolution (though they later turned against him bitterly). Back in Berlin, Born organized a workers' party before the revolution, insisting that workers "take our affairs into our own hands." Attracting mainly other skilled artisans, Born contributed a solid organizational effort to the revolution, traces of which survived into the 1850s. Born was actually somewhat suspicious of direct revolutionary violence, preferring to work through association and education. After the Berlin rising was suppressed, Born went on to Leipzig where again he organized a workers' club as part of the radical revolt of 1849. When this was crushed in turn, Born escaped to Switzerland, where he became a professor. His legacy to the workers' cause remained important, for he was basically fighting for human dignity; as he said about his Berlin organization, "We want a club in order to become men."

Such were some of the key revolutionary leaders. Many of them shared a roughly common social background, for the professions bred most of them. Except perhaps for Odilon Barrot, they shared also a certain element of ideological inspiration, whatever their other reasons for action; in some this went to the point of fanaticism. But their ideas were extremely diverse, in some ways more diverse than their other characteristics. Here was one obvious source of weakness in the revolutionary forces. Furthermore, none of the leaders, of whatever ideological stripe, proved capable of harnessing the full force of the revolutionary sentiment. They could make contact with the aspirations of the masses, but they could not express their aspirations fully. Here, in a concrete sense, is where the social and the ideological impulses behind the revolution split.

WEAKNESS AT THE TOP

Intellectual ferment helped prepare the revolutions and give them direction. Lower-class elements made the revolutions. One other ingredient must be briefly discussed, for all the revolutions could have been easily suppressed. Serious outbreaks had been beaten down in France on a number of occasions during the 1830s. The Prussian government had torn down workers' barricades in Berlin during the previous year. It is true that the system of fighting on the barricades was relatively new—it was first extensively used in Paris in 1830. Protected by mounds of torn-up street paving and other materials, revolutionaries were hard to get at.

It was also true that some uncertainty existed about the reliability of the common soldiers who had to be used against any uprising. Trained riot police were not available in any numbers, and indeed police forces of any sort were small in number. There were only a handful of police in the whole city of Berlin, and these were used against criminals. Vienna had 1200 paramilitary police, but they stood aloof in 1848, their commander believing that large-scale riots were up to the army. Paris, better supplied with a Municipal Guard of 1500 men, also depended on other forces to deal with more than minor unrest.[52] Hence most governments relied on the regular army to repress the kind of agitation that arose in 1848, and common soldiers had been known to refuse to fire on their fellow citizens. A special situation existed in Paris, where the National Guard, 80,000 strong and recruited primarily from the middle classes, had the main responsibility for keeping order. The Guard, which had performed well in the 1830s, had grown more and more disenchanted with the July Monarchy and could not be counted upon any longer. But even in Paris there were also 30,000 garrison troops. All the major governments had sufficient military force to suppress the rebellions quickly. In Berlin the troops were well on the way to a brutal but effective repression when they were called off. In Vienna and Paris the troops never received clear directives at all, and quickly became demoralized. Most governments, then, did not even try to use the force at their command. Their failure of will was remarkable.

The suddenness of the revolutionary outbreaks found most. statesmen unprepared. Governments were accustomed to lower-class unrest during hard times, so the agitation during 1846 and 1847 was not taken seriously. The fact that the middle-class groups, to which the governments did pay close attention, were not overtly revolutionary further reduced the sense of danger. Conservative statesmen from Metternich on, basing their judgments on the French Revolution, had seen the middle classes as the main threat to order. Earlier organizations, like the Italian Carbonari, that were at once revolutionary and strongly middle class in character, made statesmen actively wary. Such groups had largely disappeared, their leaders dead, in jail, or in exile, by the 1840s. It was still fashionable to speak of threats to the social fabric. Alexis de Tocqueville, a conservative though no friend to the July Monarchy, warned of revolution in a speech in January 1848, but he admitted later that he was not really so alarmed and that his warnings were a rhetorical device. The French monarch felt secure, claiming in that same month that none of the forces

52. Jean Tulard, *La Préfecture de police sous la monarchie de juillet* (Paris, 1964), 164 ff.

opposed to his regime could unseat him. Rulers in Central Europe had even more reason for confidence, for after all it was only the example of France, rather than spontaneous internal developments, that proved capable of provoking revolution at all.

Caught by surprise when the actual uprisings occurred, government reaction was affected by two other factors. The first was the personality of several of the key monarchs. Louis Philippe, wily though he was, had never firmly established the new Orleanist dynasty as he wished following his accession to power in 1830. He had long prepared for the eventuality of a change in fortune, investing heavily abroad. And he was growing old and increasingly inflexible—hence his unwillingness to compromise when the first disorder broke out. The Austrian emperor, although he had assumed the throne only in 1835, was positively feeble-minded. His advisers, including the aging Prince Metternich, resisted any change or reform, but lacked confidence that they could do more than delay an inevitable upheaval. When insurrection broke out, the council of state was divided, some urging concessions and delaying military repression, others, including Metternich, insisting on firm action. Amid such disputes the opportunity for firmness vanished.

Prussia had a newer ruler than most other states, but he too found it difficult to make effective decisions. Frederick William saw himself as the patriarch of his people. He could not believe they would rebel against him, long claiming that the rising was the work of foreign instigators. He wrote an emotional appeal "To my dear Berliners," urging them to dismantle the barricades and talk the situation over with him. But he was loath to use troops against his subjects and seized on unsubstantiated rumors that the barricades were coming down as an excuse to send his troops back to their quarters, against the urgings of most of his advisers. As a result the city was given over to the revolutionaries.

Old kings, weak kings—the weakness of most rulers owed something to accident but something perhaps to the problems of adjusting monarchical institutions to a changing world. Certainly Frederick William suffered from an outdated conception of his relations with his subjects.

Monarchs and their advisers were further hampered by the aura surrounding revolution, which derived from the powerful image of 1789 and had been fed by the periodic uprisings since the time. Unquestionably in France the mere fact of revolution had awesome implications. To any but the most confident in the existing regime, it seemed prudent to escape while escape was possible. Hence, with little ado, Louis Philippe and his ministers fled to England, avoiding the persecution and ultimate execution that had befallen their predecessors in the 1790s. The revolutionary image lacked this force elsewhere, but everywhere governments were manned by people who had lived through the great revolution and had been deeply surprised and shocked by it. They had devoted their lives to fighting against the forces of change, but for many it seemed a rearguard action. The revolution of 1789 was such an immense, searing experience that its thrust could easily seem inevitable. Faced with revolution in their own lands, many officials in 1848 found it natural to yield easily.

Unready governments, headed by indecisive rulers and doubtful about their own future, obviously facilitated the conversion of street fighting into full-scale revolution. But in many instances the weakness of the established regimes went deeper still. Everywhere the aristocracy, which was still the ruling class, was in trouble.[53] Its economic position was shaky, though by no means impossible. In Prussia the legislation of the early nineteenth century, encouraging market agriculture, created risks as well as opportunities for the landlords. Many aristocrats lacked the knowledge or capital to take advantage of the growing market for grains. Hence in eastern Prussia, the stronghold of the Junker aristocracy, a large number of estates were lost, sold out to more venturesome Junkers or to successful businessmen. In the Habsburg lands aristocrats had even greater difficulties adapting to the new conditions of agriculture. There was widespread uncertainty about the continued viability of the manorial system. Many landlords wondered if conversion to a free labor market, even at

53. Barrington Moore, *The Social Origins of Dictatorship and Democracy* (Boston, 1966), 45–61 and *passim*.

the expense of traditional dues and services, would not be to their benefit.[54] This kind of questioning about the basic social and legal order would delay the reaction of the ruling class to a revolutionary challenge.

The situation in France was even more confused. The aristocracy had made a considerable comeback economically, after 1815; much land had been reacquired. But, quite apart from the fact that France was not dominated by large estates, the aristocracy did not monopolize the big holdings. Many middle-class landlords had bought in. Similarly, at the political level, the aristocracy was no longer the undisputed ruling class. Many aristocrats had retired from government after the revolution of 1830. Others served still, but so did men from the middle classes, including many from the distinctive, nontitled landlord groups. There was the possibility here of forming a new ruling class, including elements of both new and old. But the process was far from complete. Aristocrats, or at least large numbers of them, still shunned the newer men, while the new men themselves had been unable to work out a sensible political self-definition.[55] Hence the government, despite the very limited suffrage, was compelled by the 1840s to rig elections and fill the parliament with state bureaucrats in order to assure loyalty. It depended less on a ruling class than on self-interested, corrupt cliques. As a result, when attacked by revolution, the regime found amazingly few defenders.

The states of Central Europe were not so vulnerable, but they had some comparable problems.[56] In Prussia the quality of the bureaucracy was deteriorating steadily. Senior officials, whether of aristocratic or middle-class origins, were bent on carving out a secure and prestigious place for themselves in society. They saw themselves as a distinctive class, but modeled on the landed aristocracy. Hence they thought less of service to the state than of defending, indeed expanding, the bureaucratic prerogatives. They enhanced the social gap between themselves

54. Blum, *Noble Landowners, passim.*
55. Higonnet and Higonnet, "Class, Corruption and Politics," 204 ff.
56. John Gillis, "Political Decay and the European Revolutions, 1789–1848," *World Politics* (1970), 344–370.

and junior officials. They enforced rules rigidly, without imagination. They were often lazy, devoting themselves to trivia. These developments fed revolutionary discontents, even within the bureaucracy. Also, the Prussian state was divided within itself, with hundreds of younger officials in the opposition. By the same token the response of senior officials to agitation was bound to be initially weak and ineffective.[57] A somewhat similar situation prevailed in the Habsburg lands, though here it was less a question of bureaucratic deterioration than of long-standing inefficiency.

Weakness and confusion at the top, then, were vital to the causation of the revolutions of 1848. Where regimes remained confident, revolutions did not occur. In Britain the government was sufficiently sure of itself to make concessions to middle-class demands and thereby begin the process of forming a new ruling elite. In Ireland the same government carefully positioned large military forces before trouble broke out, and showed no hesitation in using them as necessary. The Russian government was in a strongly repressive phase, which helps explain why no serious agitation occurred there in 1848. But in most other parts of Europe something of a circle had developed. Pressure from below fed uncertainties at the top, which favored still further pressure from below.

Yet some of the weakness at the top was superficial. We have all the advantages of hindsight here, in knowing that the revolutions of 1848 failed in many ways. But it is obvious that the ruling classes were not as vulnerable as their counterparts in France in 1789. Aristocrats had a sense of their own interests. They were not, in any large numbers, influenced by doctrines of political or religious dissent. Their economic situation was changing, but overall it remained solid, for agricultural production was growing in value. Existing governments, for their part, were far from paralysis. Most of them were financially solid, for example, in marked contrast to the French regime in 1789. What happened in 1848 was that most governments yielded some of the trappings of power, but did not yield its substance. This followed in part from the weaknesses and divisions within the revolu-

57. Gillis, *Prussian Bureaucracy*, 49 ff.

tionary ranks, but also in part from the continuing vitality of the established regimes.

It was perhaps a tragedy that revolution broke out in 1848, particularly in Central Europe. Governments were certainly unwilling to undertake reforms that would alter the basic social and political structure. In this they differed from England, where agitation before 1832 had produced an essentially new political system, albeit run by traditional political personnel. The unwillingness of Louis Philippe and his ministers to build even a really middle-class regime in France after 1830 was proof that revolution was necessary, and this was definitely the case in Central Europe. But governmental inefficiency had not yet gone far enough to incapacitate. The viability of the ruling class was not yet sufficiently dubious—not nearly so dubious as it would be a quarter-century later, when its economic base clearly began to erode. But there was enough weakness at the top, combined with unwillingness to grant reforms, for revolution to break out. Its ultimate failure reduced the chance of revolution later, when conditions might otherwise have been riper. But in the winter and early spring of 1848, victory seemed already at hand. Elated revolutionaries everywhere had their opponents on the run.

PART II THE REVOLUTIONARY OUTBURST

M OST OF the revolutions of 1848 broke out rather haphazardly. There was usually a brief, confused period of demands and demonstrations, during which governmental uncertainty helped prolong the tension. Street fighting by the lower classes and negotiations by middle-class elements converted agitation into some semblance of revolution. New governments were formed, and most sought a new basis of legitimacy.

As the revolutionary leaders tried to define and defend their achievements, pressure for radicalization quickly built up. This was a standard revolutionary phenomenon, but it developed with unusual rapidity during 1848. Growing ideological awareness—whether democratic, socialist, or nationalist—obviously furthered this process. Economic conditions worsened once again with the advent of revolution, for both agricultural and industrial producers reduced their output amid political uncertainty. So the lower classes were again goaded by despair.

Radicalization in its turn brought repression and the collapse or compromise of the political goals of the revolutionary leaders. This was another normal feature of revolutions, but again it was hastened during 1848. Because the lower classes were more articulate than in 1789 or even 1830, the property-owning revolutionaries took fright quickly. Their own knowledge of revolutionary "excesses" in the recent past, plus the lack of clear revolutionary targets for the owners of property, plus some ideological divisions—notably among different varieties of nationalists—strengthened their desire for repression of further disorder. Thereafter the established governing forces found maneuvering room and demonstrated great resiliencey. Increasingly they combined with the moderate revolutionaries to bring the active phase of revolution to a close.

The present narrative takes each of the major revolutions from its outbreak through the period of major activity. These were the months of high drama and high hopes, though the more prosaic period of revolutionary settlement is important as well. Although in a very general way the revolutions displayed a common dynamic, they must be discussed one by one, for each was distinctive in many respects. The nature of "radicalization," for example, differed from one case to the next. So did the speed of the whole process. In France the active revolutionary period lasted barely four months. With their rich revolutionary experience, all sides in the 1848 outbreak were able to define their positions almost immediately and the revolution moved toward a bloody climax. In Central Europe the process was slower and less definitive. In Italy and Hungary, where the revolution was really a war against foreign domination, the risings were put down only during 1849, on the field of battle.

FOUR

France: The Catalyst

REVOLUTION IN PARIS, for all its ultimate seriousness, began almost frivolously. Since the latter part of 1847, opposition political groups, led by parliamentary deputies like the lawyer Odilon Barrot, who wanted to open parliament to serious discussion and to shake the existing ministry's monopoly on political power, had sponsored a series of reform banquets in various French cities. Their particular target was François Guizot, who had controlled the ministry for almost eight years and was adept at rigging elections to obtain a docile parliament. They were supported by more radical groups, notably the *La Réforme* editors led by Ledru-Rollin. But even these groups saw the banquets as a lever for political reform, not as a first step in revolution. They wanted a more flexible political system, including an expansion of the suffrage which would enfranchise a larger segment of the middle class and would make elections harder to manipulate. A number of banquets in provincial cities drew enthusiastic support, particularly from professional people.[1] The government at first ignored the effort. Guizot was sure of parliamentary backing, having carefully engineered the election of deputies in 1846. The king rejected urgings even within his own family that Guizot be replaced with someone more flexible.

Early in 1848 the reformers scheduled a banquet for Paris, to be held on February 22, and they advertised it widely. The government feared that this was too close for comfort and refused to authorize the gathering, as they were empowered to do by a law which required permission for any meeting of more than six people. The government was particularly worried because the

1. J. J. Baughman, "The French Banquet Campaign of 1847–1848," *Journal of Modern History* (1959), 1–15; see also Georges Duveau, *1848: The Making of a Revolution* (New York, 1966).

reformers had lowered the prices for the banquet, to attract lower-middle-class attendance and create a truly massive spectacle. Then the government backed down to the extent of allowing a symbolic gathering in a well-to-do neighborhood near the Champs-Elysées. The police would close the banquet as soon as it began, allowing a test of the legality of such assemblies in the courts. At this point the bulk of the reformers wanted to call off the whole effort, lest it have unforeseen consequences, but the *La Réforme* group insisted on pressing forward. They urged the people of Paris to gather during the morning of the 22nd, on the Place de la Madeleine, and they proposed a grand procession before the banquet itself, inviting the National Guard as well as deputies, students, and journalists to parade to the banqueting hall. When they learned of these plans, most of the opposition, including many radical newspapers, urged that the whole effort be dropped. Not only did most politicians fear the possibility of revolution, but also they worried lest the government score a bloody triumph at the expense of the demonstrators. But a minority persisted, driven by their desire to challenge a government that they found repulsive. The poet Lamartine, who though an opposition deputy in parliament was aligned with no large group, declared his intention to go ahead with the parade even if he were accompanied only by his own shadow.

Posters, newspaper articles, and rumors, all circulating for many days before February 22, worked on the grievances and the simple curiosity of politically conscious Parisians. A sizable crowd gathered in the morning, despite bad weather, in the Place de la Madeleine. A group of students came over from the Left Bank, leading a contingent of parliamentary deputies, but were turned back by the police. This helped push the crowd toward acts of disorder. Individuals broke street lights, small groups overturned omnibuses, and there were some efforts to set up barricades. But all this was quite tentative still, and in the evening the troops, which had supported the police at some points, were sent back to their barracks.

On the following day, however, the crowds were larger. The weather was even worse than before, and it is no mean comment on the seriousness of the 1848 crowds that this was the first of the great revolutions in France to begin in the winter, when the common impulse was to stay at home and keep warm. The crowds also shifted ground; instead of gathering in the open streets of the new, wealthy section of Paris—the western quarters—they moved to the narrow streets of the center city, where troops could move less easily and barricades were more effective. The crowds were more aggressive as well. The day before they had shouted for reform and against Guizot; now they attacked Louis Philippe and his dynasty. The National Guard, on which the government relied for the preservation of order, refused its task and instead petitioned for reform. Even the units from the richest sections of Paris joined in, while those recruited from the poorer districts were quite radical in their demands. All insisted upon Guizot's resignation, and in the afternoon the king gave way, unceremoniously dismissing Guizot though failing to take the next logical step—appointing an opposition leader in his stead. Still the crowds surged through Paris, accompanied by National Guard units. The police and troops were confused and demoralized, particularly because of the Guard's defection. In the evening the inevitable occurred: a crowd clashed with a detachment of troops on the Boulevard des Capucines. The troops panicked and fired into the mob, killing or wounding forty or fifty people. The crowds were enraged over this "massacre" and paraded the dead through the city during the night. Rumors spread that the government planned to slaughter the working class, and as in other great revolutions rumor here both expressed and strengthened class resentments. The workers were now in full revolt. During the night they tore up over a million paving stones and cut down more than 4000 trees; by morning Paris was crisscrossed by over 1500 barricades.

Louis Philippe now tried to form a more liberal ministry, under Adolphe Thiers and Barrot. But Thiers was swept up by the crowds as he went to the Chamber of Deputies and was completely unnerved; he refused to take part in the parliamentary debates and scurried home. The crowds now insisted on more than a reform in the regime. The king tried to rally the army, but it proved impossible to communicate with some of the scattered garrisons, and many of the troops had already given their weapons to the insurgents. Louis Philippe decided to abdicate. He abandoned the royal palace in disguise, only minutes before the crowd attacked it, and was able to reach Le Havre and then England. His hope, which was taken up by Barrot and other moderates, was that his nine-year-old grandson, the Count of Paris, would be named king, with a liberal regent until the child came of age. Parliament enthusiastically accepted this scheme, but the deputies had no control over the situation. The crowds invaded the parliament building and dispersed the deputies. A radical minority of deputies remained, led by Lamartine, who proclaimed the republic and, amid great uproar, secured the approval of a provisional government. The revolution had won its first goals.

Up to this point the revolution was unusual in a number of respects. It had been remarkably bloodless. Less than four hundred people had been killed, eighty on the government side and about 290 from among the people. This reflected above all the weakness of the resistance. With the National Guard hostile to the regime and the army demoralized, there was virtually no military opposition to the crowds. Only the tough but small forces of the Municipal Guard were loyal. The regime had pitifully few natural defenders. It had failed to win the middle classes, yet, through the National Guard, it relied upon them in any crisis. It had not rallied France's natural conservatives. Many aristocrats ignored the regime entirely. Leading Catholics were lukewarm in their acceptance. Most bishops preferred the older Bourbon monarchy. Many churchmen resented restrictions which the July Monarchy had placed upon Catholic activities, notably in the field of education; a movement for "free schools"—that is, schools without government authorization—had won wide support even among conservative Catholics during the 1840s, and it was specifically directed against the educational policies of Louis Philippe's government. So, quite apart from the collapse of military resistance, the regime proved almost completely isolated. Never in France's history had a monarchy fallen so easily or with so little regret.

For its part, the crowd was unusually single-minded in its goal. Undoubtedly it was more politically aware than its counterparts in 1830 or 1789. It wanted an entirely new government. It did not set out against some of its traditional enemies. The aristocracy, at least those aristocrats visible in Paris, were no longer powerful enough to be worth attacking. The Church's antipathy toward the July Monarchy was well known, so there was no point in rushing against Catholic leaders. This was the only modern French revolution that was not fed by substantial anticlericalism. With rare exceptions the crowd attacked neither people nor property. It did invade the royal palace in the Tuileries, hurling the throne into the courtyard and wrecking the furniture. Clothing and other fineries were stolen. But this activity was obviously but an adjunct of the political focus. In the short run the crowd's political awareness was an obvious asset, for combined with the lack of resistance it enabled the crowd to win more political gains than ever before. In the longer run some questions might be raised. The old enemies were not as moribund as they seemed. And, beyond the leaders of the July Monarchy, the crowd had not clearly identified new targets. In February, and for several months thereafter, they sought major political change without directly attacking the groups, both old and new, who were bound to resist.

On February 24, the power of the crowd most obviously placed Lamartine, the self-appointed revolutionary leader, in something of a dilemma. Lamartine was a good speaker; he had a considerable reputation. But he was not one of history's leading political thinkers or tacticians. He had become convinced that a change of regime was necessary. He was not a little attracted by the chance at a major political role—how many thinkers can so suddenly become doers? But he had no clear plan for a future regime. He was not even a convinced republican or democrat, having fluctuated widely in his recommendations for suffrage reform in previous months.[2] Personal ambition and a flair for the dramatic aside, what motivated him on February 24 was above all a desire to avoid bloodshed and civil war. He spoke of leaving the decision about France's political future to "that sublime mystery of universal sovereignty." The provisional government was to arrange to consult this mystery and to tide

2. Gordon Wright, "A Poet in Politics: Lamartine in 1848," *History Today* (1958), 616–627.

things over until political issues were resolved. But the composition of this government was surprisingly moderate. Its president was the eighty-year-old Dupont de l'Eure, one of the only veterans of the great revolution available; he was only for show. Lamartine, as foreign minister, actually led the government while most other ministers were from the moderate wing of the opposition, mainly from the editorial board of the newspaper the *National*. Ledru-Rollin was the only leftist included.

The obvious question, posed during the afternoon of the 24th and repeatedly thereafter, was how a government whose goal was caretaking could manage a crowd whose goal was revolution. Late in the afternoon of February 24 Lamartine and his cohorts walked over to the Hôtel de Ville, where Parisian revolutions traditionally focused, lest the crowd set up a revolutionary government of its own. They were in time, but the crowd indisputably controlled the streets. The provisional government spent the remainder of the day and many days thereafter meeting delegations from the people and facing the milling crowds.

A number of concessions were granted, though in retrospect they seem surprisingly limited. On the 24th itself a group from *La Réforme,* headed by Louis Blanc, marched into the city hall and demanded representation in the government. It was finally agreed that Blanc and two colleagues, including a worker named Albert, would be added to the provisional government, though initially they were appointed as secretaries rather than full members. Unfortunately these appointments exacerbated divisions within the government without, as might have been expected, providing a real leadership element. Louis Blanc, though intelligent and articulate, had no clear plan for the installation of socialism and he failed to give clear direction to the crowds that supported him.

Still, for a day or so it seemed that the crowds could win genuine gains. The government proclaimed freedom of speech, association, and assembly. This was compatible with even moderately liberal political principles, but in the heady atmosphere of revolution it quickly encouraged an amazing proliferation of political organizations and newspapers. Release of former political prisoners, such as Louis Auguste Blanqui, who formed a radical club on February 28, the day he got out of jail, added to the effervescence. Even before this, the government came into conflict with the crowds about the nature of the new regime. Most of the ministers agreed that a republic was the only form of government now practical, but several, including Lamartine, were reluctant to proclaim it unilaterally; Lamartine argued that the whole country should be consulted in the matter. Not so the crowd: its delegates insisted on remaining in the council room until the government declared that it "wished" a republic now and decreed one, subject to ratification by a national vote. After this the crowd demanded adoption of the red flag, the banner of Parisian radicals in the Great Revolution and more recently the accepted color of socialism. Here Lamartine refused to back down, among other things because the government was advised that to do so would ruin their financial credit. In his finest hour he faced a hostile crowd, with muskets pointed at him, and won them to support of the tricolor which, he urged in an appeal to nationalist emotion, "has gone around the world in triumph." It was agreed that a red rosette would adorn the tricolor's flagstaff, while each member of the provisional government wore a similar rosette on his coat. With this issue settled on February 25, the worst pressure of the crowds diminished.

Other early measures established a new regime more concretely. Troops were withdrawn from the city and the hated Municipal Guard was disbanded. Marc Caussidière, a well-known member of revolutionary clubs, took over the police force and began to form a new Popular Guard from among newly released political prisoners. The government also recruited 24,000 young volunteers, who came from every section of Paris, to serve as a National Mobile Guard; each member was to be paid a franc and a half per day. The intention here was to develop an effective police force and to take some of the restless young men, many of them unemployed in any event, off the streets. Finally, the National Guard was expanded—its membership tripled between February and April—in part through the recruitment of working-class members. These new forces of order, which did prove willing to act against working-class demonstrations, were obviously a potent weapon for a government seeking to consolidate its power.

But what was to be consolidated? The situation in early March remained extremely confused. If the crowd receded, scores of radical newspapers and over a hundred clubs kept the sense of excitement high. The government was deeply divided. Its members ranged from conservative republicans who wanted only the mildest political change, through more radical types such as Ledru-Rollin, to the outright socialists. Many were personally antagonistic. Three, including Lamartine and Ledru-Rollin, paid political spies to keep tabs on their fellows. None had much administrative experience. No one was able to gain clear ascendancy, so that the various ministries operated rather separately, though often effectively.

Four principal issues, admittedly intertwined, faced the government now that the first revolutionary effervescence was over: diplomacy, finance, political consolidation, and the social question.

The diplomatic problems were not severe. Many governments expected revolutionary France, true to the traditions of the 1790s, to launch a war of conquest (or of liberation, depending on one's point of view). In fact Lamartine, as foreign minister, quite sensibly sought peace. But there was a great deal of pressure in Paris, particularly among the hordes of political émigrés, for an active foreign policy that would liberate captive nationalities like the Poles and the Italians, so Lamartine at first trod a bit warily. He issued a Manifesto to Europe which proclaimed that France did not accept the boundaries of 1815 but would abide by them in fact. He promised protection to legitimate nationalist movements but did nothing to carry this out. The Manifesto did encourage revolutionaries elsewhere, particularly in Italy, but it did not unduly disturb the established governments; and France remained passive, aside from verbal encouragement, when revolutions broke out in neighboring states. The government strengthened its armed forces, improving conditions for ordinary troops, but this did not lead to a bolder diplomacy. Correspondingly, France did not face major diplomatic problems.

The United States quickly recognized the new republic, while Britain assured France privately of support; there was no danger of foreign intervention, particularly after Russia was blocked off by the Central European risings in March. Thus France escaped one of the disturbing ingredients of many past revolutions which so often fed the fear of counterrevolution. At the same time the lack of an active diplomacy may have added to radical discontent with the new regime; the government lacked an obvious rallying point.

Financial crisis, another common revolutionary element, struck quickly. Business came to a standstill during the disorders at the end of February. Bankruptcies increased, employment fell, many banks had to close.[3] The government deficit mounted rapidly. Few in the government had much competence to deal with this problem, but, as good bourgeois, they were eager to assure the government's credit and to avoid the kind of deficit financing that had plagued France during the 1790s. So they raised taxes, levying a surtax of forty-five centimes on every franc paid in direct taxes. This meant an additional tax on the land, in fact, for only property owners paid direct taxes. Urban workers, whom the government still feared to antagonize, owned no property and so were not affected. But the financial crisis and the measures taken to meet it obviously enhanced the long-range problems of political consolidation.

From the first, Lamartine and most of his colleagues felt the need to consult the whole country about the nature of the new regime. Perhaps because the previous regime, installed basically by politicians in Paris, had failed so badly, they genuinely sought a clear basis of legitimacy. Presumably some kind of referendum was envisaged, possibly the election of a constitutional assembly, but the means were not initially clear. What the people wanted,. however, was clear, and on March 2 the government yielded to popular demand and decreed universal manhood suffrage. On March 5 elections to the Constituent Assembly were scheduled for April 9, with all males over twenty-one having the right to vote. At one sweep nine million people were enfranchised.

3. T. J. Markovitch, "La Crise de 1847–1848 dans les industries parisiennes," *Revue d'histoire économique et sociale* (1965), 256–260.

This was a historic decision, a major gain for democracy. Universal suffrage had been ordered once before in France but only briefly and without a real chance to function. Now it was definitely established and, with a few qualifications, it has existed to this day. Yet because of its novelty its real meaning was not clear. Radical politicians soon began to have doubts, as they realized that urban voters made up a scant quarter of the total. France would now be in the hands of the peasants, and Parisians had little faith in their judgment. They feared their ignorance, their domination by priests and landlords. There was no retreat from the basic principle of democracy: the people should rule—but many radicals began to seek more time to prepare them.

Ledru-Rollin, as minister of the interior, quickly developed misgivings of this sort, and he was in a position to do something about them. He established special commissioners to replace the prefects in ruling the provincial departments, and gave them wide powers to promote the cause of revolution: "Your powers are unlimited. Agents of a revolutionary government, you are revolutionary too." Specifically the commissioners worked to promote the right candidates on electoral lists and to distribute influence and patronage in order to gain support for the new regime. These efforts, the first of many in France which reflected a real understanding that the democratic republic was possible only through the political conversion of the masses, were exceedingly important, but they roused opposition from more conservative elements. Local notables feared that their influence would be undermined. Moderate newspapers—there were few that expressed an outright conservatism—protested the efforts to radicalize the people. The regular propaganda bulletins issued by the Ministry of Interior, many written by the romantic author George Sand, one of France's leading novelists and certainly the best-known female intellectual of the day, added to the controversy. Sand was a highly emotional republican who had an exalted vision of the French people ("sublime, generous, the most admirable people in the universe"). In a bulletin on the subject of the coming elections Sand urged that if the elections did not turn out in the people's interest they should again mount the barricades; this threat of renewed revolution roused a storm of controversy.

In other words, not surprisingly, the organization of elections created great uncertainty and forced a clarification of what different factions meant by revolution. The republic itself had been widely accepted. Though the revolution per se was an almost exclusively Parisian affair there was no resistance from the provinces. Almost everyone was glad to be rid of the July Monarchy. Priests, long the natural enemies of political change, sang Te Deums for the revolution and helped plant trees of liberty in town squares. Aristocrats and wealthy businessmen, who—as Flaubert suggested—were agreeably surprised to find themselves still alive, raised no protest. There was, then, no counterrevolution in a literal sense, a surprising testimony to Louis Philippe's unpopularity and to the willingness of most major groups to fight for their interests in a new political framework. As radical groups and propaganda spread in Paris, however, they began to assert themselves in the localities. They were greatly aided by the unpopularity of the increased tax on land, which burdened the peasantry severely.[4] The radicals' fears were well founded: the elections would determine the real meaning of the revolution and they were going to be vigorously contested.

In Paris and to a lesser extent in other major cities the political issue was quickly wrapped up with the social issue. Most members of the government preferred to separate the two. They believed that a proper political arrangement assured a proper social arrangement; explicit social reforms were not needed. The Parisian crowd saw no such distinction. The people were genuinely interested in politics but they expected direct social remedies to result from any new regime. The artisans and laborers who milled around the city hall on February 24 and 25 talked incessantly about the "organization of labor" and the "right to work." They wanted government action against unemployment and hunger, the forces that had most directly goaded them to revolt in the first place. One young worker burst into the council on the 25th, shouting, "Citizens, the revolution was achieved twenty-four hours ago and the people still await its results"; he insisted that the government proclaim the organization of labor within

4. Rémi Gossez, "La Résistance à l'impôt: les quarante-cinq centimes," *Études* (1953), 89–131.

the hour. With this kind of pressure, supplemented by the promptings of Louis Blanc within their own ranks, the government had to take some kind of action.

The response, outlined on February 26, was twofold. Blanc, who had asked for the establishment of a Ministry of Progress, was appointed the chairman of a Commission of Labor, which met in the Luxembourg Palace and was hence known as the Luxembourg Commission. This body had wide investigatory power concerning working conditions and ultimately assembled a wide variety of data on the workers' situation throughout France. The Commission quickly interviewed representatives of various trades in Paris and persuaded the government to enact two reforms in early March. Subcontracting, which was widely employed in the building trades and was regarded as a means of reducing wages, was abolished and the hours of work were reduced to ten a day in Paris, twelve in the provinces. The latter reform was a considerable advance in principle, for no government had previously been willing to regulate the hours of adult males, but there was no provision for enforcement. In the long run the Luxembourg Commission played some role in informing workers about their conditions and in giving them experience in public action; agents of the Commission fomented strikes and other protests. But its existence helped divert demands for outright social reform and removed Blanc from day-to-day operation of the government, which furthered the socially conservative purposes of the majority of ministers.

The second concession to the social agitation had a far more sweeping impact: national workshops (*ateliers nationaux*) were set up in various sections of Paris to provide work for the unemployed. Anyone admitted to the workshops was paid two francs a day when work was available and one and a half when no jobs could be found; this latter figure was later reduced.[5]

The goal of the workshops was in no sense unworthy. Massive unemployment cried out for relief, and while the pay offered was below even unskilled levels in Paris it could put some food on the table. But the basic conception was not at all new. Similar relief projects had been developed in earlier economic crises. The

5. Donald McKay, *The National Workshops* (Cambridge, Mass., 1965), *passim*.

jobs provided by the workshops were for the most part trivial manual labor, repairing the city walls or working on the roads. What was new was the name, which was adapted from Blanc's proposal for "social workshops." The government was trying to woo the workers with titles, not substance. The name, smacking of socialism, roused the fears of the property-owning classes, who also resented the expense involved. More important, it roused hopes among the workers which were doomed to disappointment. The workshops' director, Pierre Marie, was resolutely opposed to any form of socialism. Even suggestions that the workers apply themselves to more useful projects, such as housing construction, were ignored. Workers did grumble at the way the workshops developed; unemployed artisans, particularly, resented the menial chores they were given. The radical clubs complained even more bitterly. But by their very existence the workshops divided the working classes somewhat. Many workers were not socialist, and even some who were disappointed depended on the workshops for their livelihood. In this sense the workshops, like many of the other concessions offered to the crowd, did relieve the pressure on the provisional government.

By mid-March the situation was as follows: the government was in reasonably firm control, and its police services were improving rapidly. Crime rates, for example, declined notably as Marc Caussidière built up his uniformed police forces. But radical clubs and newspapers—there were a hundred seventy-one papers founded between February and June, producing 400,000 copies a month at their peak—directed a constant stream of criticism at the government for not going far enough in its reforms and for scheduling the national elections prematurely. Even seasoned radicals like Louis Blanc were accused of betrayal for not fighting for the postponement of elections. At a slightly different level, artisans and workers founded a number of aid societies and trade unions to press for social justice. This same outpouring of sentiment roused fears among more conservative groups. Many middle-class residents left town, fearing attack from the lower classes. Provincial elements organized to make gains in the forthcoming elections; Catholic groups, for example, campaigned actively for candidates who would support religious education. There were firm republicans campaigning as well. Ledru-Rollin's emissaries were successful in winning considerable support.[6] Artisans and workers in cities like Marseilles began forming political clubs to support the republic.[7] School teachers, who opposed any increase in Catholic educational influence and who sought more secular independence for the schools, largely wanted republican reforms. But there was a growing rift between the frenzy of the capital and the calmer, more moderate mood of the rest of France.

On March 17 a large number of workers, led by leaders from the radical clubs such as Armand Barbès and Blanqui, marched to the city hall to demand a postponement of the elections. The marchers were well disciplined and the new police forces helped keep order, but the government was intimidated. It refused to grant the demanded two-month delay, which would have given time for considerable electioneering by the radicals, but it did grant two additional weeks, to April 23, which annoyed the conservative elements. No one in the government really supported the radicals' demands. Louis Blanc helped persuade the marchers to go home despite their lack of real success. His lack of a clear program of his own, his resentment of the influence of men like Blanqui, and his sense of responsibility as a member of government drove him to a moderate stand despite the fact that privately he too would have perferred a delay in the elections until vital reforms were enacted. Ledru-Rollin also distrusted the radical leaders and was understandably concerned lest agitation in Paris undermine his propaganda in the provinces; so he tried to calm the situation too. In mid-April he used the National Guard to overawe another crowd that had gathered to demand a further postponement of the elections. Here of course was a genuinely vicious cycle. The radicals wanted a change to win the provinces, but their efforts to get it created an impression of anarchy that antagonized many provincial voters. The government antagonized the Parisian radicals by their efforts at repression

6. A. R. Calman, *Ledru-Rollin and the Second French Republic* (New York, 1922), 34 ff.
7. William Sewell, "La Classe ouvrière de Marseille sous le Seconde République: Structure sociale et comportement politique," *Mouvement social* (1971), 27–66.

but did not create a sufficient impression of firmness to win the conservatives. Yet increasingly the government resolved to steer a moderate course. Even before the elections it began to put pressure on radical leaders, trying particularly to discredit Blanqui; there was even talk of possible arrests.

The April elections confirmed the radicals' worst fears.[8] With more than 84 percent of the eligible voters voting, the provinces voted overwhelmingly for local notables—men of property, many of whom had been politically active in earlier regimes. Wealthy men of this sort won all but a hundred of the 876 slots. A hundred sixty-five had actually been in a July Monarchy parliament. Three hundred styled themselves moderate republicans while four hundred were monarchist, some favoring the Orleanist dynasty while others, as Legitimists, harked back to the Bourbons. Even in Paris, partly because the moderate ministers in the government had worked against their more radical colleagues, men like Blanc and Ledru-Rollin barely won election. Only eighty-five socialists or radicals gained seats at all; Blanqui and other prominent leaders actually went down in defeat. Not surprisingly the new assembly expelled Blanc and the two other social reformers from the new Executive Commission which replaced the provisional government, while only Lamartine's intervention kept Ledru-Rollin in his post. The assembly refused Blanc's request to create a ministry of labor and rejected a new proclamation of the right to work.

In retrospect, the election results were not surprising for a first democratic experience. Voters, even working-class people in Paris, tended to look to traditional types of leaders with recognizable names and positions. Only thirty of the new deputies were workers of any sort and there was not a single peasant elected. In Paris the election results confirmed the divisions within the lower classes. Sizable crowds could be gathered for radical causes, but

8. George W. Fasel, "The French Election of April 23, 1848: Suggestions for a Revision," *French Historical Studies* (1968), 285–298; Alfred Cobban, "Administrative Pressure in the Election of the French Constituent Assembly, April, 1848," *Bulletin of the Institute of Historical Research* (1952), 133–159; Alfred Cobban, "The Influence of the Clergy and the 'Instituteurs primaires' in the Election of the French Constituent Assembly," *English Historical Review* (1942), 334–344.

they were a minority, and doubtless many a barricade fighter, when not excited and faced with a strictly political choice, opted for moderation. In the provinces, particularly the countryside and the small towns, the results reflected even deeper traditionalism. In many villages priests led the voters to the polls, after carefully recommending appropriate candidates from the pulpits. (In many cases, bishops circulated approved lists to their priests in their diocese.) Conservative elements had campaigned widely, not only through religious groups but also through the Republican Club for Freedom of Elections. The willingness of even many monarchists to call themselves republican helped prevent an impression of inflexibility or explicit counterrevolutionary sentiment. Resentment against the tax increase weakened the popularity of government candidates. And the election was neither the first nor the last expression of provincial resentment against efforts by Parisians to run the whole French show.

As a result of the elections, a battle for Paris itself was inevitable, for the radicals had great influence and considerable organization and it was obvious that the assembly would not countenance any social reforms. On May 15 huge crowds marched to the assembly, declared the parliament dissolved, and then went on to the city hall to form a new government. This effort was not organized by the radical clubs, whose leaders participated only reluctantly because they believed the effort premature. In fact the demonstration was a godsend for the assembly. The National Guard, including many working-class members, and the Mobile Guard scattered the crowd easily and the most visible radical leaders were arrested. Barbès and Blanqui were jailed, other crowd orators fled. It was easy to believe that the workers were now powerless. The assembly dissolved the Luxembourg Commission and began to discuss the termination of the national workshops.

This last issue, which precipitated the tragic end of the active phase of the revolution, had become exceedingly complicated. On the workers' side, quite apart from the socialist hopes that some harbored, the need for unemployment relief had grown steadily. The economic crisis which the revolution exacerbated led to mounting joblessness. In 1847 about 335,000 workers had

been employed in Paris—and this itself was a year of severe recession—while in 1848 the figure fell to 147,000. Over half the
labor force lacked work, a crisis of unprecedented severity. Obviously the slump extended to the rest of France as well; ordinar-
ily this would have been of only indirect concern to Parisians, but
this time mounting unemployment in provincial cities had a direct impact, for large numbers of workers flocked to Paris if only
to seek relief in the workshops. The workshops, which had been
designed to handle ten or twelve thousand people, had over a
hundred thousand enrolled by early June. They included many
unskilled laborers but also large numbers of artisans and even unemployed professional people and artists. Despite workers' complaints about the lack of jobs and the purely unskilled labor provided by the workshops—only 10,000 men were employed on any
given day, while the rest received the small sum granted for outright unemployment—the workshops seemed essential in the pre-
vailing crisis. They provided not only a small money payment but
also extra food, cheap clothing, and free medical service. Emile
Thomas, the engineer directly in charge of the operation, had
even more elaborate projects for his charges, though the government consistently denied him support. He organized the workers
in a paramilitary fashion, with squads, brigades, and companies,
which provided some needed discipline and also gave a number of
workers who headed the various units some valuable leadership
experience.

From the standpoint of the middle class and property owners
generally, in Paris and the provinces, the workshops were an
abomination. Specific complaints were repeated regularly: the
workshops cost a vast amount of money, at a time when taxes had
been raised; they produced little useful work. It was easy to claim
that hard-working peasants and shopkeepers were paying for the
maintenance of ne'er-do-wells in the capital. The government's
refusal to allow the workshops to attempt more than menial
chores had the circular effect so common in relief projects even
in our own day, for the whole effort seemed a gigantic boondog-
gle; though in fairness it must be admitted that in the short run
more constructive work would have cost the hard-pressed government more money. By the spring of 1848 the fears of the "right-

thinking elements" went beyond financial complaints. There was the sheer image of a hundred thousand workers gathered in a single organization. The menace to social order seemed immense, and it was widely believed that socialist propaganda found a ready audience in the workshops. Given the tensions of the time and the rioting that had already occurred, it is perhaps not surprising that the worst hostilities and prejudices harbored against the lower classes were directed against the workshops' personnel. Caussidière noted: "The bourgeoisie have been in a state of alarm for some time at the imagined composition of the Workshops. Thus if we are to believe certain organs of the reactionary party, out of 120,000 workmen, one-third are liberated galley slaves, one-third idlers and men incapable of doing anything, and the remaining third only half honest, that is to say men not worth much and whom it would be wise to distrust." [9]

In this atmosphere the discussions over dissolution of the workshops dominated the assembly. As Tocqueville noted, "The National Assembly was so constantly obsessed with this thought that one felt one could see the words 'civil war' written on each of the four walls of the hall." With each passing day the situation became more tense. From mid-May onward, workers circulated in the streets every night, holding political discussions; lacking work and fearful of the assembly's intentions, there was little else to do. One of the radical clubs planned a great popular banquet for June, in imitation of the early banquet campaign.[10] These moves added to the terrors of the moderates and conservatives who controlled the assembly, for it was increasingly easy to believe that an outright socialist revolution threatened. The government named an experienced army general, Eugène Cavaignac, commander of the troops, National Guard, and police in Paris. There was some uncertainty about the loyalty of the troops and the National Guard, for the army was still demoralized and the Guard contained so many new working-class elements, but the

9. Lorenz von Stein, *History of the Social Movement in France* (Totowa, N.J., 1964), 233.
10. Peter Amann, "Prelude to Insurrection: The Banquet of the People," *French Historical Studies* (1960), 436–440.

Mobile Guard, now 15,000 strong, was disciplined and tough. The government prepared for battle.[11]

The debate over the workshops themselves proceeded rapidly. All the arguments against them were expressed repeatedly. Opponents contended that business would revive as soon as the workshops disappeared, so that even the lower classes would benefit. The chief influence in the labor committee of the assembly was the conservative Catholic Comte de Falloux, who scorned the idea, backed by moderate republicans, of a gradual dissolution in favor of an immediate contest. Falloux claimed understanding for the special problems of labor because of the charity work he had done among the poor. What he in fact represented, along with the assembly majority, was the traditional view of the poor as an inevitable part of society, to be offered charity when possible so long as they showed themselves resigned to their lot. The workshops, which so obviously went beyond this conception even with their limitations, simply had to go. On June 23 Falloux's committee presented a decree to dissolve the workshops within three days. Young workshop members were to be sent into the army, older members were to be encouraged or even compelled to go on public works projects in the provinces. The idea was to get as much of the dangerous element as possible out of town.

Reports of the committee's plans had spread among workers several days before, and in fact some workshop members had already been conscripted into the army. Hence early in the morning of June 23, before the report was presented, barricades began to go up in the narrow streets of the working-class sections of eastern Paris. They were carefully built, not the flimsy jobs of February, with only small openings for pedestrian passage. Wagons were overturned to add to the piles of stones and construction materials. Within a few hours a large section of the city was in the hands of the roughly 15,000 insurgents. (Some contemporary esti-

11. P. Chalmin, "Une institution militaire de la Seconde République: la garde nationale mobile," *Études d'histoire moderne et contemporaine* (1948), 339 ff; General Doumenc, "L'Armée et les journées de juin," *Actes du Congrès du Centenaire de la Révolution de 1848* (Paris, 1948), 255–266; Rémi Gossez, "Notes sur la composition et l'attitude de la troupe," *Études* (1955), 77–110; Louis Girard, *La Garde nationale, 1814–1871* (Paris, 1964).

mates went as high as 50,000 but the more modest figure is probably accurate.) Activity was feverish. The workers established communication lines from house to house, to minimize the danger of outdoor travel. They carried munitions to the barricades, women carrying sacks of powder under their skirts so that they looked pregnant. Civil order was assured, as the insurgents refrained from thefts, except of munitions, and many wealthy citizens, caught in the insurgents' network, were carefully released.

From the workers' standpoint the June Days constituted one of the most impressive risings in history.[12] There was little leadership from experienced radical elements, for most were in jail. Members of the Luxembourg Commission had continued to meet during June and urged a fight for a democratic and social republic, but actual leadership emerged from the workers themselves. Some leaders, like Louis Pujol, had gained experience by directing workshop groups; Pujol had a vague, almost mystical social vision and saw a personal mission in leading the people. But most leaders had even fewer links with any kind of social ideology. They sprang up spontaneously in defense of the workers' right to live. A minority of the insurgents had been in the workshops; estimates vary, going up to 40 percent. Workshop members, like Pujol, undoubtedly took an important lead in the early stages of the rising. But most barricade fighters had not been admitted to the workshops at all. Far more had gained experience in the workers' societies that had sprung up after the February rising. Hence many undoubtedly battled for a socialist republic while others fought in desperation, because they wanted some means of survival. The June Days proved to be a bloody landmark in the history of class relations in Europe, but their complexity must not be minimized. The insurrection pitted older lower-class elements against the representatives of largely rural property owners. It pitted two traditional conceptions of the social order against each other, for the workers' claim for state

12. George Rudé, *The Crowd in the French Revolution* (Oxford, 1959), Chap. XV; Rémi Gossez, "Diversités des antagonismes sociaux vers le milieu du XIXe siècle," *Revue économique* (1956), 439–457; Charles Tilly, "The Changing Place of Collective Violence," in Melvin Richter, ed., *Essays in Theory and History* (Cambridge, Mass., 1970), 139–164.

assistance in time of dire misery was almost as old as Falloux's concepts of charity. The June Days constituted one of the last, if one of the largest, popular risings of the traditional type in Western Europe; they were all the more fierce for their roots in popular desperation. They also bore the seeds of a newer conflict. A disproportionate number of the workers—particularly furniture-makers and metal workers—came from the largest shops and were concerned about the new organization of the economy.

The insurgents gained their hold over so much of eastern Paris because the government, guided by General Cavaignac, deliberately held back. Lamartine and his moderate colleagues urged that each barricade be attacked and torn down as it was built, to minimize the ultimate bloodshed, but Cavaignac refused to act until all his forces were ready and concentrated in three main centers. The National Guard was summoned in the morning, but the response was incomplete, probably because many guardsmen stayed home to protect their own property. So the government sent for contingents of National Guards in the provinces, and the response was considerable. For the first time, the railroads made possible a direct provincial intervention in a Parisian rising.[13] Thousands of provincials had arrived by June 24, and by July 1 about 100,000 had come in, eager, as Tocqueville said, "to defend society against the threat of anarchic doctrines and to put an end to the intolerable dictation of the chronically insurgent Parisian workers." Most of the provincials were too late to take part in the fighting, but they did perform guard duty and obviously bolstered the morale of the other government forces.

Cavaignac's offensive began on the 24th. There was vicious fighting, during which the workers were steady driven back. An observer described the carnage: "Near the Column of July where the most violent cannonade took place, the fronts of the houses are, as it were, taken off. . . . One of them was more completely destroyed than the others and which was still smoldering, had no part standing but the wall on which the looking glass remained unbroken over the chimney place, together with a glass

13. Jean Vidalenc, "La Province et les journées de juin," *Études d'histoire moderne et contemporaine* (1948), 83–144.

bottle and three pints. . . . Everything else, doors, windows, floors, staircases, and ceiling, had fallen into rubble." She ended by noting that she "could not imagine how anyone escaped the butchery committed there." [14] Bitter fighting continued for four days. There were atrocities on both sides. The archbishop of Paris, trying to mediate, was killed by a stray bullet. National Guardsmen showed themselves particulary vicious, in the spirit of a class war. Approximately 500 insurgents lost their lives in the fighting, as against almost 1000 soldiers and guardsmen, but after the last barricades were captured the insurgents were hunted throughout the city and almost 3000 more were killed in cold blood. In addition, over 12,000 people were arrested, and about 4500 of them were ultimately jailed or deported to labor camps in Algeria.

The June Days have been often and variously interpreted. Marx saw them as "a fight for the preservation or annihilation of the bourgeois order"; "the first great battle . . . between the two classes that split modern society." Conservatives like Tocqueville viewed the conflict somewhat more broadly, but also believed that it was an attack on the system of private property by the propertyless masses. These assessments undoubtedly reflect what many National Guardsmen thought they were fighting for, though they exaggerate the insurgents' explicit intention of challenging the existing order. Marx's terms can, as we have seen, be misleading, for the workers who led the struggle were not a real factory proletariat and the bourgeoisie was not an industrial middle class.[15] The alignment was really one of "poor" versus "rich," and even this must be qualified. The insurgents constituted only a minority (at most one twentieth) of the Parisian poor. Many workers served in the Guards and police along with shopkeepers and professional men (most Parisian factory owners did not take part in the conflict, though a few fought at their workers' side on the barricades). But the insurgents were mainly

14. Florence Bonde, *Paris in 1848* (New York, 1907).
15. Karl Marx, *The Class Struggles in France* (New York, 1924); Peter Amann, "The Changing Outlines of 1848," *American Historical Review* (1963), 938–952; Gossez, "Diversités des antagonismes," 439 ff.; Rémi Gossez, "L'Organisation ouvrière à Paris sous la Seconde République, 1848," *Revue des révolutions contemporaines* (1949), 31–45.

propertyless and their opponents, whether propertied or not, defended the established social order. It was also true that some new elements, notably a number of railwaymen, suggesting a more modern working class, took part in the rioting. Even more important, the clash helped widen the gulf between rich and poor and helped teach some among the lower classes to seek newer, more effective forms of protest. In this sense the June Days undoubtedly helped prepare for class conflict of a more modern sort.

The June Days clearly limited the revolution itself to the political sphere. The question that had hung fire for four months, of whether the revolution would have social content as well, was resolved. The defeat of the insurgents helped set a pattern that would dominate France well into the twentieth century, in which radical political forms were combined with social conservatism. The assembly gave Cavaignac dictatorial powers and suppressed the radical clubs and newspapers. The legal restrictions on working hours were repealed, and the work day returned (in those few establishments that had obeyed the law) to twelve or thirteen hours. The whole mood of France, or more properly of Paris, seemed to change. Romantic intellectuals, including Lamartine, grew disillusioned with the bloodshed and what they viewed as the fickleness of the common people. George Sand, who had idealized the masses before, wrote that "the majority of the French people are blind, credulous, ignorant, ungrateful, bad, and stupid." [16] But the drafting of a new political constitution continued through the summer. And if the more radical republicans were decimated and the intellectuals disheartened, there were plenty of political reformers still at work, inside the Assembly and without. If the essential revolution was over, its impact had yet to be fully worked out.

16. André Maurois, *Lélia: The Life of George Sand* (New York, 1953), 338–346.

FIVE

The Habsburg Lands:
The Flare-up

N EWS OF THE February revolution in Paris spread rapidly
in Central Europe. It served as the same sort of catalyst
that the banquet campaigns had in France itself, for it
induced a flood of petitions and demonstrations that aroused
the common people and could lead to outright revolt. Neither
liberalism nor radicalism was so advanced or popular as in
France, but for a time this did not seem to matter. The excitement caused by the French example is hard to recapture. Paul
Boerner, a university student in Berlin, had to walk for hours in
the cold until he was exhausted in order to calm himself. For
many evenings after he heard the news he went to a café to listen
to the newspapers being read over and over again.

A number of risings occurred in the state of southern Germany in early March. In Baden, which had a parliament already
but where overpopulation and economic distress caused great
misery, big popular meetings took place as soon as the news from
Paris arrived. Liberals demanded full freedom of the press and
the establishment of a citizen guard. The governments yielded
quickly, forming a liberal cabinet on March 2. But almost immediately peasant risings attacked Jewish money lenders and
aristocratic manor houses. Manorial records were burned and the
lords were forced to sign away their traditional privileges.[17] The

17. Theodore Hamerow, *Restoration, Revolution, Reaction* (Princeton, 1958),
Chap. IX; Günther Franz, "Die agrarische Bewegung im Jahre 1848," *Zeitschrift
für Agrargeschichte und Agrarsoziologie* (1959), 176–192; Franz Schnabel,
"Das Land Baden in der Revolution von 1848–1849," in Wilhelm Keil, ed.,
Deutschland, 1848–1948 (Stuttgart, 1948), 56–70.

army had to be called in to restore order. Similar agitation occurred in Württemberg where a veritable peasant rebellion occurred, while in Hesse-Darmstadt, Saxony, Hanover, and the Hanseatic cities there were large demonstrations and petitions for political reform accompanied by some worker and peasant unrest. By mid-March most of the governments in the smaller German states had established ministries that were responsible to parliament and had provided an array of civil liberties. Real revolution, in the sense of armed confrontation between insurgents and the forces of order, scarcely seemed necessary.

The next major revolution, in fact, was triggered in Austria. On March 3, Lajos Kossuth delivered an impassioned speech to the Hungarian diet, meeting at Pressburg. Invoking the French example, he urged the establishment of parliamentary rule throughout the empire. He professed loyalty to the ruling house, but excoriated its absolute rule and the powers of the central bureaucracy. Not only parliamentary control but also decentralization was essential, and he insisted on recognition of Hungarian autonomy. Following his speech, which roused the Hungarian diet, Kossuth came to Vienna where he spoke to large crowds and also met with middle-class leaders to whom he recommended firm action. Excited meetings and petitions for reform proliferated in the days that followed. Attention focused on the gathering of the diet of Lower Austria, scheduled for March 13. This was an essentially feudal regional chamber, dominated by the aristocracy, with few formal powers, but it could address recommendations to the government and there were enough liberal aristocrats in the body to create some hope for change.

The government, aware of the rising agitation, wallowed in uncertainty. Metternich realized that reforms were inevitable, but he wanted the government to grant them outright, not to yield to crowd pressure. Members of the Habsburg family—the emperor was feeble-minded and did not really play a role—were divided over what action to take, and many resented Metternich's influence. So nothing was really done.

On the morning of the 13th the Lower Austria diet began to discuss a reform petition. Several thousand university students marched toward the meeting. They had suffered keenly from censorship and police supervision and they were to play an unusually important revolutionary role. Their intent on the 13th was to persuade the diet to insist on really substantial reforms; and they wanted to get rid of Metternich. As crowds of onlookers swelled their number, students invaded the meeting place. The presiding officer of the diet, seeing that the meeting was out of control, appealed to the government to restore order. The response merely exacerbated the situation, for instead of sending in a large force a few squadrons of cavalry were dispatched, and they found it very difficult to operate in the narrow streets of the central city. During the afternoon some stones were thrown at the troops, and shots were fired in exchange. There was no planned repression involved, simply a reaction to the tensions of the moment, but several people were killed and the excitement of the crowd mounted. The crowd was now composed of a mixture of students and artisans, and by late afternoon it began to gain reinforcements from the suburbs outside the old city walls. For here was where a large number of artisanal shops and some factories existed, and the journeymen and laborers were eager to express their own grievances. The city gates were closed before many actually entered the city, but this merely encouraged a different kind of riot in the suburbs themselves. The workers broke a number of machines and burned and pillaged shops.

Middle-class leaders in Vienna, worried by the growing unrest, urged that the troops be withdrawn and the Citizen Guard keep order in their stead. This was done by late afternoon, but the Citizen Guard, like the National Guard in Paris, itself insisted on reform, sending a deputation to the palace to demand Metternich's dismissal. The Imperial Council decided on concessions. Metternich argued vigorously for military repression; he pointed out that Louis Philippe had dismissed Guizot but had lost his throne anyway. The governor of Bohemia, Prince Alfred von Windischgrätz, supported this position, for he had experience in putting down riots in Prague and thought that force alone could save the regime. But the council forced Metternich to resign, and the man who had served the Habsburgs for fifty years had to flee in disguise to Germany and on to England. which was fast becoming the repository for lost causes.

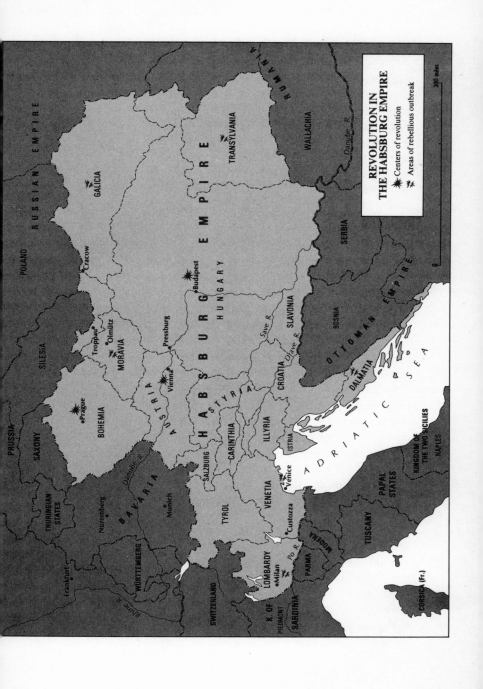

REVOLUTION IN
THE HABSBURG EMPIRE

✴ Centers of revolution
✾ Areas of rebellious outbreak

300 miles

RUSSIAN EMPIRE

POLAND

PRUSSIA

SAXONY

SILESIA

THURINGIAN STATES

Frankfurt

WÜRTTEMBERG

SWITZERLAND

BAVARIA

Nuremberg

Munich

Rhine R.

Danube R.

GALICIA

Cracow

Troppau

Olmütz

MORAVIA

BOHEMIA

Prague

AUSTRIA

Vienna

Pressburg

SALZBURG

CARINTHIA

TYROL

STYRIA

HABSBURG EMPIRE

HUNGARY

Budapest

TRANSYLVANIA

RUMANIA

WALLACHIA

Danube R.

SERBIA

BOSNIA

OTTOMAN EMPIRE

DALMATIA

SLAVONIA

CROATIA

ILLYRIA

ISTRIA

Save R.

Drave R.

VENETIA

Venice

Custozza

Po R.

Milan

LOMBARDY

PARMA

MODENA

K. OF
SARDINIA

PIEDMONT

TUSCANY

PAPAL
STATES

KINGDOM OF
THE TWO SICILIES

NAPLES

CORSICA (Fr.)

ADRIATIC SEA

The government undoubtedly hoped that a change of faces would end the unrest. It named a cabinet to replace the Imperial Council, filling the ministries with government officials, most of them aristocrats who had a vague reputation for liberalism. There was no desire to offer substantive reforms. But the government still lacked the will to put down the crowds, and in fact confirmed its loss of control over Vienna by allowing the students to arm themselves. During the evening of the 13th the students distributed several thousand muskets from the arsenal and formed patrols to keep order. Soon thereafter the government consented to the formation of a National Guard with a distinct student corps called the Academic Legion. With the troops idle in their barracks outside the city walls, this made the revolutionaries masters of the city.[18]

On March 15 the government offered more far-reaching political concessions. It guaranteed such civil rights as the freedom of speech and of the press and it announced that the diet would meet, with increased representation for the middle classes, and that a constitution would be granted. While these promises were somewhat vague, it did seem possible that some kind of parliamentary monarchy would emerge, and as a result many middle-class liberals were contented. Participation in National Guard duty declined dramatically. In the excitement of the first revolutionary days approximately 30,000 had signed up for the guard, apart from the separate Academic Legion. But while this showed the widespread satisfaction with the gains that had been made, it also left the streets open to more radical elements.

It is time to attempt a more precise description of the forces involved in the revolution. One element was the pressure of revolt elsewhere. The government was distracted by the news of agitation in other parts of the empire and in the German states. As a member of the Germanic Confederation, Austria was obviously influenced by liberal gains in Germany; by April, government actions were in part intended to conform to this pattern lest Austria lose her role in the Confederation. Risings within the Habsburg empire itself created more direct pressure, encouraging the government to try to calm the Viennese revolutionaries so

18. See R. John Rath, *The Viennese Revolution of 1848* (Austin, 1957).

that it could deal with other threats. Bohemia and Hungary were in virtual revolt by mid-March. Northern Italy rose against Austrian control on March 18, as soon as the Viennese revolution seemed successful. These risings must be discussed separately, but as far as the beleaguered government was concerned each of them abetted the others and reduced the possibility of effective counter-action.

Within Vienna, the middle-class liberals formed the largest articulate political group. It is easy to ridicule them, in the light of what ultimately happened to the Austrian revolution. They sincerely sought the classic liberal demands: freedom of press and speech, abolition of arbitrary imprisonment, and so on. But they were certainly vague about how to secure these goals and they were decidedly unrevolutionary. They can in this sense be compared unfavorably with French liberals in previous revolutions and with English liberals who won their gains by firm, if unrevolutionary, political action. The Viennese liberals wanted the imperial government to run their revolution for them. They waited for concessions from above. They took no steps to form an alternate regime. They developed no clear leaders of their own. In largely forsaking the National Guard they abandoned the most obvious revolutionary force they had created. They relied mainly on their ability to offer advice. Groups such as the Chamber of Commerce regularly sent delegations to visit government ministers to urge reform, and during the months the ministers lived in fear of further revolts they found the channels open. But this was not the same thing as gaining real control of the political apparatus. The Viennese middle class was too new, its political views too inchoate, to seek political power directly. It was quickly distracted by popular disorder, for these were people of wealth who had their own wealth to defend.

To the left of the middle class were the students, almost 5000 strong. The students were distinctly more radical and more highly politicized than the bulk of the middle class. They did form a governing committee, which essentially controlled the revolutionary forces, and they produced definite leaders. Most of the latter were young university instructors and junior members of hospital staffs, such as Dr. Adolf Fischhof and Dr. Josef Goldmark. Most of the students were of middle-class origins, though it was significant that some came from the ranks of the suburban artisans. They differed from the middle class in their youth and their lack of property, which helps explain their readiness to take to the streets. They had been among the most direct victims of the repressive policies pursued by the imperial government and so were unlikely to be lulled by promises emanating from this same government. And they were specifically activated by the crisis in professional ranks from which older, more established middle-class elements, particularly those in business, were largely exempt. So the students ran the show for many weeks. They demonstrated time and time again. They gathered around the homes of unpopular government officials, and by this kind of pressure usually got their way. Although barely acquainted with Western political doctrines, they learned from their radical leaders and formed democratic clubs and radical newspapers that attacked the whole established order, not only the political regime but also the powers of church and aristocracy.

Student action was backed by the workers during this revolutionary period. Few workers were politically articulate. They presented no clear political demands, as their Parisian counterparts were doing, for they lacked the revolutionary experience that France had so often provided. Their distance from the central city also limited their influence, for industry had increasingly fled outside the walls and while the suburbs were not far distant (they were in fact incorporated into Vienna a few decades later) they did tend to scatter the lower classes and to divert their attention from the government in Vienna. But the workers were profoundly aggrieved. They had no Louis Blanc to suggest slogans and doctrines, but their expressions of discontent were all the more direct as a result. They resented the threat of factories and machines to the artisanal economy; they hated the rich; and they wanted food. Their agitation served as an important pressure both on the government and the middle class. Student and worker action was mutually reinforcing.

Vienna in the spring and summer of 1848 in fact offered one of the rare cases of student-worker cooperation. Workers supported student initiatives at first because they so clearly challenged the status quo. The fact that some students came from lower-class homes may have added to the attachment, but the main point was that students were able to articulate a discontent that the workers found difficult to express outside of direct action. The students responded to the support, and during the spring and summer a number of them spent a great deal of time with the workers, giving them legal and medical assistance. This sort of defiance of ordinary class barriers was unusual, and not surprisingly, despite good intentions, it was incomplete. The students urged the workers to keep order, lest they jeopardize the revolution in the eyes of the moderates. One leader laid it on the line in a speech to a working-class audience: "Do you think we have thrown over our lords and nobles to let ourselves be ruled by you? Then you are much mistaken. Do you expect us to be intimidated by you? There again you are wrong. . . . You a mostly fine, sensible people. Why do you let yourselves be led by a few hotheads?" A rare suggestion that the workers strike out on their own, as in Paris, was widely criticized by the student press and its author arrested when he went on to plan for a workers' rising. There was little talk of social reform. Nor were workers integrated into student groups. A workers' democratic club finally formed on its own. But the limitations on student-worker cooperation long went unnoted. Certainly few workers criticized; they were visibly grateful for the attention they did receive. One noted, in promising to defend student political action: "If one of our men falls it is no matter, but for one of the fine young student gentlemen, to whom we owe our freedom, it would be a great pity."

By late April the government was forced to further concessions. It proclaimed a liberal constitution for the German provinces of Austria plus Bohemia, Moravia, and Galicia. This established a series of civil liberties and a two-chamber parliament, in which the upper chamber would consist of aristocrats and the higher clergy and the lower house would be indirectly elected by taxpaying citizens. The liberals were delighted with this arrangement, but the students were incensed, protesting particularly the limitation on the suffrage. The government again yielded, offering the vote to all adult males except laborers and servants, whom it said were too dependent on others to exercise a free vote. But again the students protested, mounting huge demonstrations on May 15, and again the government, still unwilling to use force, backed down. Universal manhood suffrage was proclaimed, and a single-chamber parliament decreed. The government also promised not to bring military troops into Vienna save when requested by the National Guard.

The radical triumph was enhanced during the following days. Frightened by its complete loss of control of Vienna, the imperial court organized the flight of the emperor and his advisers to Innsbruck on May 17. This was a decisive development in the long run, for it gave the Habsburgs the freedom to plan the defeat of the revolution. The moderate liberals in Vienna were shocked even at the time, for their loyalty to the dynasty ran deep and they blamed the radicals for excessive action. But when the government tried to capitalize on this sentiment by closing the university and dissolving the Academic Legion, the Viennese backed the students. Thousands of workers poured in from the suburbs and for the first time barricades were set up. The government again yielded, establishing a Committee of Citizens, National Guards, and Students of Vienna for Preservation of the Rights of the People, which was in essence a watchdog group to keep constant tabs on the government. It was headed by Dr. Adolf Fischhof, now the clear leader of the radicals. At the same time the first measures were taken to assist the lower classes, who were suffering from massive unemployment enhanced by the revolution itself. The government set up works projects and provided pay for the impoverished workers involved. So matters rested until the constituent assembly met in July; the radicals controlled Vienna though the Habsburg-appointed government retained nominal power, while the Habsburg court itself, cowed but intact, began to marshal its forces in other parts of the empire.

The Habsburgs had already taken one measure that significantly limited the spread of revolution outside Vienna. On March 20 the movement decreed the abolition of forced labor and all other manorial obligations imposed upon the peasantry.[19]

19. Jerome Blum, *Noble Landowners and Agriculture in Austria, 1818–1848* (Baltimore, 1948), 232 ff.

The abolition initially applied to Bohemia and Moravia, but it was soon extended to other areas. The abolition was to take effect in 1849, except in Galicia, where there had been serious peasant unrest just two years before; there it was made immediate. The landowners who had exercised manorial rights were to be indemnified by the government, which in turn would raise the taxes on the peasants. This was a measure of great significance. It resulted from the government's intense fear of peasant agitation, particularly in the the non-German portions of the empire. There were also grave doubts about the system of serfdom among Austrian landlords, not only because of growing peasant discontent but also because its economic utility had diminished as production for the market increased. Most landlords were willing to rely on paid labor, so the government's move created no reaction among them. For their part, the peasants were rid of some of their chief grievances and they hoped for a more favorable final settlement than the government intended; they did not realize how much the compensation to the landlords would cost them and the government did not encourage them to think about it. For the duration of the revolutionary period most peasants abandoned any interest in serious agitation, though their uneasiness still played some role. The Habsburg monarchy was overwhelmingly rural. It was not at all clear that a largely urban revolution could have any lasting success, any more than revolution could have succeeded without massive rural unrest in France sixty years before. Furthermore, peasant calm extended to loyal service in the imperial armies, which were largely composed of rural recruits. In sum, though it was not apparent in the excitement of the moment, the abolition of serfdom was an extremely clever stroke, suggesting the resiliency of the imperial government and the ruling class. A measure that could have been the product of revolution was preempted, even as it was granted in a way that would not alter the basic social structure of the countryside.

NATIONALIST REVOLTS

Outside of Vienna, and aside from Italy, which will be treated separately, the centers of revolution in the empire were Hungary and Bohemia. The Hungarian diet avidly discussed Kossuth's March 3 proposals for autonomy during the next two weeks. Kossuth's plan called for a separate self-governing Hungarian state, tied to the empire only through the Habsburgs serving as kings of Hungary. This state would include not only the historic Hungarian lands, the "Kingdom of Saint Stephen," but also the South Slav areas of Croatia and Slavonia and Transylvania, which was largely inhabited by Rumanians. Kossuth wanted a modern parliament to replace the system of diets, with a responsible ministry. Resistance to his plan came, predictably, from the diet's upper house, which was dominated by the great magnates and higher clergy, who had long been more moderate in their discussion of Hungary's links with Austria. The lower house, controlled by the Magyar gentry, were extremely enthusiastic, and when news of the Viennese uprising reached the diet the radicals easily won out.[20]

On March 15 the outlines of the new Hungarian state were adopted by the diet. This was revolution by law, but no less effective for the absence of violence. The Hungarian diet was transformed into a parliament elected by limited suffrage. A ministry responsible to it was established as the executive branch, and the whole government moved to Budapest, the traditional Hungarian capital. Hungarian units were taken out of the imperial army to form a separate force, and Hungary was to control

20. Paul Bödy, *Joseph Eötvös and the Modernization of Hungary, 1840–1870* (Philadelphia, 1972), 46–57; Coloman Benda, "La Question paysanne et la révolution hongroise en 1848," *Études d'histoire moderne et contemporaine* (1948), 231–242; Erzsebet Andics, "Kossuth en lutte contre les ennemis des réformes et de la révolution," *Studia historica* (1954), 61–67; Zoltan I. Toth, "The Nationality Problem in Hungary in 1848–1849," *Acta historica* (1955), 235–277; Günther Rothenberg, "Jelačić, the Croatian Military Border, and the Intervention against Hungary in 1848," *Austrian History Yearbook* (1965), 45–67; Erwin Szábo, "Aus den Parteien und Klassenkämpfen in der ungarischen Revolution von 1848," *Archiv für die Geschichte des Sozialismus* (1919), 258–307.

her own budget and foreign policy. The Habsburg ruler, as king of Hungary, was to appoint a viceroy to serve as his agent in Hungary, while a Hungarian minister would serve as a kind of ambassador to the court in Vienna. This was the flimsiest sort of personal union, leaving Hungary independent in all but name. The diet also incorporated the territories of Transylvania and Croatia, which had possessed their own regional diets; the fact that the Croatian diet did not consent was ignored. And the abolition of serfdom was voted for the new Hungarian state, for there were rumors of a huge serf rising near Budapest, though such did not in fact occur. Kossuth and the rest of the diet sought to protect the gentry, however, by stipulating a state-subsidized redemption.

Following this legislation a large deputation, headed by Kossuth, went to Vienna. They were enthusiastically greeted by the Viennese people, in marked contrast to later reactions to nationalist risings. After long negotiations the imperial government approved the new laws, fearful lest Hungary declare her independence outright. As king of Hungary, the emperor named a liberal magnate, Count Louis Betthyány, as prime minister.

The new government proceeded to work out the details of the regime during the last weeks of March. Its accomplishments were considerable and in many ways astonishing, for what was involved was really a revolution from above. The new government was dominated by the magnates and moderates, all with reformist credentials but naturally cautious men none the less. Count Czéchenyi was minister of public works, Baron József Eötvös was minister of education, Ferencz Deák minister of justice. Kossuth was included, as minister of finance, only because he was so popular that he could not be ignored; most of the other ministers feared and distrusted him. The parliament was controlled by the gentry, traditionally more radical than the magnates but men of property even so. Yet this government enacted a series of "March Laws" which created the basis for a genuinely modern state. They abolished preliminary censorship of the press and established jury trials for press offenses; they set up a National Guard, open to anyone with fairly modest property; they declared all religions equal. In the social sphere they carried the abolition of serfdom to its logical conclusion by abolishing all manorial rights and jurisdictions, and all church tithes, and ended the nobles' exemption from taxation. The landowners were again promised indemnification for their lost privileges, though the promise was a bit vague. Furthermore, landless serfs were not only given no land but were still compelled to labor service. This caused serious peasant unrest in April and again in the fall, when peasants seized land and destroyed gentry property. It is clear that the gentry had no intention of legislating themselves out of existence. They also enhanced their powers in local government. Yet the question as to why the gentry went as far as they did remains intriguing. They were afraid of revolution from below, particularly given the persistent rumors of peasant insurrection. A radical rising on March 15 gave rise to frightening tales of furtive sorties to inspire a peasant attack on the landlords' manor houses. Fear, then, played a major role. There was also the euphoria of revolution itself, so obvious in Vienna during the same weeks. This was an area without modern revolutionary experience; it had been touched, and in individual cases deeply influenced, by the Western ideologies of progress. It was easy to believe that a new world could be created, combining the benefits of older privilege with a new freedom and justice. And it was clear even in this reforming period that some privileges were to be enforced in new ways. The dominance of nobles over serfs was to be formally ended, but a dominance of Magyar over non-Maygar would to some extent compensate. The new state incorporated new territories, by simple fiat. Its parliament was to be elected by anyone with at least a modest amount of property, but any representative was required to speak Hungarian. Here was the beginning of a serious new rift in Hungary, between races but also to an extent between classes, for while some Magyars were peasants and workers, almost no non-Magyars were landowners.

The limits of the reform mentality were tested rather quickly. On March 15 a small number of young people, mainly university students, had rioted in Budapest itself, forcing the city council and the army commander to accept a radical platform. A local revolutionary committee was established, along with a citizen militia. The leader of this radical movement was a poet, Sándor Petöfi, a young man who had already won wide attention with his writings. He was acquainted with the romanticism of Western Europe, and with current political doctrines; he was particularly fascinated with French republican theory. Above all he had an ardent sympathy for the common people and a hatred of aristocratic exploitation. His poems had already castigated the idleness and parisitism of the landlords, and during the demonstration of March 15 he read a new "National Ode": [21]

> Up, Hungarian, your country is calling!
> Here is the time, now or never!
> Shall we be slaves or free?
> This is the question, answer—
> By the God of the Hungarians we swear,
> We swear to be slaves no more.

Petöfi and his fellows almost certainly believed that they were acting along the lines of Kossuth's own doctrines, but they were in error. When a delegation went to meet him after the rising he warned against any pressure from the lower classes on the diet. This was a strategical concern: he relied on the nobility to create a new nation and he did not want to divert them from their path of reform. He also had a nationalist concern. The young radicals of Budapest, though firmly in favor of the Hungarian nation, did not adopt an ethnic definition of this nation. They had fraternized with Jews, Slavs, and Rumanians in the Budapest rising. For Kossuth, and certainly for the moderates who controlled the diet, the new Hungary was for Magyars. The voting qualifications established for future elections made this clear: the requirement of property ownership excluded most Slavs and Rumanians, while a special religious qualification excluded the Jews. The continuing obligations required of landless serfs hit non-Magyar peasants particularly hard, and this accounted for much of the popularity of the counterrevolution among them. The laws that the diet did pass should not be lost

21. D. Mervyn Jones, *Five Hungarian Writers* (Oxford, 1966), 277. See also René Schwachhofen, *Bettelsack und Freiheit: Leben und Werk Alexander Petöfis'*(Weimar, 1954).

sight of in retrospective cynicism, but the limits were fairly clear. The terms of the legislation were more advanced than the intent; a landowning aristocracy, though unusually large and devoted to Magyar self-expression, would hardly produce a thoroughgoing upheaval.

From the standpoint of the Habsburg government, however, the menace of the Hungarian revolt was quite apparent. Social and political moderation paled before the obvious threat to the integrity of the empire. The imperial court was aghast at Hungary's arbitrary incorporation of new territory. Kossuth created another grievance when, as minister of finance, he retained all Hungarian taxes and other revenues for use in his own country. The ordered withdrawal of Hungarian regiments, many of which were vital to the defense of other Habsburg holdings, was another problem. Despite their grudging consent to autonomy, the Habsburgs were inevitably pledged to countermeasures. The only question was what measures were available.

Here, the Magyars created their own opposition. Guided by the Archduchess Sophie, who wanted to preserve the Habsburg throne intact for her son Francis Joseph, and backed by other vigorous high officials, the court began to support the minority nationalities in Hungary. On March 23 Baron Josip Jelačić, who had contacts with the Croatian nationalist movement, was appointed governor of Croatia, and soon thereafter the emperor encouraged Croatian nationalists in their resistance to Hungarian control. Jelačić ordered all Croat officials to ignore the Hungarian government and took command of all troops in Croatia. Kossuth, who was grievously disappointed by Croatian resistance, having hoped that the minority nationalities would be reconciled to Hungarian rule by the provision of liberal political institutions, reacted by refusing the government's request for more Hungarian soldiers to battle the revolution in Italy. For a time the ploy worked. In early June, when the government was at its lowest ebb, Jelačić was dismissed, though he ignored the order and continued to prepare for war against the Hungarians. But the party of resistance in the imperial court, known as the camarilla, soon restored Jelačić officially. Sophie and advisers such as Windischgrätz deplored Emperor Ferdinand's policy of concessions and openly supported the minority nationalities. Not only the Croats but also the Serbs and Rumanians organized opposition to Hungarian control, while professing their loyalty to the Habsburg dynasty. By early July the lines were clearly drawn. The imperial government only waited for the right moment to attack, while Kossuth urged the Hungarian parliament to declare his country in danger and raise 200,000 troops. In an impassioned speech on July 11 he castigated the Croats, noting that they benefited from all the liberties granted to the rest of the country; he simply could not understand that, in the Habsburg lands, one nationalist claim begat another. Efforts by the Hungarian cabinet to negotiate with the emperor failed, and at the end of August the March Laws which had created Hungarian autonomy were rescinded by the Habsburg court. In September Jelačić invaded Hungary proper, and the Hungarian moderates resigned from their government, leaving Kossuth in complete control. The Hungarian revolution turned now into outright war.

The Bohemian revolution inevitably differed from the rising in Hungary and inevitably lacked the same strength.[22] The Bohemian nobility was German and obviously loyal to the Habsburgs who protected their estates. Hence the Bohemian diet, controlled by the nobility, could not serve as an agent of resistance to Austrian domination and any change would have to come through illegal action. Hence also the revolution depended on urban elements in Bohemia. Czech peasants had grievances, particularly against the manorial system, but they were not yet nationalist and were largely satisfied by the promised abolition of serfdom. But the cities in Bohemia were small and were dominated by Germans. In fact, initial protest meetings held in Prague during early March included both German and Czech liberals, but the former withdrew when it became clear that the goal was not simply individual freedoms but also Czech autonomy. Hence the Czech revolution depended above all on a small

22. Lewis Namier, *1848: The Revolution of the Intellectuals* (New York, 1964), 116 ff.; I. I. Udalzow, *Aufzeichnungen über die Geschichte des nationalen und politischen Kampfes in Böhmen im Jahre 1848* (Berlin, 1953); Stanley Peck, *The Czech Revolution of 1848* (Chapel Hill, 1969).

number of intellectuals in Prague, many of whom had been active in promoting Czech culture during the preceding decades. Czech shopkeepers and artisans provided some support, but there was no massive rising. The Czech leaders, conscious of their position, appealed for popular backing by urging the immediate abolition of manorialism and by talking of the "organization of labor." They also phrased their initial nationalist demands in a moderate manner. Under the guidance of the historian František Palacký and Karel Havlíček, the young nationalist journalist, a petition was drawn up on March 22. It asked for the equality of the German and Czech languages in an autonomous Czech state, which was to be formed by the union of Bohemia, Moravia, and Austrian Silesia. This state was to have a position in the empire similar to that which had just been granted to Hungary.

The government replied on April 8. Recognizing the weakness of the Czechs, the court, for once in this troubled period, stopped short of complete surrender. It granted the equality of the two languages in official dealings and the establishment of a separate Bohemian administration in Prague, but it declared that any union of Bohemia with other Slavic areas must await discussion by the imperial parliament which had been called for July.

The Czechs were in fact in a difficult position. Their demands offended many leaders in Moravia and Silesia—the Moravian diet protested against the idea of merger—and began to antagonize middle-class Germans in Prague and elsewhere. The Germans supported the idea of reform and could even go along with demands for regional autonomy so long as they did not have an exclusively Czech flavor. German intellectuals and businessmen served on the National Committee which, by mid-April, had become the *de facto* government in Prague. Their numbers, position, and wealth in the cities made their support essential. But during April and May a rift opened between them and the Czech leaders, as each began to define its nationalism against the other.

In Frankfurt, Germany, a group was organizing a national assembly to prepare for German unification. As Bohemia had long been considered German territory—by Germans—Palacký was invited to attend the meeting as a Bohemian representative. He declined on April 11, in a widely publicized document that was essentially an essay on Czech politics. He asserted his devotion to the Czech nationality and renounced German claims. He professed loyalty to a Habsburg empire in which German nationalism would have no place. Only the empire protected Europe against Russian expansion, for none of the nationalities within its boundaries was strong enough to stand alone. "Assuredly, if the Austrian state had not existed for ages, it would have been necessary for us, in the interests of Europe and indeed of humanity, to endeavor to create it as soon as possible." The Germans should go ahead and unify Germany and let the peoples of the empire develop a new federation on their own, with full equality for all nationalities. Following this policy, the Czechs tried to block elections to the Frankfurt parliament, and on this issue the German liberals abandoned the provisional government, holding elections in those districts in which Germans predominated.

Palacký did not confine his effort to pronouncements of theory. As a counterweight to the Frankfurt meeting he and other Czech leaders organized a Slav Congress, designed to support his doctrines of unity among the Habsburg Slavs (a policy later called Austroslavism). This immediately angered the Germans, not only in Bohemia but also in the Viennese government, but their opposition was not at first important save as a sign of the fatal disunity of revolutionaries in the empire. The imperial court actually supported the idea of a congress as a slap at the Viennese radicals, on the principle that whatever they opposed couldn't be all bad.

But the congress did not go well. Convening in early June, it included most prominent Slavic intellectuals from the empire, with the Czechs and Slovaks in a decided majority. Poles and Ruthenians from Galicia and representatives of the South Slavs were the other main groups, while a few Slavs from outside the empire, including the Russian anarchist Mikhail Bakunin, attended as well. The tone of the majority was moderate, seeking to prepare a manifesto to the nations of Europe justifying the demands of the Austrian Slavs and to present a plan for reorganization of the empire in a petition to the emperor. But the

Slavic groups found it difficult to agree. The Poles disliked the Czechs and the Habsburg empire almost equally; what they wanted was backing for an independent Polish state. The Slovaks, though they had agreed to earlier Czech demands, were suspicious of Czech dominance. There was also general disagreement about how the empire might be converted into a federation: was it to follow ethnic divisions or should it be organized on the basis of historic lands; the Czechs, mindful of the Bohemian past, naturally favored the latter. Finally, Bakunin stirred the whole congress by his radical pronouncements, in essence disputing Palacký's leadership. For Bakunin the empire was a monstrosity to be replaced as soon as possible; what the Slavs should work for was unity under the guidance of a revolutionized Russia.

On June 12 the congress issued its manifesto, drawn up largely by Palacký. Not surprisingly the document was rather vague, papering over the considerable disagreements by an eloquent statement of liberal nationalism. The congress professed its affection and respect for all peoples, though it attacked the Germans as warlike oppressors of the Slavs. All nations, like all individuals, should live in liberty and equality. The manifesto appealed for justice for the Poles, for the Slavs in Hungary, and for the Slavs under Turkish control, but above all it insisted on a federal reorganization of the Habsburg empire. It ended with a call for a European Congress of Nations to discuss all international issues, "being thoroughly convinced that free nations will more easily come to agreement than paid diplomats." [23]

The congress, like the whole Czech revolution, was an important step forward in Slavic nationalism, but it was obvious that national feeling among the Austrian Slavs was not yet sufficiently intense or widespread to maintain a genuine revolutionary effort. There was simply not enough force to bring about the reorganization that the nationalists desired. But the congress had fired great hopes in Prague. On the day it ended, young radicals,

23. Hans Kohn, *Pan-Slavism* (Notre Dame, 1953); Josef Mačurek, "The Achievement of the Slavonic Congress," *Slavonic Review* (1948), 329–340; Otakar Odložilik, "The Slavic Congress of 1848," *Polish Review* (1959), 3–15; Peter Sugar, "The Nature of the Non-Germanic Societies under Habsburg Rule," *Slavic Review* (1963), 1–30.

mainly university students, tried to establish an independent Czech republic by revolution. They were inspired not only by the congress, and particularly Bakunin's fiery speeches, but by the proliferation of radical pamphlets since the beginning of the revolution in Prague. And they had backing from Prague workers, who suffered from the same kind of unemployment and high food prices as their counterparts in other cities. Strikes and angry meetings had multiplied among laborers and artisans in Prague since early spring. So the barricades went up for the first time in the city.

But in fact the dramatic rising put a close to the Czech revolt. It had long been obvious that the Czechs were the easiest of all dissidents to put down, because of the narrow base of their agitation. Prince Windischgrätz, the governor of Bohemia, returned to the region in mid-May. He supported a firm line throughout the empire. He had had experience in putting down popular insurrections before. And he had discussed with the court camarilla new ways of dealing with urban revolt, stressing the massing of troops in key positions of a city while avoiding entanglement in the narrow side streets; bayonets, rather than muskets, should be used against crowds, with artillery breaking down barricades if necessary. By early June, Windischgrätz, eager to translate theory into fact, had massed large numbers of troops and artillery around Prague. It was against this threat that the students and workers demonstrated, firing on the governor's palace. Hundreds of barricades were quickly erected, and several days of bitter street fighting resulted. The radicals tried to rouse the peasantry, without success, while moderate leaders like Palacký, appalled at the violence on both sides, tried to mediate, also without success. Windischgrätz let the revolt develop so that he could repress it completely. He ultimately moved his troops out of the city and on June 16 began an artillery bombardment, even though the radical leaders had already offered to surrender. With the revolt crushed, the National Committee was disbanded and martial law imposed; many insurgents were arrested.

The defeat of one revolution inevitably had an impact on the rest. The morale of the imperial court, and particularly the strong-minded camarilla group, was greatly enhanced; victory was possible without concessions. Tragically, other revolutionaries rejoiced in the Czechs' defeat. Germans both in Germany and Vienna praised Windischgrätz; some even offered to help. (In fairness, they could recall that the Czechs had rejected German overtures to discussions of unity that were not based on narrow ethnic lines; one man's nationalism was another man's oppression.) The Germans now saw the Czechs' loss as a gain for German nationalism—the Germans in Bohemia were saved from Czech persecution—and for German rule in Austria. Certainly, with the end of the Czech rising, attention reverted to Vienna, where the imperial parliament was about to meet, for moderate Czech leaders, who had intended to boycott the affair, now realized that this was the only way they could be heard.

As the constituent assembly met in July, the resurgence of the imperial government continued. The Italian armies were defeated on July 25 at Custoza. The policy of firmness against the Hungarians gained ground, though military action was still some weeks away. And the Habsburgs named a new ministry, to replace the ineffective group that had held power in name only in Vienna. The new prime minister was Wessenberg, a man with liberal sympathies and considerable ability. Also included was Alexander von Bach, a Viennese liberal whose main aim was to modernize and strengthen the government of the empire. The ministry supported the idea of a central parliament to help reinforce the integrity of the empire and it was open to other reforms, but its primary loyalty was to the maintenance of the Habsburg dynasty. The formation of the ministry in fact signaled the drift of moderate liberals away from support of the revolution.

Meanwhile conditions in Vienna were deteriorating rapidly. The economy stagnated. Many stores went for weeks without selling a thing. The regular police were too demoralized, in part because of rigorous civilian supervision provided by the revolutionaries, to maintain normal order. Crime had risen rapidly in the spring, until the committee of safety, under Dr. Fischhof, in cooperation with the National Guard, took matters in hand. Neither the committee nor the Guard had any working-class members; and the task of keeping order raised obvious potential conflicts with the desire to make further revolutionary gains. But for a time the committee held the confidence of the workers, and the crime wave receded.

The new administration assumed responsibility for ending unemployment, through the public works projects, particularly road grading and clearance of the navigable channel of the Danube River. The effort was not attended by any of the grandiose titles or hopes such as accompanied the National Workshops in Paris, but it soon encountered many of the same difficulties. Workers flocked in from the countryside to seek assistance; soon there were 20,000 enrolled, despite arrangements by the committee of safety to pay for transportation back home. As in Paris, middle-class opinion quickly turned against the workers. Employers complained that their workers found the road grading work so easy that they deserted their regular jobs, despite the fact that the committee of safety insisted that their charges must not refuse any chance of private employment. Resentment at the mounting expense of the public works spread widely. And the imperial government added fuel to the fire, for it was vigorously opposed to this modest relief effort. Army recruiters tried to enlist the workers to fight in Italy, though without much success. Government ministers tried to insist on a reduction in pay, though the committee of safety refused. Unfortunately the administration of the works projects invited growing attack. The direction was in the hands of inexperienced university students. The leader, Willner, was eloquent and energetic, talking increasingly of the "right to work," but the projects in fact seemed to promote a right to loaf. The workers enrolled grew harder and harder to control, spending much of their time drinking and playing cards. The committee of safety was fully aware of the growing hostility of public opinion, organizing a demonstration in August to urge the workers to make a more favorable impression. But the middle-class resentment of expensive social measures and their fear of the working class had already reached the breaking point.

On August 12 middle-class leaders induced the emperor to return to Vienna, as a counterpoint to the revolutionary forces in the city. On August 18 the imperial ministry of public works announced a substantial reduction in pay for the public works projects. The committee of safety protested, but it was the ministry that had the money for salaries and the government was clearly resolved on a showdown.

The workers responded, between August 21 and 23, with derisive demonstrations against the government. The government, genuinely angry at the ridicule but also eager to seize the chance to put the workers down, answered with force. Students and some elements of the National Guard backed the workers, but the resistance was badly organized and the students were unwilling to use violence, still fearing outright civil war. The National Guard units from the central city, drawn from the property owners, sided with the government, firing on unarmed workers and killing at least eighteen. Their victory was enthusiastically hailed by the middle classes, while it seriously weakened the revolutionary forces. The National Guard was put under command of the imperial government, while the committee of safety was disbanded.

The August clash, obviously reminiscent of the Parisian June Days though far less bloody, was a straightforward class conflict, with the students, uncomfortably caught in the middle, largely ineffective. Social problems increasingly overrode political goals. But the revolution was not yet crushed. The student organizations persisted still, while the workers yearned for a chance at revenge.

In this atmosphere the Constitutional Assembly met in Vienna, beginning on July 22. The voting had been by universal but indirect suffrage, with many irregularities and abstentions. Nevertheless the result was far from the French assembly that had convened three months before. Even though two key revolutionary areas, northern Italy and Hungary, had not participated in the voting, the assembly's mood was not conservative. It included only a minority of Germans—about 140 of 400 representatives; 190 were Slavs. A full quarter of the deputies were of peasant origin.

Clearly, this was not, in the main, a counterrevolutionary body. But its very composition hampered its operation. German was the only possible common language for the assembly, yet a quarter of the deputies did not understand it and depended on translations. Many of the peasants, not surprisingly, were politically unsophisticated and followed the lead of prominent landowners. Peasant delegates from Galicia, more notably, voted as they were told by Count Franz Stadion, a powerful government bureaucrat who had abolished manorial dues and labor service in the province in April. So during parliamentary debates the Galician peasants, after listening to long debates in a language they could not understand, would indicate that they wished to vote "like Mr. Stadion." Nationalities disputes further plagued the assembly. The German representatives, like Dr. Fischhof, were the most articulately liberal group involved. But they were also devoted, almost without reflection, to a strong central government over the whole of the empire exclusive of Hungary. To them centralization meant efficiency, the possibility of really modern and effective government; and of course this would pretty well assure German control. The Czech delegates stood for federalism. Although they shared many liberal views with the Germans they stood as a party apart, labeled conservatives in fact; and it was true that they had no interest in supporting the Viennese revolution, for they now thought their best hope lay with the emperor. This of course only infuriated the Viennese revolutionaries still further.

In early September, the assembly passed its most important and constructive act, ironically in so doing adding to the revolution's loss of momentum. Under the leadership of Hans Kudlich, the son of a wealthy Silesian peasant who had gone through the University of Vienna, where he served as a student leader, the assembly took up the question of the abolition of manorialism. Kudlich proposed an outright abolition, to replace the delayed emancipation that had already been decreed for several key areas. There was really no resistance to his basic proposal. Peasant agitation over delays had already troubled Bohemia and some other areas, though it fell short of outright revolt. Landlords, fearful of genuine insurrection, knew that change was essential. But Kudlich demanded emancipation as a human right, not an economic reform, which led to considerable debate over indemnification. On September 7 a compromise was agreed upon.

For the loss of their jurisdictional rights—control of local courts and of permission to marry or travel—the landlords would receive no compensation. But they would be indemnified for their loss of rights on the land, notably manorial dues and work service. Peasant delegates opposed this latter measure, which was vigorously supported by the imperial government, but their dissatisfaction was limited. The peasants had won the kind of freedom that really mattered to them, immediately and throughout the empire. Their interest in the revolution now ended completely, and they served as a conservative force, loyal to the dynasty, for many decades thereafter. Many in fact attributed their gains to the emperor rather than the assembly, for it was the local imperial officials who carried out the law.

Obviously, the assembly, while not counterrevolutionary, was not revolutionary either. It worked for changes within the existing regime. There was no talk of setting up a substitute government. At first it seemed unnecessary, for the imperial government was amenable to reform. But it meant that the assembly was dependent on official goodwill; it had no counterweight of its own. Above all, it made no real contact with the one revolutionary force remaining outside of Hungary, the student-worker coalition in Vienna. The lengthy debates in the assembly in fact exacerbated tensions in the city. The peasant reform took six weeks of discussion, and it was not of central importance to the Viennese radicals. Then the assembly got down to actual constitutional matters, which were to take many months; the revolutionary forces in Vienna lost interest. Indeed the mood among students, despite the workers' defeat in August or perhaps because of it, became more and more defiant. The radical clubs and newspapers became more assertive, coordinated by the Democratic Club. Workers' grievances mounted as the public works projects were cut back by 50 percent and employers became harsher in their treatment. Property owners, on the other hand, grew more fearful. Some fled the city. Others organized the Constitutional Club to oppose radical measures. Their activities strengthened the resolve of the imperial government to restore order.

The final confrontation occurred in October, ironically over the question of Hungary. The Viennese radicals supported Hungarian autonomy or even independence. They saw this as a complement to their own desire to set up a genuinely new regime in Austria. And they respected Magyar claims to possess a historic nation, even as they scorned the somewhat shakier Slav claims to the same effect. The radicals' position isolated them from moderate German liberals, who wanted a strong and united empire, and from Slavic nationalists, including those in the assembly, who had decided to support the emperor and who commiserated with their fellow Slavs in Hungary. But for a time this did not matter, as the radicals were in firm control of the city. The moderate elements had now definitively abandoned the National Guard, whose numbers had correspondingly shrunk still further. The radicals' mood was gay, whipped up by their clubs and newspapers. It was easy to think that action meant victory.

In early October rumors spread that the imperial minister of war, Count Latour, was supporting the army of Jelačić against the Magyars, which in fact he was. When he openly ordered reinforcements sent from the Vienna garrison, he triggered a massive rising. While a National Guard deputation pleaded with him, on October 5, to rescind his order, crowds and guardsmen began tearing up railway tracks and bridges to force the troops to remain. The radicals saw this crisis as a means of forcing Latour, a known opponent of the revolution, out of office, and they incited their working-class allies to this effect. Violence broke out on October 6, as the crowds ignored efforts by assembly representatives to restore order. Latour was seized and murdered, his body badly mutilated and his corpse hung on a lamppost while rioters shouted around it. All the frustrations of the Viennese workers burst forth. The workers involved claimed they had been incited by students, but this kind of personal violence, unusual in crowd action, was really the fruit of the workers' inability to gain relief from their suffering and their difficulty in channeling their grievances into political demands.

The violence turned many moderates against the revolution. Many more propertied people left Vienna. Some Slavic delegates left the assembly, though the majority of assembly members con-

tinued to try to restore order. The emperor fled from the city a
second time, on October 7, this time to Moravia, while promising
the assembly that he would not make war on Hungary and would
grant amnesty to the Viennese radicals. For a few days some of
the Viennese could delude themselves that negotiation could
patch things over, but by October 11 it was clear that a battle was
inevitable. Jelačić had pulled his troops out of Hungary and
camped on Vienna's outskirts. The city council announced that it
would provide for the families of any men killed in the city's
defense.

Real power in Vienna now lay in the Central Committee of
the Democratic Societies, which controlled the National Guard.
As they prepared for war, the radicals thought they had three
main sources of support. There were 18,000 men still in the
Viennese National Guard. The crowds had armed themselves
from the military arsenal during the first day of rioting; it was
believed that a total of 50,000 men could be raised if necessary,
and some artillery was available. Workers were now recruited
into the Guard. A radical journalist, Wenzel Messenhauser, was
named commander, but although he had been an army officer
he proved ineffective. University students, their numbers now
considerably depleted, helped organize the defense and maintained contact with the workers. Morale among those who remained in Vienna was quite high. Women helped build huge
barricades. Workers maintained careful discipline, not even
yielding to the temptation of pillaging the abandoned houses of
the rich.

The other two hoped-for sources of support proved illusory.
The radicals counted on help from the Hungarians. Kossuth
favored energetic action, but in fact nothing was done. The
Hungarian commander in the field was already uncomfortable at
the idea of battling the emperor, and he was concerned also
that his small forces would prove inadequate against a massed
imperial army. A tentative crossing into Austria was quickly re-
versed, and the Hungarians really marched toward Vienna only
at the end of October, when they were easily beaten by Jelačić.

The revolutionaries also counted on the peasantry. Hans
Kudlich and others went out to recruit support, pleading that

since the revolution had granted them freedom they should defend its other goals. They won no backing. In fact peasants took
advantage of the city by increasing the prices of food, so that
conditions of life deteriorated even before Vienna was surrounded.

Jelačić was ready to attack the revolutionaries as soon as he
arrived, but the imperial government ordered a delay while
Windischgrätz, who was named commander in chief, brought
troops down from the north. By October 23 approximately 70,000
soldiers had been assembled and the city was surrounded. Fighting developed in the suburbs as the troops closed in. Windischgrätz was willing to let Vienna surrender peacefully, but an armistice, briefly agreed to, was broken by popular pressure. Here,
the workers' enthusiasm carried the day, for the National Guards,
who had already taken a fearful beating and were now being led
by inexperienced students, were ready to give in. The workers
raced through the city, trying to force anyone who had put down
his weapons to take them up again.

On October 31 Windischgrätz placed the city under heavy
bombardment, after which his troops moved in against vigorous
resistance. The city was soon taken. Approximately 3000 Viennese were killed (along with 1300 troops). The army proclaimed
martial law and dissolved the National Guard, the Academic
Legion, and the political clubs; strict censorship was imposed.
About 2400 active insurgents were arrested, and twenty-five were
executed. The Austrian revolution was over.

The October rising, futile as it proved, was in many ways an
extraordinary event. The Viennese revolution had initially
seemed rather tame. Demands were moderated by the influence of
the liberals, and violence was certainly limited. But within the
city the revolution had quickly won out, for the students and
their allies really held power for a full eight months. As the
moderates dropped out of active participation, the excitement
mounted. The students, nourished on romantic literature that
thrilled to action, were euphoric. The workers, though moved
more by a bitter resentment of economic hardship, supported
them. And the revolution fed itself. Beards and long hair came to
symbolize the democratic spirit; costumes were democratized as

working-class styles spread among the students. This was a genuine revolutionary mood, reminiscent of Paris in the 1790s. It was easy to believe that victory in Vienna meant victory, period. But, aside from the silenced opposition in the city itself, not enough people had been won over. The calm of the countryside and the loyalty of the troops assured ultimate defeat. Important matters remained to be determined: Hungary was not yet subdued, Italy not entirely so; the assembly had yet to produce its constitutional proposals. But in Austria and Bohemia the real revolution was over, as clearly as in Paris after the June Days; but in contrast to France the same regime held power. Details of consolidating the revolution's defeat aside, the main question was what, if anything, had changed.

SIX

Italy: War and Revolution

To THE CONSTERNATION of Italian nationalists, Italy had remained stubbornly divided since the defeat of Napoleon in 1815. In the south was the Kingdom of the Two Sicilies, ruled in reactionary fashion by a Bourbon dynasty. To its north were the Papal States, where politics had been almost as reactionary under most of the popes who ruled since 1820. Then came a number of smaller states, such as the Duchy of Tuscany, which were heavily influenced by Austria. Northern Italy was split between the independent kingdom of Piedmont, dominated by a relatively efficient but unprogressive monarchy, and the provinces of Lombardy and Venetia, which were under Austrian control. Despite a variety of plans for some kind of unification, despite repeated revolts in central and southern Italy, the structure of the peninsula remained unchanged.

But by the middle of the 1840s there were new stirrings. Political excitement had been mounting in Italy for two years before actual revolution broke out. It had two obvious sources. The new pope, Pius IX, immediately assumed a reforming air by granting amnesty to political prisoners in the Papal States. He followed with a number of concrete if limited reforms. He created a council of state to draw on the advice of talented laymen; the council immediately demanded the right to draft a reform program. Members of the middle class and urban aristocracy, particularly in Rome itself, saw a chance to modify the authoritarian rule under which they had long chafed. They pressed also for the formation of a civic guard, which would be their own force to preserve order and, in the eyes of the more radical, might be a military weapon against Austria. The pope by himself might have pulled back against these pressures for more than he intended to grant, but the liberals began organizing banquets, popular clubs, and popular demonstrations. There was no hostility against the pope in all of this, and the crowds were indeed truly enthusiastic about a man whom they saw as a genuine reformer. However, while they flattered Pius, who was not above a desire for popularity, the meetings also served to intimidate him. Further reforms led to further demands and wilder demonstrations, until Pius finally granted a conservative constitution.[24]

With more freedom of action in the Papal States, liberals and nationalists fanned out to stir agitation elsewhere. New activity developed in Tuscany, where the grand duke, after arresting or expelling suspected troublemakers, granted some concessions. There were stirrings in the territories of Lombardy and Venetia, often under the guise of religious demonstrations in honor of the pope. But the main second center of reform activity was in Piedmont. The king, Charles Albert, had long ruled in a rigorously conservative fashion. His first reaction to appeals that he follow the lead of Tuscany and the Papal States was to stand pat, but there were reasons to change. Representatives of the middle class and enlightened aristocrats like Camillo di Cavour, a leading agriculturalist, urged a new policy.[25] They were moved not only by a desire for liberal rule but by a hope that, with reform, Piedmont could assume guidance of the nationalist movement against Austria. For with liberalism gaining throughout central and northern Italy, nationalist sentiment arose as well. This was a motive that greatly appealed to Charles Albert, who had long resented Austrian dominance in Italy. In the fall of 1847 he granted greater freedom of the press and revised the police system. He also, in January 1848, began to expand his army. With greater freedom to operate, liberals stepped up their appeals for further reforms; Cavour launched a newspaper and, with other journalists, urged a constitution. On February 13 the king yielded, promising a civilian national guard and a two-chamber parliament; he also lowered the price of salt, to benefit the lower classes. This move created great excitement in Turin, the Piedmontese capital; bells rang out, while people in the streets cried

24. E. E. Y. Hales, *Pio Nono* (New York, 1954), 49 ff.; Cesare Spellanzon, *Storia del Risorgimento e dell'unità d'Italia* (Milan, 1936), III, *passim*.
25. William R. Thayer, *The Life and Times of Cavour* (Boston, 1911), I, 87.

tears of joy. Huge demonstrations followed, which stressed the need to drive Austria out of Lombardy. The king appointed a liberal, Cesare Balbo, as prime minister, and Balbo immediately began preparing for war.

At the other end of Italy, outright revolution broke out in January 1848, when a rising took place in Palermo.[26] The rising was spurred by intense suffering among the lower classes and by Sicilian resentment against rule from Naples. Liberals sought a return of the constitution of 1812, which had granted Sicilian autonomy. The agitation caught the conservative regime of Ferdinand II unprepared, and for some months the autonomists had the upper hand. They ultimately proclaimed the fall of the royal house. It also spread, by example, to Naples, where the king was forced to grant a constitution. This victory, in the most backward of the Italian states, obviously heartened liberals throughout the peninsula.

Italy, then, was ripe for change quite apart from the examples of Paris and Vienna. Several elements stand out in this complex background to the Italian revolution. The middle class was highly politicized and, at least in the north, fervently nationalist. Their goals were focused on a new political regime; they were not attacking a hostile ruling class, for many aristocrats sided with them. But outside of the Kingdom of Naples, where what was really the first of all the 1848 revolutions was still taking shape, liberal poltical goals had already been won, without outright revolt, by March. Middle-class liberals had nothing more to ask for in Piedmont, except to let already established reforms take their course; the same seemed true in the Papal States. This meant that essentially revolutionary excitement turned all the more readily against Austria. Even in January, merchants and shopkeepers in Turin petitioned their king to aid their brothers in Lombardy. And the reforms in Piedmont and the Papal States, supplemented by eager communications among liberals through-

26. Harold Acton, *The Last Bourbons of Naples* (New York, 1961), 25 ff.; A. W. Salomone, "The Liberal Experiment and the Italian Revolution of 1848," *Journal of Central European Affairs* (1949), 267–288; Federico Curato, *La rivoluzione siciliana del 1848–1849* (Milan, 1940); Pasquale Villani, *Mezzogiorno tra riforme e rivoluzione* (Bari, 1962), 75 and *passim*.

REVOLUTION IN ITALY

✸ Centers of revolution

✸ Areas of rebellious outbreak

Danube R.

Rhine R.

SWITZERLAND

HABSBURG EMPIRE

Geneva

SAVOY

KINGDOM OF

Novara

PIEDMONT

SARDINIA

FRANCE

NICE

Nice

L. Como

LOMBARDY

Milan

Adige R.

Peschiara

Custozza

Legnago

Verona

Mantua

VENETIA

Venice

CROATIA

Po R.

PARMA

Genoa

MODENA

LUCCA

Florence

TUSCANY

PAPAL

STATES

Tiber R.

Rome

OTTOMAN

EMPIRE

ADRIATIC SEA

CORSICA
(Fr.)

K. OF
SARDINIA

SARDINIA

TYRRHENIAN

SEA

NAPLES

Naples

KINGDOM OF THE TWO SICILIES

Cosenza

Palermo

Messina

SICILY

MEDITERRANEAN

SEA

0   300 miles

out the northern half of the peninsula, stirred feelings in the Austrian-controlled provinces. When news of the Piedmontese constitution reached Milan, there was wild cheering.

There was also, particularly in northern Italy, an articulate radical republican and democratic sentiment. This was maintained by political agitators in the Mazzinian tradition, which stressed both republicanism and an uncompromising insistence on Italian unity, and by many students. It had a somewhat distinctive social base in the lower middle classes in cities like Milan. From this group came many of the demonstrators during the political agitation of 1847–48, including the riots that set off revolution itself. But the radical sentiment was weaker than its liberal counterpart. The student population, by no means uniformly radical, was more dispersed in Italy than in Austria. The lower middle class was still small—for the Italian, economy was just beginning to take the more modern form that required large numbers of clerks and shopkeepers—and it also was not united. So in most instances it was easy for the alliance of businessmen, professional people, and urban-based aristocrats to maintain control of political action.

Less is known of the sentiments of the lower classes. It is clear that there was less commitment to political radicalism than existed among the Parisian lower classes. But there was serious discontent, induced mainly by high food prices and widespread unemployment among the urban artisans. Important agitation had developed during 1847, including major riots in Milan, over such economic issues. In advance of the revolution, the Italian artisans were definitely more aroused than their counterparts in Austria. And even if the lower classes did not provide large numbers of political demonstrators, they did participate to some extent and may have increasingly learned the relevance of political goals. Particularly in cities under Austrian occupation, it was not hard to blame economic conditions on the hated foreign rulers. Unrest among the urban lower classes—the countryside remained fairly calm outside of southern Italy—may have helped induce the mood of concessions that prevailed among Italian rulers.[27]

27. Franco Valsecchi, "Le classi populari e il Risorgimento," *Cultura e scuola* (1965), 82–93; Palmiro Togliatti, "Le Classi populari nel Risorgimento,"

The rulers themselves comprised the final volatile element in the situation. Both Pius IX and Charles Albert had been carried further into reforms than they thought wise. Both, however, enjoyed popularity and both had an interest, for quite conventional diplomatic reasons, in reducing Austria's power in Italy. The papacy had long resented its dependency on Austria's troops and advice, while Charles Albert, though no Italian nationalist, undoubtedly wanted to expand Piedmont's borders at Austria's expense. In 1847 Austrian troops had marched into Ferrara, on the northern border of the Papal States, to repress a popular rising, a move which exacerbated nationalist feeling and greatly angered the pope. Negotiations for a customs union among Piedmont, the Papal States, and Tuscany began in 1847, which spurred nationalist hopes. Everyone, including the Austrian commander in Italy, Count Joseph Radetzky, expected Piedmont to attack Austria in Lombardy during the spring of 1848.

In sum, it seems obvious that there was greater potential for unrest in Italy, in advance of any news of rising elsewhere, than in most of the other areas ultimately involved in the revolutions of 1848. Nationalism was the dominant theme, among the politically articulate at least, because of the high visibility of foreign occupation and the reforms that had defused internal grievances in most key states. Ironically, in the Austrian provinces, particularly Lombardy, where revolution broke out in March, the situation was more tentative. The Austrians had ruled Lombardy with a relatively light hand. Censorship was not severe; economic prosperity was encouraged. The peasantry was relatively contented or at least unable to articulate its grievances and, unaffected by nationalism, played no real role in the revolution in Lombardy—which greatly facilitated operations by Austrian troops. The liberal upper class in Milan, composed of wealthy businessmen and progressive aristocrats, was nationalist and wanted a constitution. They hoped for the expulsion of the Austrians and the

Studi Critici (1964), III; Denis Mack Smith, "The Italian Peasants and the Risorgimento," in *Italia e Inghilterra nel Risorgimento* (London, 1954), 15–30; Albert Soboul, "Risorgimento et Révolution bourgeoise," *La Pensée* (1961), 63–73.

formation of an Italian federation. But their grievances did not drive them to revolution; they hoped that propaganda and agitation would do the trick. Tensions did increase among this group around the end of 1847, when a careful petition of complaint was presented to the Austrian administration. Relations with Austrian officials deteriorated, while the Austrian military received reinforcements in anticipation of trouble. But, within Lombardy itself, as elsewhere in the Habsburg lands, a spark from outside was needed to set off actual revolt.

News of the Viennese revolution reached Milan on March 17, and immediately young radical, republican forces—not the liberal upper class—sought to take advantage of it. They called for a massive demonstration urging full freedom of the press, replacement of the police by a civilian guard, and convocation of a national assembly. Radetzky was persuaded by worried civilian officials to keep the troops out of the way, lest they add fuel to the fire, so when the demonstrators convened on March 18 they could freely roam the streets. About 10,000 people showed up, many of them armed, and they quickly attacked the government palace, killing two guards and forcing the Austrian field marshal to agree to their demands. The revolution was on.[28]

What followed was the most intense combat of any of the initial 1848 revolutions, for Milan was the only place where the established government mounted a really active resistance. Radetzky's forces moved back into the city during the evening of March 18, and quickly recaptured several key points. Radetzky himself, eighty-one years old, had no patience with liberal or nationalist demands, believing them to be against the interest not only of the Austrian state but also of the common people; he thought force was the only proper response. He was hampered by inadequate numbers of troops; he had only 13,000 men assigned to Milan itself, with another 6,000 called in from nearby cities. When it became obvious that the Milanese were not going to cave in quickly, Radetzky was also distracted by the fear of Piedmontese intervention—Piedmont had a standing army of 45,000 men—and by defections from his own forces. Most of the Austrian troops under

28. Antonio Monti, *Il 1848 e le cinque giornate di Milano* (Milan, 1948); G. F. H. Berkeley, *Italy in the Making* (Cambridge, 1940), III, 81 ff.

his command were not Italian—there were many Slavs and Hungarians—but many of those who were, though probably not nationalist, lost little time in seizing the opportunity to flee military service.

Yet, despite his impediments, there is little doubt that Radetzky brought against Milan a force that would have been sufficient to quell the initial risings in Vienna or Prague. Milanese resistance was encouraged by the obvious target of a hated foreign enemy. This impelled even the liberals, many of whom at first opposed the rising, to support the fighting; though it was the more radical political theorist Carlo Cattaneo who headed the insurgent government established on March 18, the liberal element filled most of the other spots. The propertied cooperated with the propertyless in the actual combat. And the Milanese lower classes had an impressive tradition of protest, possessing far more experience than the lower classes of Central Europe. It was the artisans and laborers who largely manned the barricades during the first two days, when defensive action predominated.

The "Five Days" of Milan constitute one of the few real success stories in the history of street fighting. The Milanese had a minimum of weapons—only about 600 muskets. They used stones, bottles, and clubs, plus medieval pikes and swords taken from museums and from the La Scala opera house. The barricades set up in the narrow, twisting streets were unusually massive as the rich provided sofas and pianos to add to the more conventional paving stones. Violent fighting gradually drove back the scattered outposts of Austrian troops until by March 20 Radetzky decided to invest the city by pulling back to the city walls. The citizens, who picked up the guns and munitions the troops left behind, rushed to the attack. Ultimately one of the gatehouses was seized by a force under the leadership of a university student—the students formed the main offensive units. This, plus his other distractions, including now a rising in Venetia, prompted Radetzky to pull back on March 23 in what he privately described as "the most terrible decision of my life."

The victory of the Milanese opened a general attack on the Austrians. Volunteers poured in from cities through northern and central Italy—9,000 arrived from Rome alone. Milanese students quickly formed an "army" to pursue the fleeing troops, picking up support from students from other cities and from some rural brigands. The Austrians, besieged on all sides, retreated to a ring of forts on the border between Lombardy and Venetia; their Quadrilateral consisted of Peschiera and Mantua on the Mincio River and Verona and Legnago on the Adige and commanded the narrow passage between Lake Como and the Po River. Radetzky had only 35,000 men at his command from both of his provinces, and many of these had lost their weapons and were exhausted. Not surprisingly, with the Austrians so clearly on the run, the next stage of the Italian revolution consisted of outright war. Even Ferdinand of Naples was forced by radical pressure to send 14,000 troops to the north, while most of the states of central Italy sent smaller contingents.

Yet, as the war proceeded, two other important themes must be borne in mind. First, the war on the whole distracted from the establishment of an internal base of revolution throughout Italy. This was most obvious in the Papal States, where the departure of volunteers actually relieved pressure on the pope for a time. The Piedmontese government, though it had granted relatively only the most modest liberal demands, was immune from attack because all attention was riveted on the Austrian war. There were only three centers of conventional revolution at this point: the Kingdom of Naples; Venice, where a popular rising had driven the Austrians out and proclaimed a republic under the leadership of a lawyer, Daniele Manin; [29] and Milan. In Milan and soon in Naples, the war helped divide the revolutionaries into moderate and radical camps, and this is the second main theme: this split combined with the results of war to end the first, moderate phase of the Italian revolution within a few months.

The fear of social unrest developed quite quickly in Milan, and limited the social base of the revolution. Nothing was done to solidify working-class support; even radicals such as Mazzini, as we shall see, told the workers to hold off on their own demands in favor of more pressing nationalistic goals. More immediately

29. George M. Trevelyan, *Manin and the Venetian Republic of 1848* (New York, 1923).

serious was the positive rejection of potential peasant support. Peasants in Lombardy had no obvious long-term grievances, for manorialism had already been abolished, but there was considerable discontent. Peasant unrest on the outskirts of Milan plagued Radetzky's troops, and a number of peasants entered the city to enroll in the Civic Guard, in order to help drive the Austrians out. But the urban leaders, even radicals such as Cattaneo, were terrified of rural insurrection. The radicals and the liberals lacked any clear social goals and had the contempt of the city-bred for the countryside. They also were adamant in their defense of private property and depended heavily on the support of landlords, noble and middle-class, who resided in the city. So the provisional government refused to let the peasants in the city gates and barred them from the Civic Guard, ordering them to go home. An immense potential ally was thereby lost. The same fears, focused not only on the masses but on the more radical political elements, helped prompt a second early decision by the provisional government, to appeal for Piedmontese aid. The liberals correctly saw the Piedmontese intervention would not only benefit them militarily but also assure moderate leadership for the revolution itself.

For his part, Charles Albert hesitated, thus losing an excellent chance to decimate the retreating Austrian forces. He found decision difficult in the best of circumstances. He was also firmly conservative and was alarmed by the revolutionary forces that had sprung up so suddenly in France and Italy. Representatives of Britain, Prussia, and Russia urged against action. But the king did covet the Austrian provinces for his own and he was made aware, by Cavour and others, that further delay could rouse the Piedmontese liberals against him. So on March 23 Piedmont decided to intervene, the first troops reaching Milan three days later. Charles Albert's forces, supplemented by the other contingents and volunteers, easily moved through Lombardy and invested the fort at Peschiera, against only token opposition. But the Piedmontese had no real campaign plans, and there was vigorous dispute over what to do next. They were also distracted by negotiations with the Milanese, which concerned the fundamental nature of the revolution.[30]

Charles Albert wanted a fusion of Lombardy with Piedmont. His goal was territorial acquisition anyway, and he feared the existence of an independent republic on his borders. Most of the provisional government in Milan was amenable, for as wealthy nobles and merchants they feared a more radical social uprising and preferred union with a conservative state. They were opposed by a republican minority, headed by Cattaneo, the leader of the provisional government. This group detested the "backward" Piedmontese and, committed to extensive political reform, distrusted the conservative Charles Albert. The republicans were powerful enough to delay a decision, but they were too weak to prevail. They were, furthermore, divided among themselves between ardent nationalists and those, like Cattaneo, devoted to local liberties. The Cattaneo group envisaged an independent Lombard republic linked with other Italian states on a federal basis. Other republicans demurred, and they were supported by Joseph Mazzini, the most eminent radical of them all. Mazzini reached Milan soon after the revolution began, coming down from Paris. His mood was pragmatic; the first goal was to get the Austrians out. Hence he urged cooperation with the Piedmontese so long as their military support was needed. He continued to resist appeals for support of social reform; visited by Milanese tailors demanding higher pay and no Sunday work, he urged them to think only of saving Italy, trusting that the new nation would later deal with their grievances. Mazzini thus had no desire to capitalize on a potentially radical force within Milan, and he had still less patience with the federalist notions of Cattaneo. In a meeting at the end of April, in which Cattaneo raged against Charles Albert's record of hostility to liberalism, Mazzini remained unmoved. Thus divided, the republicans could not resist the sentiments of the provisional government. On May 29 a vote was held on the question of fusion with Piedmont and it carried 56,000 to 681. This was followed by similar action in two small central states, Parma and Modena, and then in early July by the Republic of Venice. Manin and his colleagues, though ardent republicans, needed Piedmontese aid, for Venice was under a blockade by the Austrian fleet; so they went along with Charles Albert's demands.

In sum, then, the pressure from moderates and the need for

Piedmontese military aid let Piedmont triumph in principle, a significant foreshadowing of the ultimate course of Italian unification. But negotiations had eaten up precious weeks and had reduced the revolutionary elan. Governments in central and southern Italy that had sent contingents to aid Piedmont under popular pressure, but which had no desire to see Charles Albert expand his kingdom, now retrenched. They urged Pius IX to take the lead in organizing resistance. Pius was now in a difficult situation. Popular enthusiasm for the war remained high. The new secular government, which the recently granted constitution called into being to deal with temporal affairs, was vigorously liberal and nationalist. So was the general in charge of the papal forces, a Piedmontese officer named Giovanni Durando, who was eager to attack the Austrians, implying in a declaration that the pope had approved a campaign "to exterminate the enemies of God and of Italy. . . . Such a war is not merely national, but highly Christian." [31] But Pius was in fact furious at this presumptuous declaration. He was torn between his position as temporal ruler and his leadership of an international Church, but he could not endorse a crusade against Austria, which was after all a Catholic power. Backed by his cardinals, the pope explicitly renounced any connivance with revolution. He specifically repudiated any desire to establish an Italian republic under his own presidency or to make war. And he clearly denied papal support for nationalism: "According to the order of Our supreme Apostolate, We seek after and embrace all races, peoples, and nations, with equal devotion of paternal love."

The pope's action stirred immediate discontent in Rome, for he was accused of betraying the national cause. His secular government resigned, radical clubs sprang up, and there was widespread agitation against churchmen. All this helped prepare a genuine, radical revolution in Rome. But in the short run the pope's statements most obviously encouraged the outright opponents of revolution throughout the peninsula.

In the Kingdom of Naples, Ferdinand now resolved on counterattack. His position had worsened steadily during the excitement of the spring. The insurgents in Sicily controlled the

31. Hales, *Pio Nono*, 73.

whole island except for the fortress of Messina, and their demands grew steadily more extreme. Offered autonomy, they now insisted on complete independence and in mid-April declared the Sicilian throne vacant. In Naples radical pressures increased as well. Mounting unemployment fueled constant agitation. A nationalist minority, buoyed by the war in the north, insisted on active participation in the battle against Austria and revision of the recently granted constitution. This the king would not tolerate; he specifically resisted radical claims that parliament had the right to revise the constitution. Learning this, the radicals organized a new rising. Backed by the lower classes and the National Guard, they established barricades and fought the royal troops. There was considerable bloodshed, but the rising was put down by the evening of May 15.

Ferdinand's policies were supported by both conservative and liberal elements of the upper class in southern Italy, which was itself an unusual amalgam of landowners and businessmen. The landlords included both aristocrats and middle-class elements, and some of them were eager for liberal political reforms. But they were property owners and they united in their fear of social unrest. Peasant outbreaks were an unusually great threat in this area because the peasants, many of them landless laborers or sharecroppers, deeply resented the large estates. With the example of revolution in Naples, peasant disorder increased. Some landlords had to barricade themselves in their houses or flee to the cities. So there was considerable backing for Ferdinand's repression of radicalism. A provisional government established in Cosenza by the radicals was put down by the royal troops, and rural agitation gradually decreased. The king was careful not to antagonize the moderate liberal element; hence he retained the constitution and allowed a new parliament to be elected. But his suppression of the radicals was complete. Insurgent leaders were driven out of Naples, and the National Guard was dissolved.

This first successful counterattack against the revolutionary element had obvious repercussions elsewhere in Italy. Freed from radical pressure, Ferdinand recalled his troops from the north, planning to turn them to the reconquest of Sicily. The general in command, Guglielmo Pepe, a veteran of the revolution of

1820, refused to obey, but only 1000 men followed his lead. The majority returned to Naples. The general in charge of the papal force similarly disobeyed his recall, but again the actual forces in his command were reduced. The contingents from several of the central Italian states were also withdrawn or inactive. In Tuscany, the grand duke hesitated, while liberals and conservatives alternated in his government. The threat of a radical rising drove the duke out of Florence, but the moderate liberals retaliated by a *coup d'état* on his behalf. In other words, outside of northern Italy itself most support of the war against Austria was withdrawn or diminished. Conservatives, including the rulers still in power, had never wanted to fight on behalf either of nationalism or of Piedmont. And nationalist sentiment was not as strong as in the north in any event. But it was also crucial that moderate liberals, who did favor nationalism, were driven by their fear of radicalism to ally with the conservatives. The fate of the nationalist cause rested clearly with the Piedmontese armies and the revolutionaries of Venice and Milan.

During May and June, while Piedmont negotiated its territorial expansion and arranged for plebiscites, the Austrians greatly improved their position. Radetzky roamed unopposed throughout the countryside of Venetia, recapturing virtually the whole province aside from the city of Venice itself. Reinforced by 30,000 new troops at the end of May, he began to plan his reentry into Lombardy. The Habsburg government was ready to concede the province, pressed as it was in all parts of the empire, but Radetzky ignored orders to arrange a truce. Diplomatic pressures were intense on both sides. The French provisional government, guided by Lamartine as foreign minister, genuinely sympathized with the Italian cause and supported the removal of Austria from the peninsula. But it resented the fusion of Lombardy with Piedmont, for it was not in France's interest to see a strengthened state on her southern border. So Lamartine pressed the Austrians to yield but also urged Charles Albert to accept French help. A military corps, called the Army of the Alps, was sent to the border, soon reaching a strength of 60,000 men. A large munitions sale was arranged with the provisional government in Milan. But, against French pressure, Charles Albert insisted that the Italians could take care of themselves; even as Piedmontese troops first entered Lombardy in March he declared that *"Italia farà da se"* against the possibility of French intervention. He was supported by the British government, which had no desire for Austria to remain but which actively resisted any French action.[32] To these diplomatic currents was added the pressure of the Italian revolutionaries themselves, who prevailed upon Charles Albert to promise to make no peace so long as Austria controlled any part of Italy. This really doomed any negotiations for a truce, for even the worst defeatists in the Habsburg court were unwilling to concede Venetia to the Italians. So after much hesitation the government sent Radetzky another 20,000 troops—the number he felt would guarantee his success. By early July the Austrian army was considerably superior to their opponents in troop numbers and firepower.

Piedmont had courageous soldiers and good artillery, but her efforts were weakened by poor leadership. Radetzky, himself a brilliant strategist, was reputed to have told his gunners, "Spare the enemy generals—they are too useful to our side." The army was also ill-supplied, particularly at the front itself. And the whole campaign was marked by Charles Albert's own indecision. He had not pursued his initial advantage. A successful effort to block Radetzky's attempt to advance beyond the Mincio, in June, was not followed up. The king hoped that French and British pressure would induce the Austrians to back down, and he had no real plan of action.

Among the actual revolutionaries in Milan and elsewhere, enthusiasm ran high but there was little concrete assistance offered. The provisional government, ill-prepared and weakened by a severe financial crisis, was partly to blame for the inadequate supplies available to the troops in Lombardy. Nationalists in Milan displayed some of the same euphoria as the radical revolutionaries in Vienna during the same period, and with still less foundation. One Piedmontese officer, asked what the civilian nationalists were doing to help, replied: "Nothing, except to drown themselves with flowers, dancing, singing, shouting, and

32. A. J. P. Taylor, *The Italian Problem in European Diplomacy 1847–1849* (Manchester, 1934).

calling each other 'sublime,' 'valorous,' 'invincible.' " [33] The judgment was harsh, but it was true that in the final weeks the decisive action was left to the trained military forces of Piedmont and the few other contingents that remained allied.

On July 23 Radetzky attacked the Italian forces in the Battle of Custoza, in which the Italians were decisively routed after four days of fighting. After a brief effort to regroup along the Mincio, the Piedmontese fell back to Milan, where the nationalists could scarcely believe the defeat. Rightly fearing that the Piedmontese would abandon them to the Austrians, the Milanese appealed to Mazzini to organize a resistance. Under his leadership arms were distributed to volunteers and barricades set up. The radicals also pressed Charles Albert to make a stand, surrounding his residence and jeering at him. The king, impressed by the people's enthusiasm and concerned that he had lost ground to the republicans, promised to fight, but in fact his troops were too demoralized and disorganized to do more than delay their retreat. The king was smuggled out of the city at night while the army moved back into Piedmont. Over 100,000 Lombards fled too, seeking refuge either in Piedmont or in Switzerland. The abandonment of Milan led to bitter charges and countercharges between the Lombards and the Piedmontese. The Piedmontese were accused of selfishness and betrayal, the Lombards of inadequate support. Meanwhile the presence of thousands of refugees in Piedmont added to the confusion caused by defeat.

Radetzky moved back to Milan, promising gentle treatment. The French government, now in the hands of Cavaignac, realized that the strength of the Austrian forces in northern Italy made intervention too risky, and tried to mediate on Piedmont's behalf. Austria at first delayed, than rejected any idea of concessions. The Italian revolution was not over. Venice and Sicily were still in the hands of the revolutionaries; a radical tide was rising in Rome. And in Piedmont itself defeat led to a heightening of radical demands. All this was to produce, in 1849, a final upsurge. But the defeat at Custoza really doomed the revolutionary effort. In its principal phase, the Italian revolution had been an unsatis-

33. Giuseppe Pasolini, *Memoirs* (London, 1885), 90.

factory amalgam of revolt and military action. The military action had distracted the revolutionaries. In Milan they had not paid sufficient attention to their own defense, while elsewhere in Italy they had not set a firm basis for internal change. The old governments still stood, backed now by the moderates. And the Austrians, now resurgent, were back in sufficient strength that only conventional military action had a hope of dislodging them.

SEVEN *Germany: Talk and Revolution*

I F 1848 IN Italy was a combination of war and revolution, the same year in Germany combined talk with revolution. There was no outside enemy to fight in Germany; rather, nationalists had to hope that discussions would weld the separate states in which revolution or agitation was taking place. Hence the Frankfurt parliament was called soon after the internal revolutions seemed established. Its members were articulate and left abundant records. The issues raised were of fundamental importance. They suggested some important aspects of Germany's future, notably the realistic definition of the nation itself. They revealed some distinctive elements of German political culture, as in the definition of legal rights. And the Frankfurt parliament pointed up, quite explicitly, some fundamental characteristics and weaknesses of the revolution itself.[34] But though the parliament demands considerable attention, it cannot preclude examination of the individual revolts, particularly the rising in Berlin. Ultimately the fate of the parliament and the individual revolutions were bound up with each other, but the individual revolutions, though abortive, had more enduring vitality than the assembly at Frankfurt. Hence a judgment of Germany in 1848 through Frankfurt alone can minimize the solidity of the revolutionary base in the major states.

The liberal demands that quickly forced reforms in the southern German states spread widely during March. Agitation in Bavaria actually antedated news of the outburst in Paris. The

34. Namier, *1848*, 152–153 and *passim*.

aging king, Louis I, had become dependent on a bright vivacious dancer, Lola Montez, who soon virtually ruled the kingdom. Lola Montez insulted leading government officials and insisted on many of her own appointments. Discontent spread, and students in Munich staged demonstrations against her in January and February 1848. The king tried to close the university, but this led to clashes between the troops and the common people. When the news of the Paris rising reached Munich, crowds surged through Munich streets demanding a republic and setting up barricades. Louis I had to grant freedom of the press and other concessions and was soon forced to banish Lola Montez from the country. Unable to accept these new pressures, he abdicated in favor of his son, Maximilian II, on March 20.[35] Revolutionary pressures spread to Saxony and to the north. Even tiny city-states like Lübeck underwent a peaceful rising. Generally the demands were everywhere the same, focusing on the key liberal goals. In Hanover, they included universal free education, improved working conditions, and guarantees of full employment, but this was an exception to the rule. In most cases the lower classes played a peripheral role, for demonstrations sufficed to win reforms and a call to the barricades was not necessary. Articulate radicals like Robert Blum in Leipzig were content to bide their time and let the liberals lead the way.

In southern Germany, however, already politically the most advanced area of the country, explicitly radical programs emerged quickly and foreshadowed the wider divisions that would develop subsequently. Taking advantage of the confusion in March, radicals led by Friedrich Hecker and Gustav Struve met to enforce a sweeping set of demands. They urged the proclamation of a republic in Baden, the separation of church and state, taxation of the rich, and the purging from the state parliament of all conservative elements. And they talked of distinctive tactics as well, discussing the possibility of establishing Jacobin-like clubs topped by a committee of public safety and of eventually proclaiming a German republic. In mid-April Hecker did announce a republic from Konstanz. He counted on defections from the established military forces and support from the common people,

35. Egon C. Corti, *Ludwig I of Bavaria* (London, 1938), Chap. X ff.

particularly the peasantry.[36] He and his colleagues were also inspired by the frenzied organizing activities of German radical exiles in Switzerland and particularly in Paris. A Communist League was set up in Paris, coming under the direction of Marx and Engels.[37] Its program for Germany, announced on April 1, demanded a united republic with a people's army, the abolition of all manorial rights and the nationalization of large estates, of banks, and of transportation companies, the separation of church and state, the recognition of the right to work and the establishment of national workshops, a program of family allowances, and provision of universal and compulsory education. This, clearly, was one of the most detailed and far-reaching proposals to issue from the early stages of any of the 1848 revolutions. And the League was soon active in sending agents to various centers in Germany. Of more immediate relevance to Hecker's republican effort was the formation of military groups among other exiles. The Parisian contingent was formed under the poet Georg Herwegh, who claimed some military skill; Hecker counted on support from his force, which was to invade Germany from Alsace. But Herwegh proved incompetent and the invasion was easily defeated. Nor was Hecker successful in gaining popular support. The grand duke of Baden appealed to the federal diet in Frankfurt—which had since 1815 represented the German states on matters of common interest. Hessian and other troops were sent, and they easily defeated Hecker's forces at Kandern.

This abortive insurrection revealed the existence of a much more self-conscious radical sentiment in Germany than in the Habsburg lands or even Italy at a comparable stage in the revolution. The radicals were clearly aware of what ought to be done to make a revolution, and they did not fear the common people. But in fact they represented a very small group and obviously lacked practical experience in revolutionary activity. They were

---

36. Jacques Droz, *Les Révolutions allemandes de 1848* (Paris, 1957), 158 ff.; Veit Valentin, *Geschichte der deutschen Revolution* (Berlin, 1930–1931), I, 240 ff. [a condensed English version is entitled *1848: Chapters in German History* (New York, 1965)]; see also Rudolf Stadelmann, *Soziale und Politische Geschichte der Revolution von 1848* (Munich, 1948).

37. Gerhard Becker, *Karl Marx und Friedrich Engels in Köln, 1848–1849* (Berlin, 1963), 12 ff.

not yet counted out of the revolution, although Hecker himself
had to flee to Switzerland. But their early failure did not bode
well, for their very articulateness could frighten the liberals.

There was one final irony in this early flurry in the southwest. Though the radicals were unable to capitalize on it, there
was massive discontent among the peasants which flared up as
soon as news of the agitation in the cities reached the countryside.[38] In several parts of Baden, where population pressure on
the land was particularly acute, peasants rose in bitter protest.
Such agitation had not been seen in the German countryside for
many generations. Interestingly, it followed the same path as the
peasant wars of 1525, beginning in the Black Forest and spreading north to Odenwald and Franconia; it later extended still
further, into Hesse, Nassau, the Rhineland, and Saxony. The
objects of the attacks included local officials, money lenders, and
above all the large landlords and their agents. Peasants invaded
the large estates and occasionally looted the landlords' castles,
forcing them to burn records of indebtedness and manorial
obligations. In Nassau the peasants explicitly demanded the end
of landlord control and the distribution of the estates among
themselves. Occasionally the peasants swarmed into the towns,
adding to the revolutionary excitement there, but for the most
part this rural rebellion, the most serious of 1848, remained
isolated from the other strands of the revolution.

Simultaneously with the peasant riots of March, journeymen
in many cities rose up against factories and modern industrial
equipment.[39] In the Rhineland and Saxony there were many
attempts to destroy machines that threatened traditional liveli-
hoods. The cutlers of Solingen, for example, destroyed one of the
iron foundries in the area. Unemployed boatmen on the Rhine
attacked steamships, while displaced wagoners in Nassau moved

---

38. Hamerow, *Restoration*, 156–172; Franz, "Die agrarische Bewegung," 176–
192.
39. Karl Obermann, "Die Rolle der Volksmassen in Deutschland zu Beginn
der Revolution von 1848," *Geschichte in der Schule* (1958), 142–157; Karl
Obermann, *Die deutschen Arbeiter in der ersten bürgerlichen Revolution*
(Berlin, 1950), 73 ff.; Hamerow, *Restoration*, 137–155; Paul Noyes, *Organization and Revolution: Working-Class Associations in the German Revolution
of 1848–1849* (Princeton, 1966), 62 ff.

REVOLUTION IN
THE GERMAN CONFEDERATION
——— Boundary of the German Confederation
✳ Centers of revolution
✳ Areas of rebellious outbreak

NORTH
SEA

BALTIC
SEA

SWEDEN

DENMARK

SCHLESWIG

HOLSTEIN

Hamburg

MECKLENBURG

POMERANIA

Danzig

Vistula R.

Warsaw

OLDEN-
BURG

HANOVER

Hanover

NETHERLANDS

Elbe R.

P R U S S I A

Berlin

Potsdam

BRANDENBURG

Oder R.

Posen

POSEN

POLAND

WESTPHALIA

(To Prussia)

Cologne

RHINELAND

BELGIUM

LUX.

NASSAU

Frankfurt

DARMSTADT

PALA-
TINATE

THURINGIAN
STATES

Leipzig

SAXONY

SILESIA

BOHEMIA

Troppau

MORAVIA

Nuremberg

BAVARIA

Danube R.

BADEN

WÜRTTEMBERG

Rhine R.

FRANCE

Munich

A U S T R I A

Vienna

Budapest

HUNGARY

Konstanz

SWITZERLAND

H A B S B U R G

SALZBURG

TYROL

E M P I R E

Danube R.

KINGDOM OF
PIEDMONT

SARDINIA

LOMBARDY

Po R.

VENETIA

ADRIATIC
SEA

0   300 miles

against the new Taunus railroad line. As with the peasants, the chief artisanal disorders had to be put down by military force. But artisanal unrest continued throughout the revolution and was to play a major role in its later stages.

The fate of the entire German revolution depended heavily on what happened in Prussia, for with the Habsburgs preoccupied with their own risings Prussia was the largest and most powerful German state and had long been an ardent defender of conservative policies throughout Germany. The first agitation in Prussia occurred in Cologne, part of the Rhineland territory acquired in 1815. The Rhineland as a whole was surging ahead as a center of modern industry, though its factory population was still small. Its people had long distrusted Prussian rule, and the rise of an industrially based liberal middle class added to the tensions. The economic crisis was keenly felt in the area, and in Cologne (which itself was still an artisanal center) a third of the population was on relief at the beginning of the year. Two members of the Communist League, Andreas Gottschalk and August von Willich, organized a giant rally on March 3 in the city, demanding not only a revolutionary government but also protection of labor and a satisfactory standard of living for the whole population. These proposals, which were not inspired by Marxist doctrine but by a more general socialist commitment, frightened liberals as well as government forces, so there was no outcry when troops were called to disperse the meeting and arrest its leaders. But local bureaucrats and businessmen renewed pressure on the Prussian government to grant liberal reforms, notably parliamentary rule and freedom of press and religion.

Radical agitation in Berlin began in the early days of March also.[40] Radical intellectuals had been organized for at least two years when Julius Berends and Friedrich Schmidt began to work through a group called the Artisans' Society and the newspaper *Zeitungshalle*. These two leaders staged a number of public meetings in an entertainment park, from which emanated a petition to the government. When this was rejected, the crowds became more aggressive, starting on March 11, and the city coun-

40. Ernst Kaeber, *Berlin 1848* (Berlin, 1948); Alfred Hermann, *Berliner Demokraten* (Berlin, 1948), 114 ff.

cil tried to form a special police force to preserve order. Popular meetings proliferated and excitement mounted. On March 13 cavalry forces brutally charged the crowds, which retaliated with insults and stones. Two days later a mass of people gathered outside the royal palace and threw rocks and bottles at the guards, shouting for the removal of the hated troops from the city. At this point a civilian police force was formed from among guild masters and other solid citizens, but it was ridiculed by the crowds and proved incapable of keeping order.

The king, Frederick William, tried largely to ignore both this popular pressure and the reform appeals that came in not only from the Rhineland but from most major cities in the country. Frederick William was firm in his belief in his divine right to rule; his one concession was to promise periodic meetings of the united diet, the estate-based assembly that had convened in 1847 and had rejected almost all reform proposals. At first the king did not even specify when the next "periodic meeting" would be, but later he promised one for the end of April. But these concessions were completely inadequate, and after a brief respite a real revolution began.

News of the Vienna rising electrified the city of Berlin, for if Metternich, the architect of conservatism throughout Central Europe, could be toppled surely Prussia could be moved. On March 18 a large crowd gathered at the royal palace to listen to a new royal decree. The crowd was unarmed and included a variety of social groups, both lower-class and middle-class, with a considerable number of students. The decree was enthusiastically received, for it moved, if only moderately, in a liberal direction: the king promised abolition of the press censorship, a constitution, convening of the united diet on April 2, and Prussian leadership in an effort to achieve German unity. But the mood changed instantly when the soldiers were seen massed in the courtyard of the palace; the crowd took up the call for the withdrawal of all military forces. At this point the kind of mutual panic occurred that turns demonstration into violence. The king, hearing the shouts and presumably disturbed by them, ordered the cavalry to clear the square. The cavalry was surrounded by the crowd and had to be rescued by an infantry detachment, during which process two musket shots were fired. Although no one was hurt, the crowd was frightened and angry as it fanned out through the city. Within a short time barricades began appearing at various points, initially in the artisanal quarters, and serious street fighting developed. Berlin's "March Days" had begun.

The rebels were hopelessly outclassed, for they had no guns and fought the troops by throwing paving stones and pouring boiling water from the tops of houses. The army blew up the barricades by cannon fire and by midnight of the 18th had the insurgents on the run. Many were arrested while others were simply killed by the angry troops. But while the insurgents had lost control of the central city they had strength at a variety of points in the outlying districts and they had made it clear that they would resist fiercely. So the commander advised the king to leave for his palace at Potsdam while the city was blockaded and bombarded into submission. This was too much for Frederick William, who was, or professed to be, convinced that the whole uproar was the work of foreign agitators and should not be repressed at such cost to the Berlin population. So the king sat up half the night composing an emotional address to his "dear Berliners" and he halted further military action. In the morning the king presented his appeal, promising to discuss the situation with the people's representatives and to withdraw the troops as soon as the barricades were dismantled; he saluted civilians killed in the fighting as they were borne before him in the palace courtyard; and then he rode in a procession through the city streets wearing the new black-red-gold colors of the German nation. In a final proclamation he declared that "Prussia is henceforth merged in Germany." Most important, the king, eager to be done with bloodshed, readily accepted rumors that the barricades were coming down and, against the advice of his military men, ordered the removal of the troops from the city. The triumph of the revolution seemed complete.

The victory had not been without cost. About 300 people were killed in the fighting, mostly journeymen and particularly cabinetmakers, tailors, and shoemakers.[41] There were only about fifteen middle-class people killed, including students, and thirty

41. Noyes, *Organization and Revolution*, 68 ff; Ruth Hoppe and Jürgen Kuczynski, "Eine Berufs-bzw. aus Klassen und Schichten-analyse der Märzgefallenen 1848 in Berlin," *Jahrbuch für Wirtschaftsgeschichte* (1964), 200–276.

master artisans. The street fighting then, as in most of the other revolutions, came from the lower classes and its vigor expressed their desperate misery, for the economic crisis had hit Berlin severely and had drawn in thousands of unemployed from other areas. There is no sign of clear political purpose or a definite reform program in this rising, although radical leaders such as Berends did participate in the fighting. The workers did not, as in Paris, press on for their own demands. So the victory went to the liberals, for the king's concessions during the next few days (the March Days lasted until the 22nd) not surprisingly went to people who were respectable enough to get close to the king or his officials and articulate enough to say what they wanted. They were, no doubt, all the fresher for not having participated in the fighting.

The king was now defenseless. His brother William, his most conservative adviser, feared the crowd's anger and fled to England. A Civic Guard was formed to keep order in the city; it even replaced the resplendent royal bodyguard at the palace. Each district of Berlin provided a hundred men to the Guard, drawn from among those with full citizen rights. Frederick William also appointed a new ministry, led by liberal businessmen from the Rhineland; Ludolf Camphausen, the banker from Cologne, headed the ministry, while David Hansemann, a merchant and financier, served as minister of finance. The united diet was convened on April 2 with the specific object of arranging for a Prussian national assembly to draw up a new constitution.

The air of harmony which so often attends the early phases of a revolution broke down rather quickly, and by the end of March three fairly distinct groupings emerged. There was a brief period of self-congratulation, in which liberal newspapers praised the workers' contribution to political reform and the political clubs admitted working-class members. Plans were drawn up for relief programs, and the city council set up a committee to consider working-class needs. But the fears among the propertied groups of further social unrest were already active, and many wealthy people left the city. Workers, for their part, complained that they were being excluded from the Civic Guard. On March

26 a mass meeting of workers demanded universal suffrage, a ministry of labor, a minimum wage and a ten-hour day. In other words, the polarization between the liberal element and the articulate workers began to take shape almost immediately. The presence of some established radical leaders plus the brutally repressed economic agitation that had occurred just the year before help explain why Berlin workers were ready to force the issue far more quickly than their counterparts in Vienna or in Italy. The middle classes were no more wary than their fellows in other cities, but they were faced with pressure from below unusually soon.

A variety of leaders appealed for working-class support in Berlin, and although it is true that the bulk of the workers remained unorganized and that the divisions among the leaders hampered their overall effort, Berlin was one of the only German cities in which new groupings developed and in which the socialist movement made definite progress. Several radical journalists, one of them urging outright and violent class warfare as the means of continuing the revolution, had a limited popularity. The most important leader was Stefan Born, a journeyman typesetter, only twenty-four years old, who had been converted to Marxism while working abroad. Born reached Berlin on March 20 and joined the radical group around the *Zeitungshalle.* In April he established a central committee of workers and the next month launched a working-class newspaper, *The People.* Born, like many Marxists after him, saw organization of the workers as a precondition for further gains, notably the establishment of genuine democracy and a socialist state. He did not believe in revolution or violence and warned the workers against rash actions or farfetched schemes. He worked for the formation of trade unions and the improvement of working conditions and wages, as well as political gains. But most Berlin workers remained aloof from socialism. Many, as artisans, looked to a restoration of the old guild system rather than to new goals. Nor was Born successful in converting most workers to disciplined action, in a period when economic hardship steadily increased. His efforts were significant nevertheless, for they established a durable base for socialism in Berlin. Not surprisingly they also encouraged the fears of the propertied classes, who could point to a definite socialist threat.[42]

The third element, in addition to the liberals and the working-class radicals, was frankly conservative. The king had backed down, but he had not been converted to the revolution. Within a short time he withdrew to Potsdam, where his conservative advisers confirmed him in opposition to the entire revolution. The aristocracy and the military leaders were not ready to accept defeat and their sway in the rural areas of Prussia was virtually unchallenged. There was tension in the countryside, where the Junkers had their real strength and where peasant conditions were extremely poor; there was undoubted fear of social unrest and some talk of concessions. But unlike the situation in Austria, most nobles saw no reason to renounce their lucrative privileges. Their tough attitude was mirrored in the emergence of an explicitly conservative group in the capital. When the united diet met in April, a young Junker, Otto von Bismarck, raised vigorous opposition to reform demands. Bismarck urged outright counter-revolution on the royal court, but his advice was rejected in the interests of avoiding further bloodshed. Nevertheless Bismarck's basic desire to organize the agrarian interests in defense of the monarchy was widely shared. Within a short time a conservative newspaper, the *Kreuzzeitung,* was established with funding from the Junkers and the court party, as well as from the Russian ambassador in Berlin. Its motto was "With God for king and fatherland," and it preached against German nationalism, liberalism, and democracy as way-stations on the road to communism and anarchy. So the Berlin revolution was marked by a more definite and vigorous conservative movement than any other of the revolutions of 1848, and the formation of an articulate conservative party proved to be one of the significant and enduring results of the agitation in Prussia.

At the meetings of the united diet, the principal debate concerned the suffrage system to be used in electing a constitu-

---

42. Obermann, *Die deutschen Arbeiter,* 107 ff.; Max Quarck, *Die erste deutsche Arbeiterbewegung* (Leipzig, 1924), *passim;* Wilhelm Friedensburg, *Stefan Born und die Organisationsbestrebungen der Berliner Arbeiterschaft bis zum Berliner Arbeiterkongress* (Leipzig, 1923), 56 ff.

ent assembly. The liberals, interested in a constitutional monarchy of the sort that had prevailed in France before the revolution, could not resist the popular pressure for universal suffrage,
but they tried to hedge it by requiring one year of residence,
which effectively barred traveling journeymen and migrant
workers, and by excluding domestic servants and people on relief. But the diet judged that even these restrictions would not
be tolerated by the crowds in Berlin, and so it limited residence
requirements to six months and excluded only people on relief or
convicted of crime. But the elections were to be indirect, for
voters chose members of electoral colleges who in turn elected
the actual members of parliament.[43]

The assembly met on May 22, the first popularly elected
body in the history of Prussia. Its composition reflected the widespread dissatisfaction of the Prussian people, even in the countryside[44]—and it contrasted markedly with the constituent assembly
recently elected in France. There were almost no landed aristocrats, and the nobles that were elected were for the most part
liberal. There were a number of middle-class landowners but
also many peasants, including some illiterate laborers. There
were many lawyers and bureaucrats, particularly but not exclusively from the lower grades; many teachers and some professors; and many ministers. These gave the assembly a rather
heavily intellectual tone. Politically the body was predominantly
liberal leaning toward radical—distinctly to the left of the liberal ministry and without any real conservative representation—
but less radical than the articulate Berlin workers, in part because few artisans and no factory workers gained election.

Unfortunately the assembly, while interesting, was not effective. The Camphausen government submitted a moderate constitution at the outset, which was quickly rejected as too illiberal.
But then the assembly bogged down in months of debate without
coming up with a clear substitute. The issues discussed ranged

43. Gerhard Schilfert, *Sieg und Niederlage des demokratischen Wahlrechts
in der deutschen Revolution, 1848–1849* (Berlin, 1952), 49 ff.
44. Ernst R. Huber, *Deutsche Verfassungsgeschichte* (Stuttgart, 1960), 610 ff;
Hans Hübner, "Die ostpreussischen Landarbeiter im Kampf gegen junker-
liche Ausbeutung und Willkür, 1848–1849," *Zeitschrift für Geschichtswissenschaft* (1963), 123–142.

from important to silly: should capital punishment be retained, should noble titles be abolished, what should the position of the army be, did the king reign "by the Grace of God." The Camphausen ministry resigned, but its successor was no more successful in giving direction to the government. Meanwhile the court conservatives became increasingly impatient as the king let the debates continue, and the crowds in Berlin became steadily more assertive.

The Camphausen government had produced, in April, a significant economic program. It urged above all a substantial expansion of credit by the government, which signaled an important reversal of traditional Prussian fiscal policies. In the long run this helped set the basis for Prussian encouragement to industrial development, as opposed to the previous use of credit and taxes to retard this process; in the not-so-long run the policy helped speed up economic recovery. But at first the credit expansion benefited banks and industry chiefly and was resented by the traditional middle-class and aristocratic elements who feared industrial capitalism. And it did not quickly aid the lower classes.

Public works had been established to alleviate unemployment in Berlin soon after the outbreak of revolution, but as usual they could not compensate for the economic confusion caused by political instability. Unemployment rose, and with it the number of workers roaming the streets. Newspapers and radical clubs churned out manifestos and calls to action, and meeting after meeting led to petitions and demonstrations. Unions formed among many artisanal groups and raised their own demands. Many asked for higher wages and shorter hours, while a group of cooks issued a condemnation of the custom of hiring French chefs. In August a workers' congress met in Berlin, with representatives of worker clubs from various parts of Germany. They produced an elaborate set of demands, including unemployment insurance, consumer cooperatives, workers' housing, equality for women, income taxes, a ten-hour day, and free secular education. This was one of the many interesting and farsighted groups that added to the excitement of the people of Berlin.

Popular agitation began to coalesce in May, when there was a large demonstration against the return of Prince William from England. A more serious outbreak occurred on June 14. Radical leaders had continued their demands for admission of workers into the Civic Guard, some of them asking that all the people receive arms. Frightened, the government began withdrawing weapons from the Berlin Arsenal. When news of this spread among the lower classes a raid on the arsenal was organized, for the possibility of popular control of the revolution seemed to be at issue. Another serious outbreak occurred in October, when the Civic Guard fired on demonstrating canal workers.

By this time disorder seemed almost endemic to Berlin, and the Civic Guard, the body the revolution had created to keep order, was obviously powerless to stop it. The Guard was in principle composed of 22,000 men, with associated groups of students, of workers, and of artists. As in Vienna, the wealthier members of the Guard tended not to participate regularly, although they did join in during crises, when the Guard clashed with lower-class crowds. Regularly participating members, including the student group, were politically radical and disliked the notion of repression. And the whole purpose of the Guard was unclear: was it to defend the revolution or serve as a surrogate police force? Amid this kind of uncertainty the resentment against disorder and threats to property grew rapidly. Relatedly, the effectiveness of the conservative forces increased by the end of the summer. Organizations such as the Fatherland Society and the Prussian Society increased their activities, while in mid-August a group of landlords met to protest proposals to end tax exemptions for the nobility and the labor obligations of peasants. These Junkers founded an Association for the Protection of Property and began angling for lower-class support by attacking the liberal government and advocating a return to the guild system. This strategy, though not entirely novel, was to be of great use to the conservatives in the future, suggesting as it did an attack on middle-class liberals from above and below.

In the short run, conservative activities led to liberal countermeasures. The Prussian parliament passed a resolution in August directing army officers either to refrain from conservative activities or resign. This measure, expressing the hatred with which liberals and radicals held the army as an instrument of repression, struck directly at the king's power, and Frederick William in response began to plan the dissolution of parliament and a government-devised constitution. But the crisis was delayed when a new liberal government was formed, under a reform-minded general, Ernst von Pfuel, and the king backed down by accepting the parliamentary resolution. In the weeks that followed, the assembly took an increasingly independent line, antagonizing Frederick William anew.

In mid-October parliament, finally reaching decisions on the constitution, voted to make the Civic Guard permanent and to move against the nobility. The ultimate intent was to abolish the class, but for the moment the use of all noble titles was banned and the hunting rights of the nobility eliminated. The king was also challenged, as the assembly voted to remove the words "by the Grace of God" from his title. This was too much for General von Pfuel to take, and his resignation removed the last hope that parliament and the monarchy could work together. A few days later, on October 26, a huge Democratic Congress convened in Berlin, with radical delegates from many German cities. The meetings, which passed a motion "that the German people by a great majority desire a republic," were rowdy and led to demonstrations in the streets around the parliament's meeting hall, on October 31, with the crowd shouting for Prussian aid to the Viennese revolutionaries then being besieged by Windischgrätz. This renewed disorder, coupled with the news of Windischgrätz' success, finally decided the king to act in his own defense.

On November 1 Friedrich Wilhelm von Brandenburg, the king's uncle and a cavalry officer with no political experience, was named prime minister. A plea by parliament that it be given a ministry with which it could cooperate was ignored, and Brandenburg was told to bring the revolution to a close. Parliament was ordered adjourned until late November and transferred to the provincial town of Brandenburg—in clear imitation of the measures taken by Windischgrätz in Vienna. Parliament voted the decree illegal by a huge majority, while the Civic Guard refused to close the meetings and the workers' clubs offered their support. But on November 10 the government moved 13,000 troops into Berlin, meeting no significant opposition. The Civic Guard was demoralized and many of its wealthier members welcomed a force that could really keep order. The lower classes were exhausted from weeks of confusion, depressed by the news of Vienna's defeat, and disillusioned by parliament's failure to come to grips with their problems.

There was one last gesture of protest. Parliament, recognizing that it would be forcibly closed, discussed the possibility of urging the Prussian people to refuse to pay taxes to the king. The protest disturbed some of the liberal leaders; the parliament's president, a minor noble and businessman named Hans von Unruh, wanted no "revolutionary" or "disrespectful" acts— even in the face of the clear defeat of the revolution. But while the resolution was passed by acclamation it received little support. Some radical students, particularly in the Rhineland, tried to drive tax officials from their duties, but for the most part the measure went unheeded. A few organized protests against the closing of the assembly in Saxony, Silesia, and Westphalia were easily put down by the army.

In Berlin the revolution was quickly wound up. The Civic Guard was dissolved and under martial law the political clubs were closed and the newspapers submitted to censorship. Again the people yielded without resistance, and although the membership lists of the citizens' militia had been burned to impede disarmament, all but 150 of the 30,000 rifles that had been issued were returned to the government, an interesting example of middle-class docility. The king, safely in residence in Potsdam, angrily told a deputation of government officials wishing him well on his birthday, in mid-October: "The assembly wished to take from me my Divine Right. Tell them that no power on earth is strong enough to do that. I shall hold it as I have inherited it from my ancestors."

THE FRANKFURT ASSEMBLY

The defeat of the revolution in Prussia pretty well doomed the risings elsewhere in Germany, but the leaders of the Frankfurt assembly, the most visible product of the German revolution, had already gone a considerable distance in destroying the bases of their own work. The idea of a popular assembly to discuss German unity antedated outright revolution. In February 1848 Heinrich and Max von Gagern, two liberal Hessian aristocrats, proposed that a parliament be elected to arrange a federated Germany, from which Austria was to be excluded as hopelessly illiberal. The von Gagerns hoped that Prussia would be converted into a constitutional regime and take the lead in submerging its identity in a larger Germany, by dividing into eight separate states. The von Gagern plan was circulated in early March, under the auspices of the duke of Nassau. Though it had originated from the widespread but peaceful concern about national unity and the inadequacy of the existing confederation diet, the plan inevitably got caught up in the tide of revolution. Few of the rulers of the small German states could resist the proposal once the revolution broke out, though many hoped that Prussia would veto the whole notion. Max von Gagern reached Berlin just as the revolutionary forces triumphed. Frederick William made it clear that he was hostile to any dismemberment of Prussia and to the exclusion of Austria, but he was open to reform. The confederation diet itself called a meeting later in March to discuss reorganization and seventeen states sent liberal representatives, who elected Heinrich von Gagern chairman.

But even before this, on March 5, fifty-one liberals and republicans met in Heidelberg and agreed to ignore their differences in order to call for a representative parliament for the entire German nation. Members of past and present legislative bodies, plus several prominent intellectuals, were invited to Frankfurt at the end of the month to draw up plans. The resulting gathering produced lively debate, but in the end the reformers—led by the ubiquitous Heinrich von Gagern—won the day over the republicans, who left the meeting in anger and thus removed direct radical influence from the deliberations. Those who remained agreed that Germany was not ready for a republic, a sensible enough conclusion but one which necessitated some means of working with existing states and their rulers in the interest of forging unity; in other words, what was desired was a revolution without a revolution.

The preliminary parliament set up elections to the national

assembly, calling for universal suffrage but implying some limitations to assure that each voter was truly "independent" and leaving details to the state governments.[45] Most states imposed residence requirements and many prevented those on relief or in menial positions from voting. And in the actual elections many eligible voters—over 30 percent in many regions—did not vote, for abstentions among the lower classes ran high. Hastily organized radical groups in the larger cities tried to nominate appropriate candidates but there was little time for electioneering. In fact urban voters often chose radical, or at least lower-class, electors, who were in turn to choose the actual delegates; and the electors, influenced by the articulate middle class in their ranks and by a general feeling of deference to their "betters," tended to select respectable and moderate representatives.

The resulting Frankfurt parliament had only four journeymen and no laborers. There was a single peasant, from Silesia. The old upper class fared badly, for there were only thirty-four landowners, but the rising new middle class did no better—thirteen businessmen won seats. This was a parliament of established, if nonnoble, notables, with local if not national eminence. There were 95 lawyers, 104 professors and secondary school teachers, 124 bureaucrats, and 100 judicial officials—in other words an extremely well-educated group with unusual intellectual qualifications. The carefully reasoned and lengthy debates which marked the parliament, particularly in its early stages when issues of general principle seemed paramount, followed from its composition. The parliament was also a moderate body, considerably more so than many of the revolutionary assemblies in individual states such as Prussia. Some moderates deliberately preferred to come to Frankfurt, believing that national issues were primary. The mode of election also helped distinguish the Frankfurt body. This means that the actions of the Frankfurt parliament should not be taken as representative of the whole German revolution. Certainly the decision taken in the spring to avoid an explicitly revolutionary approach to unification met little challenge.

A variety of political groupings did quickly form when the

45. Theodore Hamerow, "The Elections to the Frankfurt Parliament," *Journal of Modern History* (1961), 15–33.

parliament met in May in the vast hall of the Church of St. Paul. A radical group, consisting mainly of less affluent lawyers and writers, stressed political reform.[46] They wanted a democratic, centralized republic above all, and avoided discussion of social issues despite close ties to the lower classes. One of their leaders was Robert Blum of Leipzig, the son of a cooper who wore a worker's blouse to the meetings. An electrifying speaker, Blum was nevertheless open to compromise and lacked any elaborate ideological commitment—although he ultimately went to fight for the Viennese revolution, where he died in October. The centrist, liberal group wanted unification but feared political and social unrest and hence sought the protection of established states. They can easily be accused, as radicals and Marxists have done, of betraying the revolution, but they were not revolutionaries in the first place and hence had nothing to betray. They were weakened also by their choice of a leader, for Heinrich von Gagern, elected president of the assembly, was not an original thinker and moved steadily away from any contact with the radicals, professing his detestation of "mob rule." From the liberal ranks also came the assembly's leading constitutionalist, Friedrich Christoph Dahlmann, a professor of history and admirer of the British constitution who proved rather rigid and doctrinaire in the debates in Frankfurt. There was some distinct conservative representation as well, particularly in the person of Joseph Maria von Radowitz, one of Frederick William's chief advisers. Radowitz favored German unity but under Prussian leadership. Other conservatives defended Austria's interests, and even Radowitz wanted to work closely with Austria. There were other groupings that cut across the political boundaries; Catholic delegates, most notably, stood together on religious issues, foreshadowing the later Catholic Center party of the German empire. In sum, divisions within the parliament were complex and shifting, precluding any rapid decisions.

The members of parliament, from its inception, worked extremely hard, setting up two committees to deal with the leading issues: the production of a national constitution and the forma-

46. Lenore O'Boyle, "The Democratic Left in Germany, 1848," *Journal of Modern History* (1961), 374–383.

tion of some provisional government to give parliament real authority. The moderates and conservatives wanted to choose a prince, of which there were plenty in Germany, to head a provisional executive, while the radicals wanted a directory of three. In late June, Gagern resolved this issue by persuading the parliament to elect the elderly Archduke John of Austria as administrator. The archduke had married a commoner and was credited with favoring the national cause, though in fact he was an opportunist with an eye on the Habsburg throne. A ministry was appointed responsible to parliament. This done, the assembly began to assume powers to legislate on national affairs, claiming the authority of the old confederation diet which had handed over its limited powers and disbanded. The assembly adopted a national flag, the black-red-gold of the old Reich, tried to exchange ambassadors with other countries, discussed national trade policies and above all national military matters. There were lengthy debates over the merits of professional armies versus civilian militia, and the assembly sought also to gain some authority over the Prussian and Austrian military forces. In this it was unsuccessful, leaving it a government, if only a self-proclaimed one, without powers of enforcement.

Two "national" issues elicited definite decisions, which rightly have been taken as indicative of the kind of nationalist spirit that predominated in Frankfurt and of the limitations of the whole legislative effort. Both in the Polish area of Prussia and in Schleswig-Holstein, which were under the personal rule of the king of Denmark but whose inhabitants were German-speaking, nationalist agitation developed as part of the general upheaval in 1848. German liberals had a long-standing sympathy for the Polish cause. The liberal ministry installed in Prussia as a result of the revolution freed many Polish nationalist leaders from prison and persuaded the king to promise a "national reorganization" of the Grand Duchy of Posen, which Prussia had gained in 1815. Many of the Prussian liberals were willing to give up Posen for the sake of resurrecting the Polish nation, which of course would have meant war with Russia, the major beneficiary of Poland's dismemberment. The liberal government discussed cooperation with France in this matter, for the French revolutionaries were equally interested. In Posen itself, once this sympathetic framework was established, Poles began taking over local administration. Unfortunately this roused the opposition of the German minority in Posen, which consisted of about 700,000 people. And the Prussian military, secretly encouraged by the king's advisers, began to move against the Poles. Considerable fighting resulted, with the Poles soundly defeated in part because many Polish landlords, fearful of trouble, sided with the Prussians.[47] As a result Posen was reorganized on the basis of a division between Polish and German local rule; but the Germans won control of about two-thirds of the territory, which was to be included in the Germanic Confederation and was therefore to send delegates to Frankfurt. The Frankfurt assembly roundly supported this movement, despite appeals by a few radicals to sympathize with the Polish cause. A delegate from East Prussia, Wilhelm Jordan, set the tone of the debates, urging that sentiment be abandoned in favor of emphasis on German gains: "It is time to wake up to a policy of healthy national egotism." The assembly voted 342 to 31 in favor of the division of the duchy, signaling the victory of an exclusive nationalism over the more open policies that liberals had long espoused. The movement for Polish autonomy was crushed, and in fact after the revolution was over the organization of Posen returned to its previous status.

The Frankfurt parliament played a more active role in the Schleswig-Holstein question. These provinces had risen, in March 1848, against the rule of the Danish king but had been defeated. The provisional government called on the German Confederation for help, and in April the diet in Frankfurt asked the German governments for military intervention and admitted Schleswig to membership in the confederation. Nationalist sentiment vigorously supported this move, and Frederick William of Prussia, eager to regain some prestige after his setbacks in Berlin,

47. Namier, *1848*, 57 ff; R. Hepke, *Die polnische Erhebung und die deutsche Gegenbewegung in Posen im Jahre 1848* (Posen, 1948); Cyril E. Black, "Poznań and Europe in 1848," *Journal of Central European Affairs* (1948), 191–206; Stefan Kieniewicz, "The Social Visage of Poland in 1848," *Slavonic and East European Review* (1948–49), 91–105.

sent a contingent. Along with the forces of two other north German states, the Prussians easily defeated the Danes. This, however, roused British and Russian opposition; Britain was hostile because she wanted no great power to control the entrance to the Baltic Sea and Russia for this reason as well as a general indignation over the fact that Prussia had supported a revolutionary movement. This pressure induced the Prussians to pull back, and considerable negotiation followed under British and then Swedish mediation. Finally, in August, Prussia accepted a seven-month armistice, evacuated the provinces, and agreed to the replacement of the provinces' provisional government with a joint Danish-German commission whose chairman was known to be pro-Danish.

German nationalists rightly saw this agreement as a major setback. They did not realize that Prussia faced the strong possibility of military intervention by Russia and Sweden if concessions were not made. They paid no attention to the interests of others in the issue, ignoring particularly the claims of Danish nationalists for direct Danish rule of the provinces. In their minds the fact that the provinces were German by race and language decided the question (although actually the northern part of Schleswig was Danish). So when news of the truce of Malmö reached the Frankfurt assembly there were bitter and anguished debates, with the radicals in this case taking the lead. The assembly at first refused to recognize the armistice—which had after all been signed without reference to their authority, even though Prussia was in principle acting as an agent of the whole confederation—but on September 16 a small majority approved. The radicals were furious and talked of a "second revolution," and serious popular uprisings followed.

Apart from this last consequence, to which we must return, the bitter debates over the Schleswig-Holstein issue were profoundly revealing. Relative moderates like Dahlmann talked of resistance at any cost. One deputy urged a mass levy of a million and a half men to resist pressures from the foreign powers. In the Frankfurt assembly were expressed not only the yearnings for national unity but also the frustrations at Germany's longstanding weakness which nationalists felt so passionately. These were not experienced diplomats eager to play the balance of power game; these were men groping to undo the balance in Germany's favor. In the process they talked sometimes of a Greater Germany which might include parts of the Low Countries and Switzerland, for claims of German race and language could go far in Central Europe. They also wanted to incorporate non-German lands that were traditionally part of the confederation, notably Bohemia and Moravia, and even new areas to which Germans had vague claim, such as Posen. The same sentiment prompted the Frankfurt assembly to cheer the defeat of the Czechs by Windischgrätz and even Radowitz's victory at Custoza. The dominant mood was Germany over all. The assembly even devoted considerable discussion to German sea power, then virtually nonexistent. In light of more recent history, this nationalist exuberance can seem quite ominous, though it is important to recall the excitement of the times and the understandable nationalist desire to see Germany not only united but a great power. It is true that the more enthusiastic claims distressed the older great powers at the time and helped prompt their intervention in the Schleswig-Holstein affair. Germany's setback here not only shocked the nationalists but also revealed the impotence of the Frankfurt assembly to act on its own. Hence the ultimate grudging acceptance of the Malmö armistice was really an admission of powerlessness.

Throughout the summer the assembly had been engaged in receiving deputations and petitions and in establishing constitutional subcommittees. It spent many weeks discussing fundamental questions of principle, a probably inevitable occupation for a body staffed with so many intellectuals but one which sadly delayed consideration of more practical issues. The debates produced close reasoning and intelligent analysis of the huge issues involved in a reorientation of Germany toward unity and toward liberalism as well, but they did drag on, and by the time the parliament turned to concrete constitutional proposals the revolutions had ended in many of the individual German states.

Some of the most important discussions in Frankfurt concerned the treatment of the lower classes. The parliament took a moderate position on the peasant question. It sought to end all manorial obligations. The personal rights of the aristocracy, such as their privileges in hunting, were to be abolished without compensation. But the dues connected with the land, both money payments and work service, should be compensated. This was an eminently liberal position, attacking privilege but carefully defending rights of property. It echoed what several German state governments had already done in response to the revolution, and what the Habsburg monarchy had proposed in its domain. It resembled also the solution to the peasant question reached in the first phase of the French revolution of 1789. But it was not a solution designed to turn the peasantry into ardent supporters of the Frankfurt parliament, for the notion of compensation was regarded as unjust. Peasant petitions submitted during the revolution asked specifically for abolition of dues with no strings attached and, further, for a policy of land redistribution which would facilitate independent peasant ownership. Obviously Frankfurt was not willing to go so far, and the assembly harbored the same fears of rural unrest that we have seen expressed in many of the other revolutions. It was a democratic physician, K. W. Loewe, who declared: "If there is any cause at all to fear the proletariat, then it is of the agricultural proletariat that we must especially beware. . . . It has aroused the most frightful passions in the heart of man, and it has bred a barbarism which may carry all the achievement of civilization to the grave." [48]

The Frankfurt parliament's attitude toward labor and economic policy had a direct influence on its own fate. The majority of the assembly was frightened by socialist agitation. One member, speaking of the difference between liberal and proletarian goals, noted: "We are dealing here only with civic equality, not with that crude, materialistic, communistic equality which seeks to do away with all natural differences in intellectual and physical endowment and to neutralize their consequences in employment and in the acquisition of wealth." Communist agitation in the Rhineland, particularly in Cologne where Karl Marx began

48. Hamerow, *Restoration*, 162.

in June to publish the *New Rhenish Gazette,* enhanced the liberal concern about social unrest, though in fact most of the Marxist recruits in the area were middle-class intellectuals.[49]

Throughout the summer of 1848 German artisans made a number of efforts to organize beyond the local level. In midsummer a meeting of master craftsmen, mainly from southern Germany, was held in Frankfurt in an attempt to draft a national labor policy. The congress had as its main goal the restoration of an idealized artisanal system of production. It called for greater respect and dignity for the artisan, including an end to the patronizing "du" used by the upper classes in addressing inferiors. The leading specific proposal urged a restoration of the guild system. The artisans asked also for the establishment of free and compulsory primary education, a progressive income tax, a protective tariff (designed to limit competition with machine-made imports), and provision of employment by the state during economic crisis.

The position of the journeymen was somewhat different, though no more political.[50] Excluded from the masters' congress, the journeymen organized their own sessions at Frankfurt. They sought a newer kind of workers' organization, distinct from guilds and opposed to exploitation by the masters. They also wanted a variety of social legislation, not only to limit unemployment but also to provide a minimum wage and a reduction of the hours of work. Demands of this sort were echoed in countless petitions from other labor organizations throughout Germany.

The Economic Committee of the Frankfurt parliament, called upon to produce a labor policy, wanted to assist the workers and paid serious attention to the suggestions it received. But it was in an obvious bind. It was difficult enough to please the various worker groups, for the division of thinking and interest between masters and journeymen was clear. Added to this was the commitment of most representatives to a liberal economic view, which called for freedom of action against both the old-fashioned

49. Hamerow, *Restoration,* 161.
50. Noyes, *Organization and Revolution, passim.*

demand for guild restrictions and the newer calls for legal regulation of working conditions. The committee members believed their goal should be the improvement of material conditions, but they could not conceive that state action would lead to this goal. Free economic activity would eliminate poverty, which was in any event due largely to the failings of the workers themselves. So in the end no labor ordinance was produced at all, and with this the Frankfurt parliament lost its support among the urban lower classes.

This was the atmosphere in which the rioting over the Malmö armistice occurred in September. Radical leaders had no difficulty in rousing large numbers of artisans in the city. For the lower classes it seemed obvious that parliament, having ignored their specific demands, was now betraying its own professed goals; having trumpeted nationalism during the weeks of debate over Schleswig-Holstein, the assembly now caved in to a Prussian decision. On September 17 radicals and workers in Frankfurt threw up barricades and attacked the church in which parliament met. The parliament, with no troops of its own, had to call for protection by Hessian and Prussian soliders garrisoned in Mainz, which arrived just in time to prevent the mob from breaking in the front door of the church. Bitter fighting followed, during which two conservative parliamentarians were killed by the crowd. As usual the soldiers won, and there were many arrests. A few days later the radical Struve started an armed revolt in southern Baden, toward setting up a German republic, but this too was easily suppressed.

The Frankfurt parliament continued to meet, and most of its substantive proposals were yet to come. But it had failed to win popular support, the only way a revolution could be maintained, and it had demonstrated that it was impotent to defend itself against the people without assistance from the established German states. It had never intended to be a revolutionary body, of course, but now it was explicitly reduced to the position of negotiating with the established powers for any changes it might desire. Its mood, and that of many in the middle classes, became increasingly conservative. The sight of red flags during the Frank-

furt riots and attacks on private property during the Baden revolt made many wonder whether even peaceful, liberal reform
was worth the risk. When this change in mood was followed by
the suppression of revolt in Vienna and Berlin, it was obvious
that there would be no national revolution at all.

PART III THE IMPACT OF THE REVOLUTIONS

THE REVOLUTIONS were essentially over within a year, though there was a good deal of mopping up still to accomplish. Nevertheless, important questions remained unanswered. The revolutions had a significant impact on other areas of Europe and on movements that did not play a central role in the actual course of rebellion. Here was one of the areas in which their ultimate influence was greatest, for in spurring new forms of protest such as Marxism and to a lesser extent in rousing more backward areas of Europe the revolutions set the stage for later unrest. And the revolutions still had some drama left in their waning moments, particularly in France, Italy, and Hungary, for the most devoted revolutionaries had not yet abandoned hope. The final phase of the revolutions, though it saw little durable accomplishment, helped fuel the hopes of later radicals and spurred conservatives to ponder new ways to defend the established order.

EIGHT *The Revolutionary Spill-over and New Social Currents*

Attention to the narrative of the major revolutions, a complex enough matter in itself, can obscure some issues of considerable interest and potential. None seriously affected the course of the revolutions, but several deserve comment both to show the wide-ranging excitement the revolutions stirred up and to understand the long-term impact of 1848.

There was, first of all, a significant geographical spill-over. A civil war between liberals and Catholic conservatives in Switzerland had begun in 1847 and was independent of developments elsewhere. The victory of the liberal forces in 1848, resulting in a strengthening of the Swiss federal government, was nevertheless symptomatic of the kind of contest that was going on over much of Europe.[1]

Developments in Scandinavia were directly connected to the tide of revolution. Liberal nationalism had gained ground in both Sweden and Denmark prior to 1848. Under the impact of the 1848 revolutions, the Swedes forced their king to appoint a liberal ministry, which in turn vigorously supported the Danes in their struggle against Prussia over Schleswig-Holstein. Scandinavian nationalists, in other words, stood together. Danish

1. William E. Rappard, "Considérations historiques sur la constitution fédérale de 1848," *Schweizerische Hochschulzeitung*, XXI, No. 4, 21 ff.

nationalists were of course more directly involved, and they had the added advantage in that the Danish king, Frederick VIII, came to the throne only in January 1848, and had to consolidate his position with care. Under the threat of revolution Frederick promised a new constitution that would apply to the whole of the kingdom, including the disputed duchies, and rejected protests by the German nationalists in Schleswig-Holstein. A liberal ministry was appointed, which sent troops against the German nationalists and later carried on the war against the forces of the German Confederation.

The liberal movement in Sweden did not produce decisive internal political changes, but in Denmark the constitution granted in 1849 did establish a parliament which, although conservatively organized with powers carefully divided between an upper and lower house, led to a significant modification of royal power. And the nationalist pressure continued, leaving the question of the final disposition of Schleswig-Holstein in dispute until Bismarck resolved it by force in 1864.

A similar development occurred in Holland, where in October 1848 the king revised the constitution under pressure from the liberals, who freely cited the revolutionary developments elsewhere.[2] The power of parliament was greatly increased through provision of ministerial responsibility; and the upper house of parliament, previously appointed by the king, was now to be elected by the provincial assemblies. This was a clear liberal triumph, for while the king's power was reduced that of the common people was not even discussed; suffrage for the lower house of parliament remained quite restricted. The absence of major popular unrest, notable also in the Scandinavian countries, prevented a genuinely revolutionary situation from developing. But the threat of revolution, combined with a solid liberal movement, brought Holland and Denmark into rough correspondence with the political institutions of Belgium and Britain, although the suffrage was more extensive in both these countries. Belgium in fact doubled the number of eligible voters

2. G. D. Homan, "Constitutional Reform in the Netherlands in 1848," *The Historian* (1966), 405–425.

in 1848 and escaped revolutionary pressure entirely,[3] while Britain faced only the huge Chartist demonstration, largely peaceful, for democratic reforms; in the absence of agitation among the liberal middle classes there was no possibility of revolution in either country.

In Ireland, the influence of the continental revolutions did bring an attempt at insurrection, in July of 1848, but it misfired badly.[4] The very desperation of the Irish peasantry, decimated by the potato famine, inhibited organized protest. The Irish were further hampered by the death of Daniel O'Connell in 1847, for O'Connell had been the main spokesman for Irish grievances for a full generation. O'Connell's party remained, although badly weakened; it shunned acts of violence, as O'Connell himself had done, believing that petitions and political action would win the day for Ireland. With O'Connell gone, new and more radical leaders could emerge, but they could win over no more than a fraction of the politically active Irish. The radical group called itself Young Ireland, in imitation of Mazzini's earlier movement in Italy, and struggled to win national independence. The movement was composed primarily of urban intellectuals and professional people and had difficulty in approaching the mass of the Irish population. One outright revolutionary, John Mitchel, advocated peasant rebellion—but expounding his views through a newspaper, the *United Irishman,* he had no impact on the countryside, where the sheer problem of survival commanded all available energies and much of the population was illiterate. The severity of the food crisis may also explain why there were no disturbances among the urban artisans.

When the continental revolutions broke out, the British government took strict precautions, bolstering their military forces in all the major centers. The police infiltrated the ranks of the radicals, causing several arrests during the spring. By summer the government had discovered that an insurrection was definitely planned. It suspended the Habeas Corpus Act to facili-

3. See Brison Gooch, *Belgium and the February Revolution* (The Hague, 1963).
4. Denis Gwynn, *Young Ireland and 1848* (6 vols., 1949), *passim*.

tate political arrests, and this in turn prompted the radicals to launch their rising prematurely. Their military leader was a landlord named Smith O'Brien, who proved to be a self-defeatingly courteous rebel. He raised a small force from the countryside, but refused to let them seize provisions from the farms. Hence his troops deserted frequently. In a common pattern, O'Brien could rouse a village in the morning only to find that the peasants, who had discovered that no food was available, went back home by nightfall. The influence of the village priests also worked against participation in the rising. The police finally forced O'Brien into hiding on July 29, and he was later arrested.

The Irish rebellion proved only a minor incident in the history of Irish nationalism. It shows how contagious the revolutions of 1848 were among intellectual groups. But it reveals also that when the masses were quiet and the government was unwavering, preparing an armed force that was not afraid to fire on civilians, no amount of revolutionary contagion could produce a genuine insurrection. The abortive rising, combined with more general adjustments to the effects of famine, served largely to defuse nationalist agitation in Ireland for a generation.

At the other end of Europe an imitative revolution had more impact. The Danubian principalities of Moldavia and Walachia—the area that was to become Rumania—had been under Russian domination for several decades. Although the area remained technically part of the Ottoman empire, the Russians had acquired some rights of intervention in 1774, had occupied the provinces outright between 1829 and 1834, and had controlled the government thereafter by exercising veto powers over the choice of the ruling princes. Russian rule was widely resented, even among the landed gentry (the boyars). This was a period of considerable economic change in the principalities, as the production of grain for sale in Western Europe mounted steadily. This encouraged more direct ties with the West, and large numbers of landlords sent their sons west, particularly to Paris, for their education. These young boyars readily imbibed the nationalist and radical doctrines that were available in Western Europe, and it was they who stirred revolution upon their return.

News of the 1848 revolutions stimulated a series of meetings, attended by patriotic boyars, during April in Moldavia.[5] The target was the prince of the province, but the latter held firm, sure of Russian support, and arrested most of the organizers. More serious trouble broke out in Walachia in June. Paris-educated nationalists, some of whom had come home expressly to organize revolution after having participated in the February rising, met frequently without interference from the government. In one meeting they adopted a program calling for removal of Russian domination, establishment of equal rights in law, election of a parliament by universal suffrage, legal emancipation of Jews and Gypsies, abolition of manorialism and redistribution of the land (with the landlords to be compensated by the state), and establishment of universal suffrage. In short, a small number of young boyars, fired by idealism, produced one of the most radical documents to emerge from any of the revolutions. Inevitably the Walachian prince rejected their demands, upon which revolution broke out in Bucharest. The prince appointed a radical cabinet under pressure, and then fled the city on June 23.

At this point the revolutionary forces split. The majority focused on the nationalist issue, which involved both driving the Russians out and uniting the two provinces into a single Romanian nation. A minority of intellectuals insisted on basic social reform, particularly the abolition of manorial obligations and the distribution of land to the peasantry. The peasantry itself was growing very restive. The moderates were forced to establish a commission of landlords and peasants to study the agrarian problem. Meetings were held in August, and the peasants asserted their rights with surprising vigor. They not only insisted that their labor obligations be eliminated but also demanded land. The moderate government was appalled at this effrontery and

5. C. Campbell, "1848 in the Roumanian Principalities," *Journal of Central European Affairs* (1948), 181–190; Michael Roller, "Les Roumains en 1848," in F. Fetjö, ed., *Le Printemps des peuples* (Paris, 1948), 239–266; André Oțetea, "La Révolution de 1848 et les paysans roumains," *Revue d'histoire comparée* (1948), 19–34; Dan Berindei, "Les révolutionnaires roumains de 1848 et l'idée d'unité," *Revue roumaine d'histoire* (1968), 41 ff; Keith Hutchins, *The Rumanian National Movement in Transylvania 1780–1849* (Cambridge, Mass., 1969).

closed down the commission. It represented the boyars, who despite the radicalism of some of their sons and their own interest in freedom from Russia were not about to countenance social change. The Western doctrines under which the revolution had been launched were far too advanced for the Rumanian elite, which now turned against the revolution entirely. And the peasants, despite the assertiveness of their representatives, were not yet ready to mount major agitation of their own; this would in fact develop only fifty years later, when the area was undergoing pressures of population expansion and economic development more genuinely comparable to those existing in Western and Central Europe by midcentury. With the upper class now actively hostile and the absence of mass support, the revolution was doomed.

The revolutionary leaders appealed to the Western powers for support, but they were turned away. France, in the grips of the reaction to the June Days and afraid of antagonizing Russia and Britain, wanted no disruption of any sort in the Ottoman empire. Russia had delayed at first, until the attitude of the Western powers was clear and until military arrangements all along the western border were completed.

Russia was the only major country of Europe completely immune from significant unrest in 1848, aside from a bit of nationalist agitation in her Polish territory.[6] Russia had been largely spared the crop failures that afflicted Western Europe, so there was no cause for special popular unrest at this time. And there was no real middle class to raise liberal or nationalist demands. Some intellectuals, many of aristocratic origin, were hostile to the regime but they could not accomplish much by themselves, particularly in the face of active police repression; many were in fact in exile. Czar Nicholas, always a staunch opponent of revolution, had begun to prepare for intervention as soon as he heard of the February insurrection in Paris. The German revolution prevented any active Russian role in France, but enhanced Nicholas's desire to stem a tide that was now reaching Russia's borders. So massive troop movements were ordered to

6. A. S. Nifontow, *Russland im Jahre 1848* (Berlin, 1954); Isaiah Berlin, "Russia and 1848," *Slavonic and East European Review* (1948), 341–360.

the western front and the czar repeatedly offered to help the monarchs of Central Europe restore order. Obviously he would not hesitate to move troops into his own protectorate. In July the Russians invaded Moldavia, which prompted the Turks to send forces into Walachia (in early September). Russian forces moved in as well, and by October the revolutionary leaders had fled and the rising was over. A new agreement was signed between Russia and Turkey, providing joint control of the governments of the principalities, and the occupying forces remained for three years.

The Rumanian revolution produced dramatic statements of purpose, not only from the intellectuals but also from the peasantry. Yet the revolution itself was a rather shallow affair, because of the split between the moderate nationalists and the bulk of the population. The masses were not interested in fighting for national independence and the nationalists, for the most part afraid of social unrest in any event, could not defend themselves. The revolution was more than a sign that change was beginning to occur in southeastern Europe. It called widespread attention to the existence of a Rumanian cause; nationalists in Western Europe found it particularly easy to sympathize with the Rumanians because their enemy was the reactionary Russian czar and their independence threatened no self-interest in the West. This sympathy in turn helped produce the diplomatic intervention that only a decade after the revolution created an independent Rumania.

The influence of the revolutions of 1848 thus essentially confirmed the power, and in some cases the predominance, of liberal political elements in Western Europe—the region that had been most affected by the French Revolution of 1789 and the English industrial revolution. At the same time the impact of 1848 spread steadily eastward on the continent, beyond the areas previously involved in revolutionary contagion. In this sense the revolutions, although the last in the great series that had begun in the eighteenth century, heralded further political and social change, for the new influences at work in eastern Central Europe would not be digested easily.

The revolutions correspondingly heightened certain new

developments within the countries of Western and Central Europe themselves. All major revolutions, because of the varied implications of the ideology involved and the intense excitement engendered by participation in conflict, produce a variety of subsidiary currents. The English and French revolutions had both generated socialist demands, which extended some of the implications of Protestant thought, in the English case, and Enlightenment thought in the French. Both had encouraged new activities and demands on the part of women. The revolutions of 1848 had a similar effect, but in this case some of the excitement was translated into more durable political and social movements. Two groups, the women and the Jews, demonstrated a heightened consciousness of their importance in the mainstream of European politics, while the newest socialist ideology, Marxism, first tested itself during the revolutions. These developments are related only in the sense that they all benefited from the period of revolutionary enthusiasm and at the same time helped support this enthusiasm.

Profound changes had begun to take place in the Jewish communities of Western and Central Europe at the end of the eighteenth century. On the one hand, legislation derived from the Enlightenment belief in the fundamental equality of all men broke down some traditional barriers. Jews gained legal equality in France in 1791. In Central Europe, restrictions were reduced but not eliminated before 1848. In response to new laws and to the direct influence of Enlightenment thought, many Jews began to adopt new ways in an effort to integrate themselves more fully into their national community. Some converted to Christianity, like Marx's father; many more of them modified traditional customs in an effort to appear less distinctive. They were encouraged in this endeavor by the social and economic changes taking place during the first half of the nineteenth century. Many Jews left small towns and moved toward the larger cities, as the importance of agriculture declined; a sizable Jewish community built up, for example, in Budapest for the first time. The revolutions of 1848 both reflected and furthered the modernization of European Jews.[7]

7. Adolf Kober, "Jews in the Revolution of 1848 in Germany," *Jewish Social Studies* (1948), 135–164.

A number of individual Jews, or men of Jewish origin, played a significant role as revolutionary leaders, the first time in Europe's history that Jews had entered the political mainstream. Marx has been mentioned. Daniele Manin, the revolutionary leader in Venice, was the son of a converted Jew and sponsored legislation granting full religious tolerance and legal equality in his city. The radical leader Adolf Fischhof, in Vienna, was Jewish, and the list could be lengthened. Revolutionaries in general were, for their part, eager to grant legal equality to the Jews. This was one provision of the constitution drawn up by the Frankfurt assembly. Late in the Hungarian Revolution the diet, pressed by Lajos Kossuth, emancipated the Jews. The student regime in Vienna managed to abolish the special tax on Jews resident in that city. In other words, even nationalist revolutionaries remained sufficiently liberal in their definition of the nation, avoiding racial criteria, to seek equality under the law. Jewish communities naturally supported the revolutions with enthusiasm. Jewish students played an active role in the initial Vienna uprising. Jewish militia companies were formed during the first agitation in Budapest and were joined by Magyar revolutionaries to symbolize the disappearance of race prejudice. Jews actively backed the Magyar armies with money and men, and gained great credit in the process. Thus in Central Europe generally, and particularly in Hungary, the revolutions advanced Jewish assimilation. Some of the specific achievements were undone as the revolutions were defeated; full legal equality was not actually put into effect in Central Europe for another twenty years. And even in the revolutions themselves there were adverse developments. German peasants, in their unrest, singled out Jewish money lenders on many occasions. The Habsburg forces that finally put down the Hungarian revolt levied special fines on the Jews, in punishment for their revolutionary activities. Nevertheless, the revolutions marked an important stage in the interaction between Jews and the dominant peoples of Europe. Certainly they furthered the association of modernized Jews with the political left.

The revolutionaries in France faced no legal issues concerning the Jews, but they did confront the continuation of slavery in the French colonies. Here was an issue that even the provisional government was willing to tackle, and the abolition of slavery in all French colonies, with compensation to the owners, was one of the significant and durable achievements of the revolution.

The appearance of women in the revolutions of 1848 has been noted already.[8] A few achieved positions of some authority, notably George Sand in France. Among the lower classes, women were elected as representatives of some industries, to appear before the Luxembourg Commission. A few women workers, such as Parisian laundresses, conducted strikes during the revolution period; there was some agitation among women in the National Workshops for equal pay and greater power. A number of Italian women, particularly noblewomen, were enthusiastic liberals and nationalists. Most supported the revolution by influencing their husbands and sons; Manin's wife, for example, sent her teen-aged boy to attack the Austrian arsenal despite her fears that he would be killed. But in Rome, during the eventual rising, Princess Belgioioso organized hospitals for the wounded, recruiting 6000 women for her staff. In other words there were suggestions of new roles for women during the revolution, in the middle class and, at least in France, in the working class as well, of the sort that developed more permanently during the calmer decades that followed. Women participated vigorously during some of the revolutionary fighting, and although there was precedent for this among lower-class women during the French Revolution of 1789 the extent and enthusiasm may have been greater than before. Women supported the barricade fighting in Vienna during October and some carried weapons. Women volunteered for the Hungarian army. Kossuth, nonplussed at the appearance of two regiments of women, sent one to work in the hospitals and another to make cartridges. But individual women served, in disguise, in the regular forces, and two were reputed to have earned the rank of captain before they were discovered. In Paris, a few women fought on the barricades in February, while more gathered at the entrance of narrow streets "talking anxiously and urging the men on to deeds of valour."[9] They were far more

8. Edith Thomas, *Les Femmes de 1848* (Paris, 1948), *passim*.
9. Percy B. St. John, *The Three Days of February 1848* (New York, 1848), 93.

bitter in June, and many carried weapons, some leading the men. Others loaded and cleaned guns and tried to discourage the at-tacking soldiers. Victor Hugo tells of two prostitutes who climbed a barricade, lifted their skirts, and dared the soldiers to shoot; unfortunately the soldiers took them up on it. The combat role of Parisian women was less significant than in the Commune of 1870, but far greater than in 1830, suggesting some develop-ments in the position and outlook of lower-class women that historians have yet to articulate.

The revolutions produced a few efforts by men to improve the situation of women, though most were tentative and infor-mal; here was an obvious limitation on the revolutionary ideol-ogy. The workers' congress that met in Berlin in August asked for equal rights for women. Caussidière, who took over the Paris police, tried to reduce the exploitation of prostitutes ·by dis-couraging pimps and amateur efforts; he favored large, legalized houses, each run by a matron, where the women would be regu-larly inspected for disease. More tentatively still, Viennese stu-dents, during their revolutionary euphoria, treated women on a more equal basis and with greater informality.

In a few areas women demanded new rights for themselves. There was little activity of this sort in the Habsburg lands or Italy; women who had political interests there, and they were probably few in number, thought in terms of the general goals of the revolution. A Democratic Women's Club was founded in Berlin, but despite the political implications of the title—and the fact that with one brief exception no man was allowed to attend meetings—the club raised few specific demands, spending most of its time discussing remedies to social problems, such as the pro-vision of respectable employment for jobless servants.

But in Paris, where the democratic and revolutionary tra-dition was strongest and where social changes among middle-class women had probably gone further than in any other con-tinental coutry, a large number of feminist organizations were founded during the active phase of the revolution.[10] The high political awareness of many middle-class women was indicated in their avid attendance at the meetings of radical clubs, where they

10. Thomas, *Les Femmes*, *passim*.

were allowed in the audience, and in the parliamentary galleries. Posters on yellow paper advocated women's rights. A number of feminist newspapers were launched, the first being the *Voice of Women*, which advocated some of the general radical demands, such as a delay in the parliamentary elections, but also the establishment of divorce, the elimination of discrimination by sex in the workshops, and the establishment of daycare centers for working women. At least six women's organizations sprang up after several radical clubs run by men rejected their demands for new rights. One, led by the *Voice of Women*'s editor, Eugénie Niboyet, ultimately banned men from the meetings because they so often jeered. Most demanded a vote for women and one supported a woman running for political office. The clubs' membership was not large. They drew particularly on the handful of women intellectuals in Paris and on related groups of professional women, most of them unmarried, such as schoolteachers.

The significance of this general movement should not be exaggerated, even in Paris. It resulted from the revolutionary excitement but it did not play a major role in the upheaval. It was easily crushed along with the general defeat of the revolutions. On July 26 the French assembly ruled that women could not belong to or attend the meetings of political clubs. The radical women's papers were closed down. Yet the assembly ruling indicates, along with male traditionalism, a certain fear of women's political efforts. Even so, it is impossible at this point to determine how serious and extensive were the causes of the feminist unrest, or whether there was significant continuity with later efforts. Too much of women's history, particularly for countries like France and Germany, remains unexplored. What is certain is that the demands for specific rights were substantially new on the continent, yet related to some of the broader revolutionary activities undertaken by women in the 1848 risings.

Abou the in eraction between Marxism and the revolutions far more is known.[11] Again, however, we must be careful not to

11. Peter Amann, "Karl Marx: 'Quarante-huitard français,'" *International Review of Social History* (1961), 249–255; Samuel Bernstein, "Marx in Paris, 1848," *Science and Society* (1939), 323–355; Gerhard Becker, *Karl Marx und Friedrich Engels in Köln* (Berlin, 1963); Auguste Cornu, "Karl Marx et la révolution de 1848 en Allemagne," *Europe* (1948), 238–252; M. A. Kotschet-

exaggerate, for though the revolutions played a significant role in the early history of Marxism, the converse does not hold true. Marxism, a very new doctrine known only to a handful of socialist agitators at the outset of the revolutions, was far less significant than some of the varieties of utopian socialism in the revolutions; and, with some qualifications for Paris and Berlin, socialism of any sort cannot qualify as a major revolutionary ingredient. The revolutions brought an increase in socialist agitation, not only in France and Germany but also in Italy, but this was still a tentative period, mainly because the socialists found it difficult to make contact with large numbers of workers.

Karl Marx spent several weeks in France during March, as the revolutions unfolded, and arranged to transfer the headquarters of the Communist League from London to Paris. He began drafting a program called "The Seventeen Demands of the Communist Party in Germany" that set the tone for most of his revolutionary activity during the remainder of the year. The goals he set forward were at least as much political as socialist. He sought a united German republic as his first demand. He also advocated the abolition of manorialism without compensation to the landlords, the separation of church and state, free and equal education, and the distribution of weapons to the people. German exiles in Paris took this program to a number of cities in Germany, attempting to found communist cells. One such apostle, Stefan Born, did very well, as we have seen, but he stressed workers' organizations that would win immediate gains. Most others, who stuck more closely to Marx's program, had little success.

Marx himself took a more direct role in April, when he moved to Cologne. His purpose was not to shape a workers' rebellion, for he was convinced that this would be premature, given the disorganization of the lower classes. Rather he hoped to win workers' support for the radical middle-class politicians, and it was for this reason that he concentrated on reviving the

---

kowa, "Die Tätigkeit von Marx und Engels in der Kölner Demokratischen Gesellschaft, April bis Oktober, 1848," *Sowjetwissenschaft: Gesellschaftswissenschaftliche Beiträge*, No. 11 (1960), 1155–1167; Isaiah Berlin, *Karl Marx* (Oxford, 1948), 152–172.

Rhenish Gazette as an outlet for his opinions. He had a difficult time obtaining the necessary capital. Workers could offer little and were unfamiliar with Marx in any event, while the radicals proved extremely suspicious. Engels, writing to Marx from Elberfeld, noted: "They shy away from any discussion of social problems as from the plague; the heart of the matter is this, that even the radical bourgeois see in us their chief enemies of the future and therefore refuse to put any weapons in our hands that we would turn against them." Ultimately Marx and particularly Engels had to put up some of their own money, though they won some backing from liberal industrialists as well, and the *New Rhenish Gazette* began to appear on June 1. It soon attained a circulation of 5000, which was quite high for the period. The success resulted in large part from Marx's careful concentration on the political issues, particularly during his first weeks as editor, for he continued to see political gains as most achievable in the short run and the basis for more successful social agitation in the future, as the working class matured. Marx dissolved the Communist League, arguing that a secret organization would only antagonize potential allies. He also did not wish to conflict with other workers' organizations, such as the large Workers' Society in Cologne headed by a socially minded but undoctrinaire physician, Andreas Gottschalk, which was devoted to direct action toward the goal of improving the workers' lot and establishing a democratic republic. Marx himself founded a Democratic Society to cooperate with the radicals in the parliamentary elections and later, in the autumn, after Gottschalk and other leaders had been arrested, took over the presidency of the Workers' Society. In his paper Marx stressed the importance of winning a genuine democracy, playing down specific communist goals. He vigorously supported the nationalist cause, including the invasion of Schleswig-Holstein, not because he was a nationalist but because he was convinced that only a united Germany could industrialize rapidly and thus provide the basis for a proletarian revolution. An ardent Russophobe, he also advocated war against Russia because of his certainty that the czar would intervene against a progressive Germany. In internal politics Marx vigorously criticized the timidity of the liberals in the

Prussian government and in Frankfurt, accusing them of seeking deals with the royalists and betraying the German masses. His tone, albeit largely political, was strident and uncompromising, and he could not stay away from social comment altogether. He was electrified by the news of the June Days in Paris, writing that "the clashes that spontaneously arise out of the conditions of bourgeois society must be fought to the bitter end; they cannot be conjured out of existence."

This frank advocacy of class warfare frightened many subscribers, and the *New Rhenish Gazette* soon began to lose money. Marx thus, despite some efforts at self-restraint, contributed to the growing fear of radicalism among the German middle class, though other, more visible movements played a larger role here. Following the suppression of the Berlin revolution, the Prussian government closed down the *Gazette* and arrested Marx for sedition. Marx used the occasion to deliver a long, erudite speech about the social and political situation in Germany and abroad, and, surprisingly, he was acquitted; the foreman of the jury thanked him for his unusually instructive lecture. The Prussian government subsequently expelled him from the Rhineland, in July 1849, and Marx returned to Paris, hoping for a chance to play a role in the still-confused situation in France. He was soon pressed to leave France by the conservative and apprehensive republican government, and he began his permanent London exile. He retaliated against the French bourgeoisie by writing a brilliant analysis of the 1848 revolution and the regimes that followed.[12]

Marx had won a few supporters in Cologne, mainly among middle-class intellectuals. He and his followers had founded some organizations elsewhere in Germany, and if few of them survived they did provide a precedent for later action. Without question Marx increased his reputation in the socialist movement by his 1848 activities. He played some role in advancing the level of working-class agitation, a topic to which we will return in assessing the broader impact of the revolutions. But the revolution did not launch a full-fledged Marxist movement and Marx made little headway among the workers. Nevertheless, the 1848 revolu-

12. Marx, *Class Struggles;* Marx, *Eighteenth Brumaire.*

tions did serve as a testing ground for Marx himself; they provided the only personal involvement with direct action that he ever had. As a result of his experience, he developed his belief that the proper revolutionary approach was the formation of an open revolutionary party proceeding by recognized political methods. This involved him in growing conflict with other revolutionaries, such as Bakunin, who thought that the revolutions showed the need for secret, terrorist groups. Marx was true to his conviction that history could not be rushed. Germany needed a bourgeois victory before it could have a proletarian victory. The revolution and its aftermath forced Marx to reconsider his relationships with many socialist colleagues. As defeat and disillusionment took their toll of radical enthusiasms, and as many socialists suffered arrest and exile, Marx developed a more isolated attitude, preserving contact only with men who had demonstrated their personal loyalty to his cause. Engels became his avowed chief of staff, and Marx treated other followers as definite subordinates. Conceptually, 1848 had its greatest impact on Marx in encouraging him to think more of tactics. He remained convinced that the proletarian revolution was inevitable and would succeed, but his experience in Germany suggested the need for far more careful planning. He was appalled by what he termed the stupidity of most radical leaders and also by the political gullibility of the masses, who seemed so readily deceived by their own worst enemies. Hence his future work was devoted as much to considerations of what methods revolutionary leaders should adopt in the interests of their uncomprehending followers as in the analysis of the condition of society.

The revolutions of 1848 thus radiated an influence that affected the development of eastern Central Europe, of Marxism, of the European Jews, and possibly of feminism. All these areas, movements, and peoples were to assume a major role in the mainstream of European history within at most two generations. Through them, the revolutions exerted a continuing, if sometimes unexpected, impact.

NINE *The Revolutionary*

Aftermath

THE AFTEREFFECTS OF revolution lasted until 1851. During this three-year span, two developments occurred in all the major revolutionary centers, and a third in most. There was the final mopping up of agitation everywhere. Accompanying this was the production of constitutional proposals by moderate revolutionaries and the granting of some concessions (in a few cases very transitory) by the reestablished governments. In other words, by 1851 the permanent visible achievements of the revolutions, if any, had been worked out. In a number of cases, the mopping-up phase was accompanied by renewed efforts at radical risings, which breathed a semblance of life into the revolutions well into 1849. Repression, brief but radical rebuttal, and some constitutional compromise—these are the themes to follow in exploring the waning phases of the revolution. There is no intent to provide a comprehensive narrative of the three postrevolutionary years, but rather to focus specifically on the termination process.

The revolutionary aftermath was considerably more complex in some areas than in others. In Germany, though there were some final radical risings, the process was fairly straightforward, for once the Prussian revolution had been undermined and the Frankfurt parliament had tacitly admitted its impotence there were few barriers to the restoration of order. Prussia had the strongest, most self-conscious conservative movement. In most of the Habsburg monarchy the process was similar, indeed more completely repressive; but the Habsburgs had still to contend with the Hungarian revolt, which was in full swing at the end of 1848. The revolutionary aftermath in Italy included a renewed attempt by Piedmont to war with Austria over Lombardy; this quickly proved abortive, and the spark had gone out of the Italian revolution as a whole. But the revolutionaries in Venice held out bravely and a new rising in Rome, the most interesting of all the later radical efforts, lasted well into 1849. But it was in France that the postrevolutionary years were most frenetic, with recurrent unrest lasting until 1851. Only in France was there a new regime to construct, even if most of the members of the constituent assembly did not intend it to differ greatly from its predecessor. Only in France was repression modified by continued political uncertainty, leaving some leeway for political and social agitation. France in fact went through a truncated version of the classic revolutionary cycle. There was no radical phase of the revolution, for this had been cut off by the workers' defeat in the June Days. But continued economic hardship, enhanced by political uncertainty, combined with active proselytizing by many radical and socialist leaders to produce new expressions of discontent, especially in the provinces. And this threat of radical outbreaks helped induce a final authoritarian phase under the leadership of Louis Napoleon, the nephew of the erstwhile revolutionary dictator of France.

GERMANY

The Frankfurt parliament opened its discussion of a draft constitution in October 1848.[13] It had previously approved a series of Fundamental Rights which were meant to apply to all German people. These included freedom of speech, press, and religion, trial by jury, abolition of all manorial rights and other privileges, and equality under the law. There was also to be local self-government, with democratic and responsible government in each of the German states. Despite the selfishness of the nation-

---

13. Gustav Radbruch, "Die Frankfurter Grundrechte," in Wilhelm Keil, ed., *Deutschland 1848–1948* (Stuttgart, 1948), 80–88; Herbert Strauss, *Staat, Bürger, Mensch: die Debatten der deutschen Nationalversammlung über die Grundrechte* (Aarau, 1947).

alism so often displayed in Frankfurt, in the final constitutional draft the cultural freedom of non-German citizens was to be assured. In short, after much debate, particularly on such matters as the relations between church and state, the assembly had produced an admirably liberal statement. But on the constitution itself, the parliament quickly encountered two practical problems of great magnitude: what to do about Austria in a united Germany and how to organize the executive branch of the new government. The delegates decided without great difficulty that the states of Germany would survive, but without sovereign powers; they would give their rights of diplomatic representation over to the new government and would also lose much of their authority in legislative, military, and economic affairs. Firmly nationalist, the Frankfurt assembly rejected complaints from the smaller states that their powers were being unduly curtailed. The liberal motif was continued in the provision of a two-house national parliament, the upper house representing the states, the lower to be elected by universal suffrage. The head of the state could suspend parliamentary legislation for a time, but his ministers were to be responsible to representatives of parliament. Several of the German states asked for an absolute veto for the head of state, because they feared the actions of a democratically elected assembly, but on this too the Frankfurt delegates stood firm.

Yet the real question was the attitude of the great German states, Prussia and Austria. The Frankfurt assembly was divided, in theory, about whether Austria should be included at all.[14] Advocates of a *grossdeutsch,* or greater German, policy wanted its inclusion; these included many Catholics and others fearful of Prussian predominance. The constitutional committee on the subject in fact recommended inclusion, but on condition that Austria separate the rule of her German and non-German lands. *Kleindeutsch* delegates naturally emphasized the difficulty of integrating a state with so many non-German peoples. Austria herself finally settled the question by refusing any concessions. The new

14. Heidrun von Möller, *Grossdeutsch und Kleindeutsch; die Entstehung der Wörter in dem Jahr 1848–1849* (Berlin, 1937); Jacques Droz, *L'Europe centrale: évolution historique de l'idée de 'Mitteleuropa'* (Paris, 1960).

conservative regime proclaimed, in March 1849, that Austria would unite with Germany only if the Austrian state were recognized as indivisible and that no national German parliament were formed (for it might endanger internal peace in the Habsburg lands). Frankfurt could not accept this, so the *kleindeutsch* advocates won by default, and it was at the least symbolically important in terms of future German unification that this first concrete attempt left Austria out; without doubt increasing numbers of German nationalists now thought in terms of excluding Austria in any further unity effort. On March 28 the Frankfurt assembly offered the hereditary headship of a united Germany to the king of Prussia. This forced Frederick William to declare himself openly, and he predictably refused what he called a "crown from the gutter," commenting that "it would be a dog-collar fastened round my neck by the sovereign German people."

This left Frankfurt effectively bankrupt. They had already conceded a great deal to a realistic unification effort by offering the position to Frederick William, who was now an open enemy of liberal and democratic principles. Almost half the delegates had in fact abstained from voting on the issue, but this merely meant that they had no solution either. Now Frankfurt had no head for what was a nonexistent nation. The leading states, led by Austria, withdrew their delegates from the assembly, and other moderates, including Gagern, retired on their own. This left a rump parliament of radicals, mainly from southern Germany, who tried to carry on, first in Frankfurt, then in Stuttgart, only to be dispersed by troops from Württemberg on June 18.

The Prussian revolutionary parliament died its final death at about the same time. The most radical members of the parliament were not on hand when the body reconvened in late November 1848, in the provincial city of Brandenburg. Even so, the government vowed to preempt its efforts. The conservative court camarilla wished to abolish the parliament entirely, but the ministry under General von Brandenburg feared to precipitate another crisis. It prevailed upon the king to grant a liberal constitution in December, undoubtedly intending the document as a stopgap measure to be rescinded or revised as soon as the country calmed down. The constitution utilized many proposals from the revolutionary parliament: it assured civil rights to all, including freedom of religion and of the press, and it established a two-house parliament, with the lower house indirectly elected by universal suffrage. Parliament had the right to initiate legislation and its agreement was required on any taxes levied, though there was no precise stipulation of ministerial responsibility. At the king's insistence, he was given an absolute veto over legislation and the power to rule by decree in an emergency. This suggested a recurrent problem in German constitutional history—the unwillingness to create a real separation of powers—just as 1848 in France played its role in the persistence of the difficulty of balancing legislature with executive in creating a modern political state.

The revolutionary parliament was dissolved and elections to the new assembly were held in January 1849. To the government's displeasure, the elections produced a strong radical contingent; although conservatives and moderates held 184 seats, the radicals won 160. This development forced the government to consider ways of conciliating some of the dissident elements in the population. There was no desire to offer further concessions to the liberals, but the more perceptive conservatives did see a way of winning important segments of the lower classes. To woo the artisans, some of the controls of the guild system were restored; to satisfy the peasantry, manorial jurisdiction, the system of courts run by local landlords, was abolished outright.

But this still left the problem of what to do with a dangerous parliament and a constitution that the government had not intended to be permanent. In April the parliament voted that the government should approve the liberal constitution devised by the Frankfurt assembly; to the conservatives, this was the last straw. The parliament was dissolved and a new election system was established that was guaranteed to produce a more amenable body. The new law established three classes of voters, according to the amount of taxes paid. The first class paid a third of all direct taxes but included only the wealthiest 5 percent of the population; it elected a third of the deputies. The second class, about four times as numerous, elected the second third, and the final class, which included the vast majority (approximately 75 percent) of the taxpayers, along with those who paid no direct tax, elected the remaining third. This ingenious voting system, satisfactory to many liberals as well as conservatives, since neither group had ever favored a democracy, endured until 1918, a testimony to the meager political gains the revolution had won in Prussia. The first parliament elected under the new system, in June 1849, was quite conservative. Large numbers of eligible lower-class voters, disgusted with the new system, did not even bother to cast a ballot, so the government's triumph was complete. And during the summer this new body further amended the constitution: the ministers were made specifically responsible to the king; the upper House of Lords was to be composed of hereditary members (nobles and princes), church and state officials, and life members nominated by the king; and the power of the lower house over legislation and finance was strictly limited.

The Prussian political system was thus permanently changed by the revolution, but the changes were carefully restricted and challenged the social order of the old regime not at all. The new institutions did provide some outlet for liberal sentiment, and although the liberal movement retreated during the early 1850s as a result of their failures in the revolution it proved capable of playing a significant political role later. But the source of ultimate political power was not changed. The king held this power, and he was supported by an assertive aristocracy. The power of this conservative combination, plus the timidity of the liberals who were disillusioned by 1848 and attracted by the limited gains that had been made, prevented any further revolutionary challenge to the Prussian system until it was defeated in war.

The final flicker of revolution in Germany occurred outside traditional Prussia, in several of the smaller states where hopes for results from the Frankfurt assembly had run high and in the western territories that Prussia had gained only four decades earlier. As the radical minority of the assembly tried to press for acceptance of the constitution, and as the assembly itself began to dissolve under the firm resistance of the larger states, insurgents in various areas decided on direct action. The radicals were aided by the continuing discontent of the lower classes, who suffered still from massive unemployment and resented the rejection of their fundamental demands by the liberal assemblies, including Frankfurt itself. But against them the insurgents had arrayed not only local opposition but also the power of Prussia, for on April 28, as the Prussian government dissolved its last freely elected parliament, Frederick William promised military support to any German king who needed help in resisting the Frankfurt constitution.

Disorders began early in May in the Rhineland, when the civilian militia proclaimed their support of the Frankfurt constitution and their refusal to obey orders from the Prussian government. The unrest was supported not only by journeymen but also by factory workers, who were participating in this sort of effort for the first time. A revolutionary government seized the city of Elberfeld for some days, but here and elsewhere the radicals encountered solid opposition. The middle-class Civic Guard worked to restore order, while property owners, even shopkeepers and master artisans, opposed the extremists. In other words the liberals and the vast majority of the middle class were tired of revolution and tacitly sided with the conservative repression. The radicals were also hampered by the intervention of socialist and communist agitators. These frightened the middle-class elements and bothered the radicals themselves, who still shunned outright social revolution. The revolutionary committee in Elberfeld asked Engels to leave, lest he create a false impression of their goals. Amid this confusion and opposition, Prussian troops had little difficulty suppressing any remaining disorder. It was as a result of their action against Cologne radicals that Marx's *New Rhenish Gazette* was closed down.[15]

A serious rising took place in the Bavarian Palatinate, the westernmost extension of the Bavarian kingdom. Some of the troops rallied to the support of a provisional government, which proclaimed an independent democratic republic. The Bavarian government was unable to suppress this revolt, but the Prussian army, having cleaned up the Rhineland, moved in without being asked and drove the provisional government out by mid-June.

The most important insurrection took place in Baden,

15. Friedrich Engels, *The German Revolution* (Chicago, 1967), Chap. XVII.

where the radicals had conducted two abortive efforts earlier in the revolution. Democratic clubs had been forming since the end of 1848, when the defeat of the Prussian revolution made the danger of complete collapse quite obvious. A large portion of the population was politicized, for Baden had long been the most liberal state in Germany and ideas circulated without great impediment; so the clubs' membership soared. Radical leaders formed a coordinating committee of the revolutionary clubs, which issued a call to arms early in May. A popular congress was held in the middle of the month, which voted to support the Frankfurt constitution. And the Baden army mutinied, for many soldiers had been converted to the radical cause. The grand duke fled and a revolutionary governing committee was selected, which organized general elections and established a pension fund for sick and injured workers—one of many such measures that marked the uprisings of 1849 and the growing interest of radicals in winning the masses by offering social reforms. The revolutionaries also hastily organized a military force, for Prussia declared war on the new regime almost immediately. Radical leaders from other parts of Europe, particularly Poland and Hungary, came in to help; some of them served as officers in the new army, the regular officers having remained loyal to the grand duke. But the revolutionary government was extremely disorganized and could put up little resistance to the Prussian troops, which continued their counterrevolutionary tour by invading from the Palatinate. The rebel forces were penned in the fortress of Rastatt by the end of June, and although they held out valiantly they had to surrender on July 23. The Prussians then submitted many of the rebels to courts-martial, ignoring the jurisdiction and the more lenient impulses of the grand duke. About a thousand people were convicted, and twenty-seven of these were shot by firing squads. But even larger numbers of the insurgents escaped. Over 10,000 reached Switzerland, from which many later emigrated to the United States. Carl Schurz, who had been a student before the revolution and had played a prominent role in the Baden rising, was one of these. He and other emigrants were to contribute notably to the political development of the United States. The departure of people like this seriously weakened liberal and democratic leadership in Germany in the years to come.[16] It was literally a century before the German southwest could again play the political role that it had attempted in 1848–49.

The final center of disorder in 1849 was in Saxony. There had been little unrest here before, but the king had been forced to install a liberal government. In the spring he tried to counterattack, by forbidding the diet to discuss the Frankfurt constitution and then dissolving the assembly in April. The diet insisted on a final cheer for the Frankfurt constitution; the Leipzig militia voted unanimously for the same document; and there was widespread popular unrest. On May 3 the citizens of Dresden tried to storm the arsenal, and they were backed by the militia. Government troops held the arsenal, however, and fired into the unarmed crowd. Even so, barricades were set up and a Committee of Public Safety established, and the king fled, while appealing for Prussian aid. The revolutionaries were supported by Bakunin [17] and also by Richard Wagner, who had been director of the Dresden Opera and who somewhat obscurely saw the revolution as a means of purifying art from commercialism and bad taste. Far more important was the intensity of popular support. The Dresden insurgents fought the invading Prussian troops four full days before surrendering. Again the punishments were severe. The Saxon government brought large numbers of insurgents to court. Bakunin himself was arrested and turned over to the Russian government. Wagner escaped to Switzerland where he turned away from politics completely.[18]

This final flurry of radical agitation thus ended quickly and tragically. There was strength to the movement, despite the opposition of most middle-class elements. But the failure of the revolutionaries to win in Prussia, with its massive army, doomed

16. Marcus Hansen, "The Revolutions of 1848 and German Emigration," *Journal of Economic and Business History* (1930), 630 ff; Carl Wittke, "The German Forty-Eighters in America: A Centennial Appraisal," *American Historical Review* (1948), 711–725.
17. Frederick Barghorn, "Russian Radicals and the West European Revolutions of 1848," *Review of Politics* (1949), 338–354.
18. Maurice Boucher, *The Political Concepts of Richard Wagner* (New York, 1950).

the efforts elsewhere. The radicals suffered also from the division of effort, for without unity from one center to the next the Prussians could take them on in series. There was, again, no national revolution at all. And despite the passion of the final outburst, there was irony in its cause. The radicals were fighting for a Frankfurt constitution that they long had criticized as being too respectful of existing governments and vested interests and not sufficiently democratic. Their desire to save the constitution from failure showed how forlorn their own hopes had become.

The revolution now definitively over, many of the smaller German states were left with new, reasonably liberal constitutions. But during the next few years most state governments repealed the political reforms. Only in Bavaria, where the reforms had been fairly limited, were the revolutionary achievements left intact. The Elector of Hesse-Cassel repudiated the constitution outright and reinstated his prerevolutionary prime minister, who was widely hated; with some military assistance from Prussia and Austria, he succeeded. The king of Hanover recovered his former powers; the old upper chamber was restored to the parliament of Hesse-Darmstadt. And everywhere, as in Prussia itself, revolutionary leaders were brought to trial.

As to the cause of German unity, there was only a feeble postscript. Frederick William of Prussia decided that, if organized from above, a more unified Germany under Prussian leadership might not be a bad idea after all. He proposed a more conservative national constitution than the one Frankfurt had produced, but with Austria still excluded. The Prussian government pushed its scheme for a year and a half, winning support from most of the smaller states and backing from liberals like Gagern, who met in June 1849 and decided that this kind of unity was better than nothing. But Austria intervened decisively in 1850, supported by Russia, and Prussia backed down. The old German Confederation was restored under Austrian leadership, and the confederation diet set up a Reaction Committee to undo the work of the Frankfurt assembly. The Fundamental Rights of the Frankfurt constitution were declared abolished in 1851. Nothing was left of its efforts, as German nationalism died down for a decade, save perhaps the realization among some Prussian statesmen that, if used properly, national unity might be a good thing for Prussia.[19]

THE HABSBURG MONARCHY

In contrast to Germany, radicalism had won almost no hold in Austria prior to the revolution, in terms of ideology or organization. And during the revolution itself, the lower classes in the cities had displayed less sophistication, less ability to form their own movements, than their German counterparts. So it is reasonable to assume that the chances of a final radical outburst were not great in Austria, quite apart from the power of the repressive forces. Whatever they were, the military occupation of Prague and Vienna made the situation definite: there was no possibility of further agitation. A new government was formed under Prince Felix von Schwarzenberg, a tough-minded statesman who was determined to put an end to revolution. At his urging, the emperor Ferdinand abdicated in December 1848, in favor of his nephew Francis Joseph; [20] the old emperor was demonstrably incompetent to provide the necessary leadership, as this insistence on a change in emperors indicated. The Schwarzenberg cabinet was not vowed to a restoration of the old order pure and simple. Though a member of the upper aristocracy, Schwarzenberg believed that some change was necessary to prevent further revolutionary challenge, and he wanted to integrate the upper middle class into the regime. He included several liberals in his cabinet, including the lawyer Alexander von Bach and a big businessman from the Rhineland. This was a group determined to modernize the Austrian state.

The only remaining revolutionary institution outside of Hungary was the constituent assembly. When the Viennese rev-

19. See Henry L. Meyer, *Mitteleuropa in German Thought and Action* (The Hague, 1955) and W. E. Mosse, *The European Powers and the German Question 1848–71* (Cambridge, 1958).
20. Rudolf Kiszling, *Die Revolution im Kaisertum Oesterreich* (Vienna, 1948), I, 206 ff; for biographies of two principals, see Rudolf Kiszling, *Fürst Felix zu Schwarzenberg* (Graz, 1952), and Josef Redlich, *Emperor Francis Joseph of Austria* (New York, 1928).

olution was suppressed, the assembly was moved to the provincial town of Kremsier, to insulate it from popular pressure. Schwarzenberg initially expressed his intention of cooperating with the parliament: "We honestly and unreservedly desire the constitutional monarchy." This was merely a tactic to win liberal approval, but it was true that the assembly was allowed to continue its constitutional discussions for a time. The debates focused on the problem of organizing a state with so many different nationalities, with the Czech delegates continuing to oppose all notions of centralization, which they viewed as a strategy for German domination. The constitution that the assembly unanimously approved in March 1849 was a statesmanlike compromise which, if put into effect, just might have created the basis for a durable multinational state. In Austria, at least, nationalism was still sufficiently tempered by liberalism to allow consideration for the rights of others. The constitution provided for a parliament, to which a minister, though appointed by the emperor, would be responsible. The emperor was to have only a suspensive veto over parliamentary legislation, and while he could dissolve a parliament a new assembly would meet within a minimum of three months. The lower house of the parliament was to be democratically elected; as in the Frankfurt constitution, this indicated that sentiment for universal manhood suffrage was gaining ground among liberals, which was an interesting development. The upper house was to consist of delegations from local diets. All peoples were to have equal rights as to language and administration, and to put these principles into effect the monarchy was to be organized on a federal basis. Each province would have its own diet, with considerable authority particularly in such matters as education, and each area was to be further subdivided into districts based on nationality. Each district would have a democratically elected council. This was the most dispassionate solution for the nationalities question ever put forward by an Austrian political body.[21]

The constitution was completely ignored. Schwarzenberg disbanded the parliament in March and the government issued its own constitution, terming it a provisional document. The document itself was not illiberal, though it restricted the vote to men who paid taxes and granted greater powers to the emperor; the government was still reluctant to offend liberal opinion too brutally. But there were no concessions to the minority nationalities. The entire empire was described as "the free, indivisible, indissoluble, constitutional hereditary monarchy." Provincial diets were confirmed for the major national areas, but the powers of the central state precluded any genuine federal organization. Furthermore, while many German liberals, tired of revolution in any case, doubtless accepted the constitution as a marked advance in terms of their principal goals, the fact was that it was granted from above and qualified the absolute sovereignty of the emperor only so long as the emperor allowed. And even this constitution was never put into effect, for the government withdrew it at the end of 1851 when even the need for a liberal façade had disappeared.

The 1849 document was intended as a direct challenge to the Hungarians. Hungary was fully included in the constitution's provisions, whereas the Kremsier assembly had ignored it. This meant that Hungary was to be treated just like any other area of the empire. It lost the Slavic and Rumanian territories it had annexed, for Croatia, Slavonia, Voivodina, and Transylvania were each given the status of individual crown lands, each with its own diet. And the Hungarian constitution was to be valid only insofar as it did not conflict with the imperial constitution. The intent of the government was clear: the Hungarian revolution was to be suppressed. It remained only to translate intent into fact.[22]

At the time of the final rising in Vienna, the fate of the Hungarian revolution had looked rather grim, for under Jelačić the Croatian troops had begun an advance on Budapest. The imperial government had declared the Hungarian diet dissolved, declared the country under martial law, and named Jelačić civil and military governor—a deliberate insult, because the general

---

22. C. M. Knatchbull-Hugessen, *The Political Evolution of the Hungarian Nation* (London, 1908), II, 108 ff.

belonged himself to the hated Croatian minority. The Viennese rising diverted the Croatian army, but the belated sortie by Hungarian troops in an effort to relieve Vienna was soundly defeated. Furthermore the Hungarians were divided. Under the pressure of war they named Kossuth president of a committee of defense, and although he maintained for a few months the pretense of subordination to the emperor, in fact he behaved as ruler of an independent nation. The Hungarian government refused to recognize Francis Joseph as the new emperor on grounds that the change of ruler had not been submitted to the Hungarian diet. But Kossuth was too radical for much of the Magyar gentry, the initial supporters of the independence movement. Many wealthy families fled from Budapest; even the moderate members of the government, such as Ferencz Deák, retired from the scene.[23]

Nevertheless, despite all these difficulties, the Hungarian revolution went on for months and the Austrians proved incapable of suppressing it by themselves. Kossuth was an inspirational leader. He roamed through the countryside with incredible energy, calling on the Hungarian people—particularly the peasants—to defend their country. His appeals enhanced the peasants' gratitude to the revolutionary government for ending manorial obligations; many volunteers went into the army. Kossuth also won support from the urban lower classes, from Jews, from women. He appealed to Hungarian soldiers serving elsewhere (many were in Italy, in Radetzky's army) to come home, and some did. The Hungarian diet levied a draft to provide soldiers, should volunteers prove insufficient. It conscripted nineteen-year-olds first, then twenty-year-olds, and so on, into a force called the Home Defenders, which had a four-year term of service. National Guard duty was required of other adult males. So an army was raised, though its numbers filled out only during the winter and early spring of 1849. There were some experienced troops, including the famous Hungarian cavalry, but other units,

23. Otto Zarek, *Kossuth* (London, 1937); Erzsebet Andić, "Kossuth en lutte contre les ennemis de réformes et de la révolution," *Studia historica* (1954), 82 ff; Györö Ember, "Louis Kossuth à la tête du Comité de la Défense Nationale," *Studia historica* (1953), 40 ff; Fritz Valjevic, "Ungarn und die Frage des oesterreichischen Gesamtstaates zu Beginn des Jahres 1849," *Historische Zeitschrift* (1941), 81–98.

notably the artillery force, were trained hastily and equipment was an obvious problem. The Hungarians benefited greatly from the strategic genius of their military leader, Arthur von Görgey, a minor nobleman who had served in the Austrian army. Görgey was no radical and distrusted Kossuth; he was also a cranky, difficult person. But he inspired loyalty among his officers and he knew how to fight.

The Austrian government ordered a new advance on Hungary in December 1848, under that redoubted repressor of revolt, Windischgrätz. The Hungarian forces pulled back. Kossuth wanted Görgey to attack the Austrians, but the general refused, having only 30,000 men in the field. The government had to move east, to Debrecem, because Görgey did not believe it wise to try to defend Budapest, which fell to the Austrians in January. The first real clash with Hungarian troops came in February, at Kapolna, and the Austrians won handily.

Only in March did the tide begin to turn. Windischgrätz had delayed his progress, giving Görgey time to organize properly and join forces with new troop levies. The Hungarians won successive victories in March and April, while another force drove the Austrians out of Transylvania. Everywhere the Austrians were severely hampered by a lack of supplies, for the Hungarian population was actively hostile. There was a constant danger of guerrilla attacks, and in many areas the Austrians were afraid to light fires lest they disclose their presence.

Emboldened by the victories, Kossuth induced the diet to declare Hungary's independence on April 14, dissolving the Committee of National Defense. Kossuth became governor-president of the new nation, which specifically included Transylvania and the other minority territories. Hungarian success continued in May, as Görgey advanced to Budapest and ultimately captured the city. The Austrians were in a panic, afraid of an invasion of Vienna. Their generals judged the situation hopeless. But at this point Görgey hesitated, for he—like many other nobles—was not enthusiastic about outright Hungarian independence and retained a loyalty to the emperor. The Austrians had time to regroup, and to call for help from Russia, and this finally did the trick.

The czar's willingness to attack revolutions was well known.

He felt particular attachment to Austria, as a bulwark against revolutionary contagion from the west and as a counterweight to Prussia in Germany. He did require a formal request from the emperor, which cost the Austrian government a blow to their pride; but they were capable of recognizing necessity, and the appeal went out at the end of April.[24]

Early in June the Russians sent 100,000 troops into Hungary and another 30,000 into Transylvania. A cholera epidemic and a lack of supplies delayed any real progress, but the czar kept adding to the force, ultimately dispatching about 360,000 troops. The Hungarians, who had outnumbered the Austrian forces, never had a chance. Morale remained high among the common people during the summer, and volunteers poured in, but Kossuth knew that Hungary's days were numbered. He tried to negotiate separately with the Russians, but the czar would have nothing to do with a revolutionary. Kossuth appealed for help to the Frankfurt assembly and to Britain and France, but got no support; the established governments wanted a strong Habsburg monarchy for purposes of diplomatic balance and they were conservative anyway, and while some radical politicians voiced their sympathy they had nothing concrete to offer.[25] The Hungarians moved the government out of Budapest again in July. Görgey managed to avoid battle for some time, but the Russians retook Transylvania and a strong Austrian force moved in from the west. Hemmed in, Görgey insisted on Kossuth's resignation in August, hoping to make a favorable deal with the Russians, to whom he surrendered his forces on August 13. The Russians did indeed appeal for Austrian restraint, but they were largely ignored. Görgey was spared, and Kossuth and a few other leaders made their own way to Turkey, Kossuth ultimately spending the

---

24. Eugene Horvath, "Russia and the Hungarian Revolution," *Slavonic Review* (1934), 628–659; Nifontow, *Russland, passim.*
25. On the military and diplomatic action see Max Schlesinger, *The War in Hungary* (London, 1850); Arthur Gorgei, *My Life and Acts in Hungary in the Years 1848–1849* (2v., London, 1852); Charles Sproxton, *Palmerston and the Hungarian Revolution* (Cambridge, 1919); Eugene Horvath, "Kossuth and Palmerston, 1848–1849," *Slavonic Review* (1931), 612–631; Denes Janossy, "Great Britain and Kossuth," *Archivum Europae Centro-Orientalis* (1937), 53–190.

rest of his life in exile in England, Italy, and the United States. But the bulk of the Hungarian armies were exposed to the full force of Austrian repression.

The Austrian government had already shown little mercy in dealing with failed revolutionaries, and they had now the added incentive of responding to the defeats the Hungarians has administered. They were making up for an international humiliation. Thirteen generals and one civilian official were executed. Thousands of other Hungarians were sentenced to long prison terms. Common soldiers were pressed into the Austrian army, where they were divided among other forces to prevent any retention of Hungarian unity. The country was ruled for several years under martial law, by German officials sent out from Vienna. Ironically the minority lands, including Croatia, were ruled in the same manner. The freedom of peasants was confirmed in Hungary, but they were forced to pay a higher indemnity payment to escape the manorial obligations than their counterparts in Austria.

So Hungary emerged with little but misery to show for the year of revolution. It was under stricter central control than ever before. Austria itself fared little better, in terms of institutional gains. The abolition of manorialism was an extremely important reform, to be sure, and it opened the way to further changes, if only because the government could introduce a more modern, efficient bureaucracy to replace manorial officials. But politically the country was back to absolute monarchy, which growing government efficiency could make more rigorous than ever, particularly in the imposition of German officials over all the other nationalities. The abolition of the imperial constitution in 1851 was accompanied by the establishment of an appointed council, but this was purely advisory and in fact interfered with the emperor's ministers and the bureaucracy not at all.

ITALY

The defeat at Custoza and the surrender of Lombardy marked the failure not only of Piedmont but of liberal revolution in general. But the disillusionment of the liberals left the way open to radical leaders, some of them veterans of the agitation for national unity and others cast up by the excitement of the earlier risings. With its background of radical unrest and the visible presence of a foreign occupation, Italy was much more fertile ground for a second wave of insurrections than Germany had been. The Austrian military, occupying Lombardy, was able to keep the lid on there, but it initially lacked the force to impose similar limitations on the smaller Italian states, and it feared hostility from the other great powers if it tried to move too fast. So in several centers the radicals had leeway, for the governments in the small states had scant forces of their own. They benefited also from the continued economic depression that oppressed the lower classes in the cities. The radical risings antagonized many in the propertied classes. They failed to win much peasant support, because the radicals themselves were interested primarily in political change and feared a social upheaval. So the long-term prospects of the revolutionary regimes may have been cloudy. In fact, despite their enthusiasm and, in some cases, impressive organization, the regimes succumbed, like Hungary, to the regular military forces sent by two great powers.

The final phase of the Italian revolution included a renewed outbreak of war between Piedmont and Austria.[26] The armistice which had followed the battle of Custoza was extended several times, but negotiations for a definitive peace got nowhere. Austria was in no hurry, being eager to finish off unrest at home and thus strengthen her bargaining position, and the other great powers were not helpful. The French government grew increasingly wary of Piedmont, warning against further adventure. In Piedmont itself, there was an active war party, composed of radical nationalists, but the government was pressed even more by growing popular unrest. Economic conditions deteriorated, leading to growing unemployment. Revolution threatened in Genoa, while democratic clubs and newspapers became increasingly assertive in Turin. The democrats criticized the king and his aristocratic advisers for the loss of the war, asking for political

26. A. J. Whyte, *The Political Life and Letters of Cavour, 1848–1861* (London, 1930), 14 ff; Rosario Romeo, *Dal Piemonte sabaudo all'Italia liberale* (Turin, 1963), 108–120.

reform and another attack on Austria. Many of them believed that the French republic would have to aid the Italian cause once battle was joined. Most liberals, including Cavour, urged patience, at least to see if Austria would be distracted by fighting in Hungary. But the war party had a large minority of the votes in the new parliament, which increased taxes on property to provide resources for the military without harming the common people. In December, when negotiations seemed hopeless, Charles Albert yielded to popular pressure by appointing a democratic war cabinet, which dissolved the parliament; the new elections in January 1849 produced a democratic majority. The radical government hesitated, as some of its members began to realize that the Piedmontese army was not in fact prepared for war and that the diplomatic situation was hostile. But in March the government renounced the armistice and reopened the conflict.

The Piedmontese forces moved into Lombardy, but Radetzky was ready for them. The Austrians won a decisive victory at Novara, on March 23, and the Piedmontese had to sue for peace after less than a week of fighting. Charles Albert abdicated, realizing that the Austrians would be more lenient if he was out of the picture. The new king, Victor Emmanuel, resisted Austrian pressure to abandon the Piedmontese constitution, for he was convinced that revolution would result. He was thus wedded to a liberal political structure, as a matter of tactics if not of principle, and this was one of the genuine changes the revolution had produced. The new king was resolved to regain control of his parliament from the democrats. He appointed a moderate liberal, Massimo d'Azeglio, as prime minister with the task of reestablishing order in the country. The government twice disbanded the parliament before elections returned a stable, moderate majority, for the democrats long refused to recognize Piedmont's defeat. The Piedmontese obtained quite moderate terms from Radetzky, who wanted to reduce the animosity with his former enemy; Radetzky specifically resisted pressure from the Austrian government to march on to Turin and impose a punitive peace. He asked for no Piedmontese territory, occupying a frontier fortress at Alessandria pending payment of a high indemnity. Details were worked out only by early August, when a final peace treaty was signed in Milan. It was the Piedmontese radicals' refusal to ratify the document which led to the dissolution of parliament in the king's successful quest to find a more workable majority.

Moderate liberalism was thus in command in Piedmont by the autumn of 1849; the radical threat had been beaten back, based as it was on false hopes of nationalist victories. Austria was in firm control of the rest of northern Italy, except for Venice. Radetzky's forces continued to hunt out and arrest dissidents, preventing any revival of unrest. There was no barrier to an extension of Austrian repression to central Italy, where serious insurrections had taken place.

Piedmont had fought alone in the second campaign. Diplomatic efforts to win cooperation from other Italian states broke down. For although nationalist leaders talked of a genuine federation, the Piedmontese government was unwilling to sacrifice any of its sovereignty and suggested only a common military alliance that in essence would have provided extra troops for Piedmont's own use. None of the other governments found this approach attractive. Nor was there an outpouring of volunteers, as in the first campaigns. Radicals in central Italy, though they had not abandoned their nationalism, wanted to establish the revolution locally first; they abandoned the tactic, urged by Mazzini earlier in 1848, of holding back on political reform in favor of unity in the nationalist cause.[27] And the common people, uninterested in nationalism anyway, became increasingly assertive as unemployment and hunger increased steadily. So the dream of a national revolution faded in Italy too.[28]

Unrest broke out in Tuscany in August 1848. This was a popular rising pure and simple, without explicit political over-

27. Franco della Peruta, *I democratici e la rivoluzione italiana* (Milan, 1958).
28. John Cammett, "Two Recent Polemics on the Character of the Italian Risorgimento," *Science and Society* (1963), 433–457; Rosario Romeo, *Risorgimento e capitalismo* (Bari, 1959); Franco Valsecchi, "Le classi populari e il Risorgimento," *Cultura e scuola* (1965), 82–93; Palmiro Togliatti, "Le classi populari nel Risorgimento," *Studi storici* (1964), III; Gino Luzatto, "Aspects sociaux de la révolution de 1848 en Italie," *Revue socialiste* (1948), 80–86; Franco Catalano, "Socialismo e communismo in Italia del 1846 al 1849," *Rassegna storica del Risorgimento* (1951), 306–316; Guido Quazza, *La lotta sociale nel Risorgimento* (Turin, 1951).

tones. The lower classes rose in the seaport of Livorno, forcing government officials and troops to flee the city. They asked for higher wages, a public works program to reduce unemployment, and limitations on the introduction of machinery—a classic if barebones set of artisanal demands. Reflecting the misery of the peasantry, the demands included land redistribution and reduced obligations to the landlords. There were in addition a few indications that socialist doctrines were becoming known, in pleas for the recognition of the right to work and the organization of labor, but this was not a well-organized or ideologically informed movement. The insurgents were not in fact able to exercise political power, even when they controlled the city; in a short time the rising was suppressed by a newly established middle-class Civic Guard. The Tuscan parliament remained in the hands of moderate liberals, who proposed the formation of a national constituent assembly to draw up a plan for Italian unification which in turn came to naught when the Piedmontese government rejected the nation in favor of its own war plans.

During the summer of 1848 unrest spread also in the Papal States, for the usual reasons.[29] Economic difficulties caused large-scale unemployment, and the government, in unusual fiscal difficulties because of the chronic financial disorder of the papal regime, could provide only a limited number of public works jobs. In August an outbreak in Bologna against an Austrian effort to occupy the city led to three weeks of disorder by unemployed workers, with a great deal of theft and personal violence. Here, as in Tuscany, there was little sense of precise program, and the government ultimately managed to restore order. The situation was different in Rome, for here social unrest took a more political direction because of the intense popular disappointment with the growing conservatism of Pius IX, particularly after the papal troops were prevented from participating in the first war

29. E. E. Y. Hales, *Pio Nono* (New York, 1954), 97 ff.; R. M. Johnson, *The Roman Theocracy and the Republic, 1846–1859* (New York, 1901); Domenico Demarco, *Pio Nono e la rivoluzione romana de 1848* (Modena, 1947); Georges Bourgin, "L'Oeuvre sociale de la République Romaine de 1849," *Actes du Congrès du Centenaire de la Révolution de 1848* (Paris, 1948), 149–156; Luigi Rodelli, *La Repubblica Romana del 1849* (Pisa, 1955); Domenico Demarco, *Una rivoluzione sociale; la Repubblica romana del 1849* (Naples, 1944).

against the Austrians in Lombardy. A number of radical clubs formed, some with lower-class leadership. The Circolo Popolare was headed by Angelo Brunetti, a baker, who advocated state guarantees of the right to work and the abolition of want through heavy taxation on the rich. Liberal forces were extremely weak in the city. The cabinet was liberal but was distrusted by the pope because it sought to separate the government of the Papal States from the administration of the Church. A parliament, elected in May 1848, under restricted suffrage, demonstrated little support for liberalism, for even many in the upper classes refrained from voting and their representatives in the assembly, though in a majority, lacked a sense of direction. Clearly, the economic backwardness of central Italy plus the impediments to the circulation of ideas before the revolution had retarded the political awareness of the property-owning classes. But members of the small radical movement, led by followers of Mazzini, suffered no such disabilities, as they proved aggressive from the outset, egged on by crowds in and around the meeting hall.

Both moderates and radicals favored participation in the war against Austria, but the pope, conscious of his position as leader of a church to which Austrians as well as Italians belonged, adamantly refused. A new government appointed by the pope in September worked for a variety of reforms in the judicial system and the economic administration, but did nothing to satisfy the demands for war. The radicals were now bolstered by the return of many volunteers from the war in Lombardy, and a group of these in November assassinated the leading liberal minister. This symbolically destroyed the middle ground of politics in the Papal States, and the polarization between the conservatives, clustered around Pius IX, and the radicals now dominated the scene.

Huge crowds gathered in the streets on November 16, the day after the assassination, demanding war on Austria and the appointment of a democratic cabinet. Units of the Civic Guard and the armed forces sympathized with the crowd, and as the masses pressed into the papal palace the pope reluctantly agreed to appoint a cabinet including prominent radical leaders. The new government promptly called for a popularly elected constituent assembly. Pius IX left Rome in disguise on November 24 and took refuge in a castle at Gaeta, in the Kingdom of Naples. He promptly condemned the revolutionary government in Rome and appealed for European aid to restore his rule.

The Roman radicals took immediate steps to meet some leading popular demands, thus making the Roman revolution the most genuinely "social" in character of all the many risings of the period. The revolutionary government abolished the tax on flour and organized a variety of public works, including a railroad building program initially planned by the liberals. Church properties were nationalized; many buildings were turned into cheap housing, while lands were divided among the peasants. The constituent assembly was elected in January 1849 by universal suffrage. Large numbers of people abstained from voting, particularly among conservatives and moderates; Pius IX encouraged abstentions by calling the elections "abominable, monstrous, illegal, impious, absurd, sacrilegious, and outrageous to every law, human and divine." As a result the democrats won an easy victory, and in February the assembly proclaimed the overthrow of papal temporal authority and the establishment of the Roman Republic. Clerical control of the university was ended, the inquisition suppressed, and censorship abolished.

The pope easily won diplomatic support, but it was difficult to translate this into concrete assistance. The French offered him asylum; the government under Cavaignac hoped to win support among Catholic voters in advance of France's presidential elections. But Pius did not wish to become enmeshed in this situation, and for the time declined French aid. Spain tried to organize a Catholic coalition. Austria was tied up by the prospect of the new war in the north. Piedmont offered to help, but Pius distrusted this state's intentions. So the matter rested for some months, although on February 18, 1849, Pius officially appealed to the Catholic powers, with Piedmont omitted. The delay gave the Roman government a chance to organize. It was supported by radical leaders from many parts of Italy, who flocked to the defense of the new regime; the Roman Republic was in this sense the climax of the whole Italian revolution, for if it could hold out it could serve as the basis for a unified Italy. On

March 5 Mazzini came to Rome, giving the moral support of the father of Italian radicalism to the new regime. Mazzini believed that the establishment of a republic was the only possible approach toward creating an Italian nation, for federation of the established governments, with their kings and princes, simply would not work. He spoke to the Roman parliament about creating a Third Rome as the symbol of a new order for humanity, and he urged a union of Rome with Tuscany and the convocation of a constituent assembly to create an Italian Republic and to organize a new war against the Austrians. Although this plan came to nothing, because the Tuscan liberals feared a union with the Roman radicals, Mazzini's presence in the Roman government served as a constant inspiration to the insurgents.

The republic was, however, in bad shape. It lacked funds and was unable to control a rampant inflation that heightened the general misery and prevented implementation of key social reforms. During March the government struggled to keep food prices down, forbidding hoarding and threatening confiscation of goods on which prices were raised; it also printed increasing amounts of paper money, which guaranteed that the inflation would continue. A forced loan from the upper classes did not yield much money, and although the regime managed to buy some munitions abroad, the Roman army was ill prepared. It is possible that the republic would have fallen under the weight of economic problems, but it is certain that it was in no position to resist the military pressure that was bound to come. With their usual enthusiasm the radicals voted on March 29 to send troops to aid the Piedmontese against Austria, but they learned the next day of the disaster at Novara. The republic was on the defensive from that time onward.

The attack came, ironically, from French forces. The French government, now firmly in conservative hands with Louis Napoleon as president, wanted to win Catholic support, and the Catholics in France as elsewhere were vigorous in their insistence that the pope should be restored to his temporal rule. The French had long been concerned about developments in Italy, wanting to avoid both a unified state on France's southern border and an increase in Austrian influence; this led to the desire to

defeat the Roman nationalists and to preempt Austrian intervention by a single stroke. On April 16 the French assembly voted
credits for an expedition to Rome, and on April 24 a force of
10,000 men, under General Nicolas Oudinot, landed on the coast,
about thirty-five miles from Rome.

The radicals offered no resistance until the French forces
reached the gates of the city, but they had vowed to fight hero-
ically. As the French approached, a legion of 1200 veteran nationalists under Garibaldi reached the city, and another group of 600
Lombard volunteers came as well; both groups had considerable
experience in fighting in the north. The Garibaldians drove the
French back in their first attempt to enter the city, but this unexpected reverse simply prompted the government in Paris to send
more men and supplies. And early in May Austrian forces took
control of most cities in the northern section of the Papal States,
meeting fierce resistance only in Bologna. Troops from Naples
moved up from the south, and Spanish soldiers landed near
Rome. The French had to hurry if they were to get in first, and
once reinforcements arrived at the end of May they attacked vigorously. The Roman government had made some preparations
in the meantime, building barricades and setting up military hospitals. And morale was high as the siege began on June 2. Artisanal leaders like Angelo Brunetti urged on the soldiers and
workers building fortifications. Garibaldi, Mazzini, and many
other patriots constantly exhorted the Roman forces. But the
Roman army was a mixture of Civic Guards, volunteers, students, conscripts, and some experienced soldiers from the north
and some former papal troops. The French had 30,000 men and
abundant artillery. For almost the entire month of June, Oudinot's forces bombarded the city, while building approach
trenches preparatory to an invasion. Under this pressure many
Romans advocated surrender. The lower classes wanted to suffer
no longer. Garibaldi, convinced by the end of June that it was
impossible to hold out, urged that the army leave the city and
conduct guerrilla operations from the countryside. Of the major
leaders only Mazzini, who had always realized that Rome could
not repel the kind of attack France was mounting, held out for
a final battle. His romantic soul yearned for a glorious ending.

Finally, on June 30, the Roman parliament voted against Mazzini's position, and he resigned from the government. Garibaldi, with several thousand troops, tried to fight his way north to help Venice, but his army was decimated by Austrian forces though Garibaldi himself escaped.[30]

The French forces occupied Rome on July 3, dissolving the parliament and the political clubs. Oudinot turned the government back over to papal officials who arrived a few days later. The French appealed for liberal measures, but the pope was bent on a complete suppression of all the revolutionary achievements and a return to the institutions of the past. Mazzini, who could sum up the feelings of revolutionaries even if he was somewhat wanting in concrete organizing ability, expressed the general disappointment: "I feel from time to time emotions of rage rising within me at this triumph of brutal force, all throughout the world, over right and justice."

Indeed the forces of reaction were in full command. Ferdinand of Naples had attacked in Sicily in March, refusing to consent to Sicilian autonomy. His forces had regained the island by mid-May, despite a bitter popular rising in Palermo.[31] The grand duke of Tuscany was restored on July 28 with Austrian help. This left only Venice, and its days were numbered.

Under the leadership of Daniele Manin, the Venetian republic had been proclaimed in March 1848.[32] News of revolutions elsewhere had provided the usual spark. Crowds freed Manin from prison, to which the Austrians had confined him for his nationalist agitation, and later seized the arsenal, killing one of the Aus-

30. George M. Trevelyan, *Garibaldi's Defense of the Roman Republic* (London, 1908): R. W. Collins, *Catholicisim and the Second French Republic* (New York, 1923), 212 ff; Emile Bourgeois and Emile Clermont, *Rome et Napoléon III* (Paris, 1907); Denis Mack Smith, *Garibaldi* (New York, 1956); Christopher Hibbert, *Garibaldi and His Enemies* (Boston, 1966); Arturo Codignola, *Mazzini* (Turin, 1946); Alberto Ghisalberti, "Popolo e politica nell' 49 romano," in *Giuseppe Mazzini e la Repubblica Romana* (Florence, 1953), 79–102.

31. Federico Curato, *La rivoluzione siciliana del 1848–1859* (Milan, 1940), 207 ff.

32. See George M. Trevelyan, *Manin and the Venetian Republic of 1848* (New York, 1923) and Vincenzo Manchesi, *Storia documentata della rivoluzione e della difesa di Venezia negli anni 1848–1849* (Venice, 1913).

trian officials. Manin, a lawyer who valued order and feared the mob, quickly established a civic guard and worked to prevent socialist agitation among the lower classes. His regime was to be radical, but only in the sphere of politics. The new government instituted reforms in the system of justice, abolishing secret trials, and established civil and religious freedom. Italian history was to be stressed in the schools, where corporal punishment was eliminated. For the lower classes the government lowered the salt tax. Relations with the rest of Italy were a problem. In July the newly established assembly voted to merge Venetia with Piedmont, which so distressed the republican Manin that he resigned, his hope resting in the possibility of a constituent assembly for the whole of Italy. But the loss at Custoza effectively destroyed the merger notion, and Manin returned to the government and began organizing resistance to the inevitable Austrian attack. The city was blockaded throughout the winter. Manin arranged for stockpiles of food, but as the city had never been self-sufficient the resources were limited. The Venetians refused an Austrian appeal to surrender after the battle of Novara, and on May 4 the Austrians began to bombard the city's garrisons. The Venetians stood up well under the siege; Manin instituted a rationing program and tried to prevent price increases. As in Rome, the morale of the lower classes dropped rather quickly, for they were not inspired by nationalist hopes and simply could not withstand prolonged additional suffering. Food riots broke out in June, though they were quickly put down. In July Austrian gunners managed to bombard the city itself. Famine increased, and epidemics of cholera and typhus broke out. On August 6 the assembly granted Manin the power to negotiate with the Austrians, and the city surrendered finally on August 22. Manin and other leaders were permitted to leave.

The Venetian revolution was a thing unto itself, one of the most remarkable achievements of the period. Its persistence owed much to Manin, who was a good organizer and also a patently fair man, inspiring confidence. Manin's limitations were also clear, for like most of the Italian radicals he offered little that would specifically benefit the lower classes. The radical movement in general rose on the basis of popular unrest but the radicals, when in power, immediately set about controlling the people. Efforts at defense, as in Rome and Venice, helped maintain a unity for a time, and here the Italian cities displayed undoubted courage. But the gap between the vision of the radicals, which precluded a genuine social revolution, and the demands of the common people was real and it showed through even during the resistance efforts. The radicals also ignored the countryside, for they had no understanding of the peasants' situation and they reflected the traditional urban orientation of Italian life. Thus even while the Austrians were on the run, in the spring of 1848, Manin concentrated his organizing efforts on the city of Venice alone. Whether the peasants in the surrounding countryside could have been roused into becoming useful allies of the revolution is admittedly doubtful, but it is revealing that no attempt was made. The radical phase of the revolution in central Italy, and the whole Venetian rising, pitted individual cities against the military might of the great powers. Retarded by diplomatic considerations and Piedmont's second intervention, the regular armies nonetheless swept away the radical governments one by one. With Radetzky reestablishing Austrian rule in Venice at the end of August, the revolutionary period of Italian history had definitively ended.

FRANCE

The situation in France during the summer and fall of 1848 was not unlike that in Germany and Austria around the turn of the year: the revolution was over, but a constituent assembly created by the revolution continued to struggle to produce a new political charter. But in Central Europe, the assemblies produced admirable documents only to see them completely ignored. In France, the anomaly was more subtle. The constituent assembly prepared another admirable constitution but, in its fear of disorder, itself created the mechanism for the constitution's destruction. The contradiction between professed intent and result was suggested during the preparation period, for as the assembly debated, it entrusted the provisional government to General Cavaignac as military dictator. Cavaignac kept order, and in practice order was preferred to liberty.[33]

The long constitution of the Second Republic, completed in the autumn of 1848, promised a variety of benefits to French citizens. It offered education, freedom of association and petition, and relief and public works. It specifically did not mention any right to work, and it listed a number of obligations that the citizens owed the state, including love, loyalty, morality, work, taxes, and service to the death. The constitution's approach thus suggested a fear of anarchy and of undue individualism, and was far less interested in individual rights than the constitutions being produced in Central Europe at the same time. The constitution was nevertheless liberal in its basic orientation; it made real efforts to remedy the weaknesses of the previous parliamentary structure, which had set off the revolution in the first place. Parliamentary deputies were to receive a wage and only in special cases could they hold jobs in the state bureaucracy; this was meant to assure parliament's independence and avoid control by the executive branch. The constitution also created a democracy. Universal manhood suffrage would elect the single-chamber parliament every three years.

The key constitutional debate concerned the structure of the executive branch. The assembly ultimately decided on a strong president, elected every four years by universal suffrage. The president was to have wide executive authority, with the ministers responsible to him. The reasons for creating a powerful presidency were numerous. France had failed to resolve problems of executive-legislative relationships ever since Louis XVI refused to fulfill the duties of a constitutional monarch, during the Revolution of 1789. This new effort proved even less successful than most of its predecessors, but it suited the mood of the assembly. There were references to the American presidency, which seemed to work well.[34] Many representatives were mon-

33. For general treatment see Paul Bastid, *Doctrines et constitutions politiques de la Seconde République* (2v, Paris, 1945); Frederick de Luna, *The French Republic under Cavaignac, 1848* (Princeton, 1969); Roger Price, *The French Second Republic, a Social History* (Ithaca, 1972).
34. Eugene Curtis, *The French Assembly of 1848 and American Constitutional Doctrines* (New York, 1918), 186 ff.

archists, and although they agreed to a republican form they wanted some of the stability they believed a strong executive assured. But above all the assembly opted for a powerful presidency because the June Days convinced them that only concentrated authority, of the sort Cavaignac had exercised, could prevent social disorder. Hence a revolution that, at the political level, had occurred because of abuses of executive power by Louis Philippe's government emerged with a president every whit as powerful, during his term of office, as Louis Philippe had sought to be.

The decision to base the presidency on popular election was almost as important as the determination of the scope of the office. Many in the assembly feared democracy still. Lamartine argued for popular election in idealistic terms, calling the nation "incorruptible." Others opted for democracy mainly because French voters had proved themselves socially conservative. Various moderates and some of the radical faction, including Ledru-Rollin, warned that a powerful president, elected by a majority, could turn into a popular dictator. They pointed to the example of Napoleon, and to his nephew, who was already gaining political support in France. But the desire for security was paramount, and the warnings went unheeded. The assembly did build in a variety of safeguards against abuse, for in no sense did they desire a dictatorship (though many of the monarchists in the assembly hoped for a *coup d'état* which would replace the president with a king). The president could not succeed himself, nor could any members of his family; he could not command the army in person or make war or peace without parliamentary approval. He had no final veto over legislation and could neither dissolve the assembly nor suspend the constitution. A genuine balance between executive and legislature was intended; that it was not achieved was due to the character of the first president and the nature of his support. Yet in the absence of a firm tradition of separation of powers in France, the office that had been created almost begged for conversion into personal rule. All the constitution did was to prevent such conversion save by illegal means.

Presidential elections were held in December 1848.[35] The candidates included the radical, semisocialist Raspail, Cavaignac, Lamartine, Ledru-Rollin, and Louis Napoleon. Napoleon won in a landslide. He polled 5,534,520 votes; Cavaignac won 1,442,302; Ledru-Rollin 371,421; Raspail 36,920; and Lamartine a mere 17,910. Some of the reasons for this surprising vote were clear enough. The majority of the French people had not wanted revolution; their votes in April made this obvious. The known republicans split what radical vote there was. Many workers and artisans, who remained seriously aggrieved, did not know how to translate their discontent into political terms, at least in a presidential contest—hence the low support for Raspail and even Ledru-Rollin. Even among these groups there was a backlash from the June Days, which made a cautious choice seem best. Lamartine had not advocated the workers' cause and had not kept order, so he won support from no one. Most convinced republicans probably voted for Cavaignac, because he seemed capable of strong government without monarchy. But the massive vote for Louis Napoleon was not simply the result of his rivals' weaknesses. It climaxed a rising tide of support that had been developing for half a year. It followed some careful organization by Napoleon's advisers and some widely disseminated campaign promises that were masterpieces of unclarity. Yet the real meaning of the vote defies complete explanation even today.

Louis Napoleon had sought power in France for almost twenty years, with complete lack of success. Two efforts at a military rising ended in failure. Napoleon had lived in France very little and was not widely known until the revolution gave him his opportunity. When the disorder broke out he prudently held back, remaining in London until after the June Days. This was his first piece of luck, for it meant that he was not discredited by being associated with any of the divisions that developed dur-

35. André-Jean Tudesq, *L'Election présidentielle de Louis-Napoléon Bonaparte* (Paris, 1965), *passim*. For biography, see F. A. Simpson, *The Rise of Louis Napoleon* (London, 1909) and Albert Guerard, *Napoleon III* (Cambridge, 1943).

ing the active phase of the revolution. Workers could not fault him as an oppressor, conservatives could not identify him with the radical cause. Supplementary elections to the constituent assembly in June and September gave Napoleon a place in the parliament, where his speeches suggested an interest in national conciliation—he advocated an amnesty for the victims of the June Days—and in social reform; he attacked economic injustice and vainly urged approval of the right to work. He received the support of some industralists, particularly from advocates of rapid economic growth under government encouragement. He gained Catholic backing with hints of giving the Church new powers in education. Monarchists supported him because, divided between Legitimist and Orleanist factions, they could not agree on a candidate of their own; many undoubtedly saw Napoleon as a stalking-horse for a genuine monarchy, believing that his unprepossessing speech and appearance bespoke a character that could be easily manipulated. Hence Napoleon had the support of the notables, above all because he, and the tradition his name represented, stood for good order.

Many common people voted for Napoleon simply because of his name. To many, as new voters, this was the only candidate's name that they had heard of before. Some undoubtedly cherished what the Napoleonic tradition had come to stand for: prosperity, national glory, and social order as well. The same tradition had also come to mean social improvements and a defense of some aspects of the revolutionary heritage; Napoleon did not represent the old regime, and Louis Napoleon's propaganda carefully fostered his image as a reformer. Peasants came to believe that Napoleon would support their interests; there were rumors that he would repeal the hated surtax on property. So there were a host of reasons for the vote. Some historians have argued that the vote proved the common people's rejection of the revolution, their fear of urban radicalism. This is too simple an explanation. Napoleon could be seen as a defender of important aspects of the revolution. His tradition, and his ultimate accomplishments, were to be sure not liberal ones; the elections did confirm the disinterest of the common people in specifically liberal institutions. But his popular vote was not an expression of pure traditionalism in politics, and his regime ultimately helped foster, in part intentionally, a sense of active political participation among the French people, a sense that could ultimately be used against Napoleon himself.

In May 1849, elections for the parliament were held.[36] They produced a parliament very like that of the July Monarchy. This resulted from the activities of the departmental prefects; most of the prefects from the July Monarchy had returned to their jobs and proved adept at managing the new electorate, at least in the countryside. Their goal was to assure the election of conservative deputies, particularly though not exclusively monarchists. They were aided by the local notables, who still exercised great influence over the peasantry, and by the undoubtedly widespread desire for social order. Hence what was called the Party of Order, a loose amalgam of Legitimists, Orleanists, and Bonapartists, won two-thirds of the seats. Liberal republicans elected a mere fifth of their previous number of deputies. But radical republicans revived strongly in the cities and also in some departments of the south. They polled a third of the national vote, and 180 radicals entered the parliament, under the leadership of Ledru-Rollin. But the radicals' strength was quickly reduced. In June, they attacked the government for its support of the papacy, moving for the impeachment of Louis Napoleon. Their motion was defeated and they left the assembly to launch an insurrection. The radicals seized a technical school in the working-class section of Paris and urged the masses to build barricades. Few people followed their lead. Memories of the suppression of the June Days were still powerful, and although the common people had voted for the radicals they were not vigorously committed to their political goals. Their strength was also sapped by a fierce cholera epidemic, which was killing several hundred people a day. The government moved in quickly to prevent serious disorder, proclaiming martial law. The radical leaders were chased out of the school and the demonstration suppressed, and the whole movement served chiefly to give the government a fine excuse to annul the most frightening results of the elections. About thirty radi-

36. Theodore Zeldin, "Government Policy in the French General Election of 1849," *English Historical Review* (1959), 240–248.

cals lost their seats in parliament, martial law was maintained in Paris and Lyons, political clubs were suppressed, newspapers were closely watched, and working-class units of the National Guard were disbanded.

Henceforward, during the short life of the Second Republic, the parliament devoted itself to a campaign against radicalism. The government led in the suppression of the revolution in Rome. In March 1850, the Falloux Law was passed, giving Catholics the right to establish schools at all levels without state authorization; the state system itself was submitted to a series of councils dominated by the clergy. The Party of Order, backed by the vast majority of the French middle class, saw an extension of religious education as a vital measure to counteract radical influences. The radicals were of course deeply angered, seeing Catholics as the avowed enemies of the revolutionary heritage. The battle between the two traditions, briefly interrupted during 1848, became once more a part of French political life. The conservative parliament also sought to modify the consequences of democracy. In May 1850, radical republicans had won twenty of thirty seats in special elections. Parliament responded by passing a law denying the vote to citizens who could not prove three years' continuous residence in one locality; it also disenfranchised people convicted of political agitation. The net effect was to deprive about three million people, almost entirely from the lower classes, of the right to vote. The assembly, clearly, was working to restore the type of regime that had existed during the July Monarchy, though with increased Catholic influence. Only the continuing disagreement between Legitimists and Orleanists about which royal family to support prevented an outright effort to return to a monarchy.[37]

Louis Napoleon, for his part, was working on a different plan for the future.[38] He wanted to create a new Napoleonic

37. Collins, *Catholicism*, 271–272; René Rémond, *The Right Wing in France from 1815 to de Gaulle* (Philadelphia, 1966), 79 ff; John K. Huckaby, "Roman Catholic Reaction to the Falloux Law," *French Historical Studies* (1965), 320 ff.
38. T. A. B. Corley, *Democratic Despot; a Life of Napoleon III* (London, 1961); Howard C. Payne, "Preparation of a Coup d'État," *Studies in Modern European History in Honor of Franklin Charles Palm* (New York, 1956), 175–

Empire. He had considerable support from Catholics, who gave him credit for the support to the Church. Businessmen favored him because he obviously served the interests of stability. Napoleon also appealed for continued popular backing. He toured the provinces to rouse enthusiasm, talking of his desire to encourage economic prosperity. He attacked the parliament with increasing openness, condemning its disenfranchisement of the masses.

Finally the government, though conservative, did not devise methods of repression adequate to stem the new kind of unrest that was brewing. Radical political ideas and organizers circulated surprisingly freely in the provinces; even when arrested many leaders were acquitted by sympathetic juries.[39] In a number of cities, lower-middle-class elements entered municipal government in the wake of the 1848 revolution. Small businessmen, clerks, and modest professional people thus got their first taste of political power, and though they were later shunted aside by the traditional ruling elites they retained an active attachment to the republic.

Workers of many kinds, including factory workers, were drawn into new activities. Proudhonist ideas gained ground, leading to the formation of a number of production cooperatives. Trade unions (usually called resistance societies) proliferated, some of them clandestine. Unions were not new among artisans, but they had never spread so widely, and they were genuinely novel among groups such as Parisian metallurgical workers and gas stokers, who formed organizations for the first time. Strikes increased markedly, in 1848–49 and again in 1852. And workers gained new political interests. In Marseilles, the working classes had been apathetic before the revolution. But in the spring of 1848, political clubs and demonstrations multiplied, and workers frequently shouted republican and socialist slogans. A major rising occurred in June, following which political agitation declined, but it revived again through 1851. The workers most

---

202; Marx, *Eighteenth Brumaire;* Henri Guillemin, *Le Coup d'état du 2 décembre* (Paris, 1951).

39. Thomas Forstenzer, *Bureaucrats under Stress: French Prosecutors and Prefects, 1848–1852* (Unpublished doctoral dissertation, Stanford, 1973).

active politically were artisans who had moved to Marseilles from smaller towns; having moved, they were most open to innovation, and some were frustrated by the difficulties they encountered in trying to better themselves. But some other kinds of workers were involved in the political organizatios as well.[40] Throughout the years of the Second Republic radical agitators were active in most French cities, so that the spread of political consciousness was not confined to unusual centers like Marseilles, or to artisans alone. By 1849 a loose party had formed, often called the Mountain, in recollection of the radical Jacobins of the 1790s, with its members labeling themselves democratic socialists. The party, in speeches and pamphlets, identified the republican cause with social reform, teaching many workers that politics—specifically, republican politics—was relevant to their interests.

The radicals also made converts in the countryside. Their progress was not uniform; they did not dent the heavily Catholic regions. They had their greatest success in the south and center, particularly along market routes.[41] These were areas of small peasant plots and cohesive villages, where peasants—even agricultural laborers—had a sense of independence but where at the same time intercommunication was common. In the winegrowing areas of the south, peasant awareness was first stirred by the famous forty-five centime tax, imposed by the provisional government in 1848. Protests against the tax, which took the form of riots during June 1848, gradually developed a political character, which the radicals were able to capitalize upon. Their

40. Georges Duveau, La Vie ouvière en France sous le Second Empire (Paris, 1956), 39–104; Edouard Dolléans and Gerard Dehove, Histoire du travail en France (Paris, 1953), 253; William Sewell, "La Classe ouvrière de Marseille sous la Seconde République: structure sociale et comportement politique," Mouvement social (1971), 27–66.

41. Pierre Dominique, Louis Napoléon et le coup d'état du 2 décembre (Paris, 1951); Albert Soboul, "La question paysanne en 1848," La Pensée, Nos. 18–20 (1948); Marcel Dessal, "Le Complot de Lyon et la résistance au coup d'état dans les départements du Sud-Est," 1848: Revue des révolutions contemporaines (1951), 83–96; Charles Tilly, "The Changing Place of Collective Violence," in Melvin Richter, ed., Essays in Theory and History (Cambridge, Mass., 1970), 159–161; Leo Loubère, "The Emergence of the Extreme Left in Lower Languedoc, 1848–1851," American Historical Review (1968), 1019–1051.

continuing effort to associate social grievances with their political cause is shown in a campaign song, the "Song of the Vine-growers," written in 1850: [42]

> Good villagers, vote for the Mountain,
> There is the hope of poor vine-growers,
> For with it, good countrymen,
> Will disappear the taxes on drinks.
> In the hamlets, agricultural banks
> Will be especially for you, good peasants,
> Without charge also you will have schools
> And money at most at three per cent.

As economic problems continued, involving (particularly in the south) high interest rates and peasant hostility toward their middle-class creditors, the republican propaganda found a considerable audience.

Napoleon's *coup d'état* in December 1851 revealed the extent of republican gains. Napoleon now overturned the constitution of the Second Republic, proclaiming himself president for life and effectively disbanding parliament; here was a clear challenge to republican strength. Violent risings occurred in the center and the south, particularly the southeast. They were called by the urban republican leaders, but affected both towns and countryside in an unusual coalition which resulted from the growing politicization of protest. Several cities and towns were taken over by the insurgents, who included professional people, journeymen, and agricultural workers. In all, 100,000 people were involved in the insurrections. Large military forces were required to suppress the rebellion; five hundred people were killed and 26,000 ultimately arrested. The large cities, including major factory centers, were not involved in this violent protest, in part because of the large concentrations of troops in advance of the coup. But important segments of the lower middle class and working class expressed their republicanism in the plebiscite which Napoleon organized to ratify his seizure of power. A number of working-class areas voted against the take-over—this was true of Mulhouse, a major factory center, for example—while others produced a large minority opposition. Equally instructive

42. Price, *Second French Republic,* 251.

is the roughly 20 percent of all voters who abstained, despite considerable pressure to vote. In major cities like Lyons, Bordeaux, Strasbourg, and Paris negative votes and abstentions together outnumbered the affirmative votes. The areas in which the actual insurrections had taken place voted heavily in favor of Napoleon, to curry favor with the regime. But the combination of the vote, the abstentions, and the insurrection demonstrates that a significant minority of Frenchmen had been won to the republican cause.

So Napoleon's triumph was more difficult than expected, but its very brutality helped solidify his regime; thousands of troublemakers were killed, jailed, or exiled. And it was a triumph. Napoleon won practically 92 percent of the votes cast in his plebiscite. Quite apart from the fact that there was no clear alternative, most Frenchmen rejoiced at the assurance of stability. The insurrections themselves had stirred wild fears of a huge conspiracy. They particularly roused that strange fear of the countryside, leading to stories of murder and rape by the rural barbarians. All this the government played up, partly because officials themselves were convinced that a revolutionary plot did exist. The vote was a vote for order, for an end to any possibility of further revolt. The regime naturally seized the opportunity to close down the unions, the cooperatives, and the political clubs. Governments throughout Europe expressed relief. The Austrian ambassador to France saw Napoleon as "the chosen instrument of Providence to deal the mortal blow to parliamentarianism on the Continent." Within another year—by the end of 1852—Napoleon had established himself as emperor. Everywhere, the revolutions of 1848 were now officially over.

PART IV · A BALANCE SHEET

THE VIRTUAL COLLAPSE of each of the major revolutions of 1848 within less than a year, and their defeat even in Hungary and Italy soon thereafter, stemmed from several common causes. The fundamental flaws in each of the risings consisted of the liberal mentality of the revolutionary leaders and the profound social cleavage between the liberal and lower-class forces involved in the revolution. Tragically, as we have seen, each of these elements was essential to a revolution's success. The lower classes, even in France, were not yet sufficiently articulate politically to produce an overall revolutionary leadership, but everywhere they had provided the physical strength the revolutions also required.

With rare exceptions none of the men who assumed control of the revolutionary governments had ever been a revolutionary. They accepted the upheaval that had brought them to power, but they wanted no further disorder. Lamartine, who can be seen as a starry-eyed romantic idealist, did have visions of a better world, but he had not even been a convinced democrat before the revolution and became one only as he sought both legitimization and a conservative social orientation for the new regime. Leaders of the new governments in Central Europe were still more respectful of orderly political process.

Many historians have seen 1848 as the point at which liberalism had a final idealistic fling before becoming pragmatic and venal. There is some truth in this, but even before 1848 liberals preferred to petition and discuss than to organize illegal action. The liberal belief in persuasion and sweet reason was an ideological weakness from the standpoint of making a revolution, even though liberal goals might be genuinely revolutionary.

Furthermore, liberals had already won some of their goals

in many of the countries in which revolution occurred, which limited their rebellion against the status quo. In France, the July Monarchy had departed from liberal principles, but it was not a conservative regime in the Metternichian sense. Most of the deputies elected to the constituent assembly did not want a government that was much different, even when they accepted the abolition of monarchy. The case of Prussia is even more interesting. The old regime had not offered liberals a genuine parliament or constitutional rights; liberals therefore had great cause for discontent. But the government was efficient; it encouraged some economic modernization, spread education widely, offered some opportunities to middle-class bureaucrats, permitted a considerable degree of religious freedom, and granted substantial powers to city governments. This was not, then, an old regime of the pre-1789 French variety. German liberals have been roundly criticized for their lack of success in 1848. Some historians take 1848 as a sign that liberalism never had a chance in Germany, while others accuse the liberals of a failure of nerve. It is unquestionably true that the collapse of the revolution left in power an authoritarian government and an aristocratic upper class. It is also possible to see why liberals did not feel a need to press too hard. The same was even more obviously true in the smaller German states where liberal political institutions had made some headway. Only in the Habsburg monarchy and central and southern Italy were liberals faced with regimes which were completely unacceptable in principle, but liberalism itself was not as strong in these areas, if only because of the impediments to the exchange of ideas and the lack of rapid economic development; and even in these cases the liberals quickly displayed their preference for evolutionary reform over a genuine revolution.

The liberals of course represented men of position and property, and this also moderated their behavior. The affluent bureaucrats were rarely interested in jeopardizing their achievements by carrying revolution too far. There is no need to be completely cynical about their behavior, for their interest in reform was genuine and considerable. But it is obvious that the societies in which revolution occurred were not closed. The barriers to advancement were far less great than in France during the latter half of the eighteenth century. Many of the prominent liberals had already gained success in personal terms. Not only in Paris but also in Vienna a substantially new upper middle class had emerged during the previous generation. It undoubtedly sought a regime more compatible with its achievements and interests but it would hardly countenance rash behavior.

Hence for a variety of reasons the liberal leaders did not do what they would have had to do to make revolution a success. They did not form their own military forces. They were often misled by their initial success, and their own belief in persuasion, to think that this was not necessary; it was easy to pretend that the old order had seen the light and would not use the regular military force in a repressive way. The typical liberal desire to establish a civilian militia, which was manifest in every major center, was not an adequate substitute. It did not train in a military manner; many of its members, who had their own interests to pursue, took only irregular part in guard activities; and the main purpose was to keep internal order anyway. As a result nothing . was really available to oppose the regular military. Whenever the latter decided to act vigorously it was successful; and in such cases the civilian guard usually either offered no resistance or, having realized its own inability to keep order, joined in attacking lower-class insurgents.

The liberals were also incapable of maintaining an alliance with the lower classes. This was the real tragedy of 1848, leading to the substantial defeat of both elements, but it is hard to see how it could have been avoided. Middle-class liberals were incapable of consenting to the kind of unemployment relief that the lower classes so desperately needed and demanded. Many had barely emerged from the traditional idea that poverty is inevitable and that the only palliative is outright charity.[1] As liberals they were not only hostile to government intervention in the economy but also inclined to attribute poverty to the fault

1. Reinhard Bendix, *Work and Authority in Industry; Ideologies of Management in the Course of Industrialization* (New York, 1956), 46–85; Charles Morazé, *La France bourgeoise* (Paris, 1952), 84–95; Charles Morazé, *The Triumph of the Middle Classes* (Cleveland, 1966), 100–135.

of the poor themselves. So the government aid programs that were established to provide jobs or relief were halfhearted efforts that the liberals distrusted from the outset. That the programs proved unexpectedly expensive and attracted fearsome numbers of poor people only added to the objections. The liberals could envisage long-term improvements for the poor and they could try to stimulate the economy to alleviate the suffering which the recession brought; again the liberals in the Prussian ministry undertook the most concrete measures in this direction. But liberalism had nothing to offer in the short run except counsels of patience.

For the more fundamental grievances of the urban lower classes the liberals were equally lacking. They simply did not look at society in the same way. They could not countenance socialism, which sought to abolish private property. They also could not accept a return to an older social order. One historian, writing of the German revolution, has suggested that the liberals' fundamental problem was their failure to come to terms with artisanal demands.[2] Yet it is difficult to see how they could have done so, since the artisans were opposed to modern industry while the liberals were trying to establish the kind of society that would further it. There was of course the middle ground offered by the journeymen's demands. In theory the liberals could go along with the idea of spreading education and treating each individual with dignity. But the journeymen also asked for government intervention in matters of wages and hours, and this the liberals could not accept in theory or in terms of middle-class self-interest.

The conflict was heightened by the persistent disorder of the lower classes during the active phase of the revolutions. The liberals, barely able to accept revolution itself, had no desire to tolerate further unrest. Yet to the lower classes agitation remained essential to express basic grievances and to take advantage of the freedom they assumed the revolution had brought them. So tension mounted, and news of social conflict in one revolution—

2. Theodore Hamerow, *Restoration, Revolution, Reaction: Economics and Politics in Germany, 1815–1848* (Princeton, 1958), 153–156.

most obviously the June Days in Paris—heightened the probability of social conflict elsewhere.

In all this the key point was that class antagonisms were articulated so quickly. In France after 1789 there were early signs of potential conflicts, but they became explicit only slowly.[3] Middle-class leaders of the revolution preached a stirring rhetoric that promised gains to all citizens; although these same leaders introduced class legislation, including property qualifications for the vote, they believed in what they said. The lower classes, without much experience politically, believed in the rhetoric as well. There were at least three years of grace, sufficient time for substantial achievements, before class hostilities helped bring the active phase of the revolution to an end. In 1848 middle-class leaders offered fewer promises. Their liberalism was a narrower ideology than the Enlightenment-based ideals of 1789. They had learned the dangers of lower-class unrest in part from the history of the French Revolution itself and from recurrent agitation since that time. There was little of the enthusiasm for lower-class allies that had marked even the first months after the revolutions of 1830, when liberal newspapers commended the fighters on the barricades and urged cooperation among the classes. And the lower classes had learned from the past too. Particularly in France and Italy, disappointments in earlier revolutions, when the lower classes had done the fighting only to find that the benefits went to the middle class, helped prompt an early articulation of separate demands. Where they were politically sophisticated, as in Paris, the lower classes asked directly for a share in government, and almost everywhere they made it clear that liberal goals were not enough. The early stages of industrialization helped radicalize the lower classes also, compared to their French counterparts of 1789. There were deeper grievances about the nature of society and they were directed, at least implicitly, at the middle class itself, which was

3. Georges Lefebvre, *The Coming of the French Revolution* (Princeton, 1947); on the general urban pattern of revolt, see William Langer, "The Pattern of Urban Revolution in 1848," in E. M. Acomb and M. L. Brown, eds., *French Society and Culture since the Old Regime* (New York, 1966), 90–118.

creating the new industrial order. So class conflict paralyzed the revolution everywhere. It was slowest to develop in Vienna, where the workers lacked revolutionary experience and industrialization was not far advanced; the long contentment with middle-class leadership, particularly of course the guidance of the radical students, had no counterpart elsewhere. But even here class conflict weakened the unity of the revolution and made repression easier. Above all, nowhere did the middle-class liberals and the urban lower classes find a durable common enemy. The aristocracy was simply not enough in evidence for the urban lower classes to be greatly concerned. The Church—the other standby of revolutionary unity even in 1830—was also not a common enemy. Liberals wanted some changes in church-state relations but did not urge an all out attack on the Church, while among the lower classes anticlericalism was at a low ebb. Liberals and the lower classes could unite in disliking certain old-regime statesmen, but once these were chased out this link was gone. They could unite in dislike of the military, but this lasted only until the middle class realized that it needed soldiers to keep order.

The failure of liberal and even many radical leaders to take advantage of peasant unrest is perhaps more revealing than their inability to ally durably with the urban lower classes. For, on the surface at least, the peasants' enemies were also the liberals' enemies, if for different reasons, and the peasants' grievances did not jeopardize the liberals' main interests. It should be noted that even had the liberals supported peasant unrest the revolutions might still have failed, for peasant risings were limited in area and intensity. There was nothing on the scale of the Great Fear of 1789 in which large numbers of French peasants had attacked aristocratic landlords and, through them, the remnants of the manorial system. Nevertheless the contrast with 1789, where middle-class revolutionaries and peasant insurgents worked —separately and for different reasons—toward some similar revolutionary goals, confirms the moderation, even timidity, of the leaders in 1848.

The liberals' almost uniform definition of manorial rights as private property, to be compensated if taken away, prevented them from capitalizing on peasant unrest. The rapid increase in the number of middle-class landowners during the first half of the nineteenth century helps explain the liberals' reluctance actively to side with the peasantry. A heavy dosage of contempt and fear of the rural masses was certainly involved. Even in France, where the revolutionary leaders hoped to be able to educate the peasants politically, there was little immediate concern about rural conditions—hence the politically damaging increase in land taxes. Elsewhere, particularly in contrast to France, where the peasants were truly restive in the early phases of the revolution, urban leaders openly expressed their hostility, and this obviously conditioned their reaction to peasant demands. Most important, in contrast to 1789, the middle-class leaders were not directly attacking the aristocracy. Their liberal principles unquestionably opposed key bases of the aristocratic order; they did attack manorialism, they did believe in equality under the law as opposed to privilege of birth. But they had little sense of direct class conflict, and this limited their ability to respond to peasants who, in southern Italy and southern Germany particularly, explicitly attacked the landlords. Liberal constitution makers in Germany and Austria did propose major legal changes in the rural world, some of which would have benefited the peasantry. But they attached a number of strings, notably in the form of compensation provisions, and they positively shunned the rural insurgents, supporting military repression wherever necessary. In fact the liberals offered the peasants no more than most conservatives did, except for a time in Prussia, for the latter turned out to be willing to abandon manorialism readily enough. And the peasants had no other reason to support liberal goals, for the political demands were not yet relevant to them and the economic principles of free market competition were antithetical to peasant economic traditions.

In the final analysis, it is the absence of explicit class conflict on the part of the liberals that most marks the revolutions of 1848. Again, we can grant, with Marx and many other interpreters,[4] that the middle class was bent on using the revolutions

4. V. I. Lenin, "Two Tactics of Social Democracy in the Democratic Revolution," in *Collected Works* (Moscow, 1962), IX, 17–140; Karl Marx, *The Class*

for its own class interest and that, particularly in Central Europe, this had to involve a conflict with the aristocratic order. Obviously also the aristocrats, particularly those in Prussia, were aware of the challenge and led the conservative counterattack. But there was little sense of direct clash, for the middle-class order had already advanced enough, and the aristocrats yielded enough, that an all-out struggle seemed unnecessary.

The absence of struggle is obvious in France and Italy. Aristocrats in France were not politically predominant under the July Monarchy; individual aristocrats held political office but there was no monopoly and the aristocrats did not cluster on any given portion of the political spectrum.[5] Aristocrats in northern Italy had long been urbanized and accustomed to working with wealthy members of the middle class. They were almost as likely to be nationalist as were middle-class people and participated actively, as moderates, in the revolution. This does not mean that aristocracy had lost its meaning in either country. Indeed the continued prestige of the class helped shape middle-class opinion. The zeal for acquiring land, displayed by successful businessmen and professional people in both France and Italy, and in Central Europe as well, reflected a desire to imitate the aristocracy.[6] But the point is that imitation was now possible. There were no legal barriers and, with advancing industrial and commercial wealth, the economic barriers steadily declined. It may be that the middle class should have sought to extinguish the aristocratic influence still more completely, but the fact is that most did not see it that way.

The situation was more complex in Central Europe, but even here the aristocracy did not have complete political control or the ability to block economic and social advances by the middle class. The Prussian Junkers retained largely traditional status attitudes and enforced them with vigor; at dances, for

Struggles in France (New York, 1924); Karl Marx, *The Eighteenth Brumaire of Louis Napoleon* (London, 1852).

5. Patrick Higonnet and Trevor Higonnet, "Class, Corruption and Politics in the French Chamber of Deputies, 1846–1848," *French Historical Studies* (1967), 204–224.

6. David Landes, "French Entrepreneurship in the Nineteenth Century," *Journal of Economic History* (1949), 43–56.

example, a rope separated aristocrats from other social elements. But in western Germany, where the power of the rising middle class lay, the Junkers had only a remote influence. Even the trouble within the Prussian bureaucracy did not pit class against class, for older middle-class bureaucrats were just as hidebound as their aristocratic counterparts. We can easily see, in retrospect, that the middle class should have struggled harder to break the political and economic power of the aristocracy, for this power exercised a strong and on the whole deleterious influence in Central Europe for a full century after 1848.[7] But the middle class simply did not feel hemmed in. The kind of frustration that had developed in eighteenth-century France was absent. And without this frustration the middle class, property-owning and not a little deferential to their social superiors, was unlikely to undertake anything remotely resembling explicit class war. And without class war, a revolution could not be made.

Nowhere, then, did middle-class liberals undertake a root and branch campaign against the aristocracy. Even when aristocrats formed the major opposition to the revolution, as in Prussia, there was little impulse to counterattack. The Prussian parliament's measures against reactionary generals were relatively mild in the circumstances, and further moves were not discussed. Most middle-class concerns about gut issues related in large measure to middle-class society itself. Professional people worried about their future; businessmen concerned about recurrent economic crisis might blame governments for part of their misfortune, but they could hardly turn against the aristocracy. If anything, their grievances related most directly to other elements of the middle class. Professional people were somewhat concerned about the rising wealth and prestige of the most successful businessmen; shopkeepers had to wonder about the stagnation of their fortunes while larger business units prospered. But none of this had coalesced yet into clear intraclass rivalries that could substitute for more traditional class conflict. At most, the penchant of students for radical political action suggested a tension within the middle class, though rarely did the students

7. Alexander Gerschenkron, *Bread and Democracy in Germany* (Berkeley, 1943), *passim*.

attack other middle-class elements directly and the tension was at least as much generational as social. The middle-class liberals in 1848 were in essence trying to effect a political revolution without a full-scale social revolution, but they could not pull it off. The political targets did not concern enough people intensely enough to motivate a real revolutionary effort, and unless the social bases of the regimes were attacked explicitly—unless the Prussian middle class, say, had moved directly against the Junkers' influence at court and in the military and ultimately against the economic power that lay behind it—the regimes themselves were strong enough to survive. Even in France, where the political regime did change, the basic ruling class, a combination of noble and middle-class landowners, the local *notables,* emerged unscathed, dominating the Second Republic and to a considerable extent the Second Empire that followed.

Given the weakness of middle-class liberalism as a revolutionary force, the most potent and persistent revolutions were those with a nationalist element as well. There is no doubt that many of the representatives in the Frankfurt parliament, or the liberal advisers around Charles Albert in Piedmont, or the Magyar gentry, were drawn into the revolution almost exclusively because of their nationalist feeling. Where there was a foreign ruler to expel, as in Hungary and Italy, the revolutions proved most durable, for the enemy was very clear. But nationalism was also incapable of cementing a bond between the middle and the lower classes. Briefly in Milan, perhaps for a few days in Frankfurt, the lower classes seemed roused by a nationalist excitement, but for the most part the issue was irrelevant to them. Hence the nationalist revolutions were no more successful in providing an alternative force to the armies of the established order than the risings led by liberals alone. And even for the middle class, the enemy had to be clearly identified if nationalism was to rouse an unusual revolutionary intensity. Vigorous nationalism in Austria and Germany lacked focus. Nationalists were tempted to protect the established order as part of national strength, which distracted them from fomenting revolution, consolidating internal reforms, or forming alliances with other nationalist revolutions.

But if the liberals or liberal nationalists suffered such severe limitations as revolutionary leaders, why did the revolutions not pass into the hands of that amorphous group we have labeled radicals? Leaving aside the outright socialists, whose doctrine was not yet sufficiently widespread to play a major role, there were in most of the major revolutionary centers a large group of people who were sincerely democratic, open to social reform, and often vigorously nationalist as well. Why didn't the Ledru-Rollins, the Struves, the Mazzinis, play a larger role in the active phase of the revolution?

Some radicals, whose ideology shaded off from liberal sentiment, found it difficult to avoid some of the liberal concern about pressing revolution too far. Although radicals like Kudlich hoped to gain peasant backing, others—like Caetano in Milan—shunned it. Ledru-Rollin, although firm in his support of the revolution, found it difficult to maintain any rapport with the urban masses. A famous anecdote concerning an incident in 1849 tells of him looking out on the street from his apartment window, and suddenly exclaiming to a friend, as he saw a crowd pass by: "There go my people, and I must follow them for I am their leader." The story, if improbable in fact, is true in spirit. Few of the radicals had a genuinely popular touch. Even those who tried to work among the people, like the Vienna students during the summer of 1848 or the radicals in Rome, were unable to close the gap between classes.

Although the radical message clearly had more appeal to the urban lower classes than purely liberal doctrine, there remained at the least a vast difference in emphasis between the radicals and the crowds. Elements of the lower classes, most obviously in Paris but also elsewhere, were devoted to political goals, but most of the people who manned the barricades did not see a republic or democracy as the main purpose of the revolution. Their economic grievances were not foremost in the minds of the radicals, who could therefore attract them but not weld them into a solid revolutionary force. All the risings which radicals fomented, such as the attack on the Frankfurt assembly, were put down relatively easily—more easily than some of the massive efforts which were, to all intents and purposes, conducted by the lower classes alone over economic demands. Radical-led military campaigns perished quickly for lack of support.

And at the other extreme, radicalism roused far more hostility than liberalism did. It soured not only wealthy businessmen but also many clerks and shopkeepers on revolution in general. It smacked of the big city, and tended to antagonize opinion in the smaller centers that distrusted the metropolis in any event. It could easily be confused with socialism and the lower classes. In theory the radicals might have been able to appeal to a middle ground between the wealthy businessmen and professional people and the urban crowds. The promise of democracy undoubtedly attracted some of the fringe elements of the middle class, who did not own enough to qualify for a vote if property criteria were introduced. There was a suggestion in Milan that liberalism appealed mainly to the upper segment of the middle class (and many aristocrats), while radicalism attracted the lower middle class. But the lower middle class, though large, was of recent vintage in the big cities; it had not acquired much group identity as yet. Sixty percent of Parisian shopkeepers, for example, were of rural origin. Many brought in religious values or an esteem for the traditional social hierarchy which disqualified them from support of radical causes.[8] Nor, obviously, had radicals identified this group explicitly; there was no campaigning directed at lower-middle-class problems or aspirations.

And for large segments of the poorer segment of the middle class, particularly those who lived in smaller towns, radicalism had no attraction at all. Even liberalism might be held suspect. In Germany, where this group has been studied particularly, the revolution initially brought forth a mass of petitions from small businessmen, teachers, and minor officials in the towns.[9] But the grievances these people expressed were grievances against the changes that were already engulfing them—against industry, against new wealth disrupting the established social hierarchy, against the growing restiveness of the lower classes. These people

8. Adeline Daumard, *La Bourgeoisie parisienne* (Paris, 1963), 250–256 and *passim*.
9. Edward Shorter, "Middle-Class Anxiety in the German Revolution of 1848," *Journal of Social History* (1969), 189–215.

did not want progress of the sort the liberals and, even more, the radicals advocated. They quickly decided that they did not want new political rights at all, but rather returned to their traditional faith in the aristocratic ruling class and the monarchy.

In short, radicalism, despite its genuine potential as a revolutionary doctrine, lacked a real constituency. The group it most consistently attracted was the students, who played a role in several revolutions far greater than their numbers warranted. But the students were not sufficiently numerous to form a solid base for a revolutionary movement. In many cases they lacked independent means of financial support, and so tended to drift back to their home towns when economic conditions deteriorated or the universities shut down. And many students shared with some of the radical leaders a romantic enthusiasm which, though obviously inspirational, militated against careful, realistic revolutionary planning. The radicals did not organize well. They tended to overrate the potential success of spontaneous action. Rarely able to reach outside a major city, the radicals were too easily caught up in the excitement of months of revolution in the city itself, heedless of the forces that were building up outside. Successful revolutions are often directed by groups that began without a large constituency but which compensate by careful planning and organization; no such grouping emerged in 1848.

The revolutions of 1848 failed, then, because the dynamic segment of the middle class no longer had cause to commit itself to a revolutionary course and because no other social group was yet prepared to wrest revolutionary leadership from it. Once the revolutions were launched much of their activity in fact revolved around disputes over the revolutionary direction rather than attacks on the opponents of the uprisings. In a few cases the radicals, with lower-class support, briefly gained the upper hand, but they could not prevail for long. For all the liberals had to do was to call upon the forces of the established order, which had steadily built up strength outside the centers of revolutionary ferment. This was a painful decision, but it was taken in every instance. But the story did not end there. Lessons learned during the active phase of the revolution and decisions taken during the period of repression reshaped all of the major elements involved, from conservatives through urban rioters. It is impossible to imagine that the revolutions of 1848 could have avoided defeat; this is the contribution a study of the revolutions can make to an understanding of the revolutionary dynamic and its evolution in a modernizing society. None of the many historians who have lamented the defeat have suggested realistic alternatives. Perhaps if romanticism had been less in vogue the intellectual revolutionaries might have been more hardheaded in their approach; but without this kind of inspiration radicalism might not have developed at all. There is no way to envisage a reshuffling of the key social elements involved in the revolution to come out with a winning combination. But this in itself helped change the nature of social protest, as some groups began to experiment with new approaches even as the revolutionary glow began to fade.

ELEVEN *The Legacy of 1848*

THERE IS NO need to further belabor the failures of the revolutions of 1848. The leading demands of the working-class revolutionaries were not met, save insofar as economic recovery finally relieved the worst material miseries. Artisans did not win a halt to mechanization. They did not obtain expanded systems of education or shorter hours. There were in fact no social reforms that appreciably benefited the urban masses. The middle classes did gain, but with the exception of Piedmont none of the regimes that emerged from the revolutions met either liberal or radical criteria of acceptability. By the standards of great revolutions, such as those of 1789 or 1917, the revolutions of 1848 were short and very nearly stillborn. Movements generated in Hungary and in parts of Italy might have succeeded without foreign intervention; but revolutionaries have to count on foreign intervention, and here again the risings of 1848 can be found wanting.

The aura of failure was heightened by the policies of reaction that dominated much of the 1850s. Censorship, political arrests, weak or nonexistent parliaments—these were the order of the day.[10] Many regimes renewed an alliance with the Catholic Church, as a wave of concordats gave the Church new powers in education and censorship. And under Pius IX the Church itself seemed locked in resistance to all modern developments. The power of the Prussian aristocracy increased as Junkers regained police, though not judicial, rights over their estates. There was little resistance to the reactionary regimes, and this cannot be explained entirely by the activities of political police. Europe seemed sunk in political apathy now that the revolutionary hopes were dashed.

10. Howard Payne, *The Police State of Louis Napoleon Bonaparte, 1851–1860* (Seattle, 1966), 41–71 and *passim;* Hales, *Pio Nono,* 68 ff.

Yet the revolutions had changed a great deal, in politics and in society at large, which assured among other things that reactionary politics could not endure. France gained democracy, and though this was perverted by the plebiscites and controlled elections of the Second Empire, the political awareness of the population had increased. Most active political forces in France were coming to terms with universal suffrage. Republicans had learned to make contact with the common people, and they were to put these lessons to good use in the 1860s and 1870s. Louis Napoleon made contacts of his own, creating the first authoritarian regime that rested (at least in part) on active popular consent. Though much of Italy sank back into prerevolutionary political conditions, the Piedmontese government continued on its path of moderate liberalism. The constitution and parliament were maintained and the powers of the Catholic Church, particularly in matters of justice and education, were reduced. Under the leadership of Cavour, the government favored economic development by lowering tariffs and building railroads. These policies were designed to enhance Piedmont's image in the rest of Italy, and the government formed active links with liberal and nationalist groups elsewhere. Within a decade, of course, it sponsored a new diplomatic and military effort against the Austrians, with the result that Italy won her unity only a few years after the revolutions had failed.[11]

The revolutions had their deepest effects in Central Europe. Some of the increased freedoms for Jews remained in effect. The abolition of manorialism was a major step. Quite apart from the changes in peasant conditions, it forced major bureaucratic reforms in the Habsburg monarchy. During the 1850s the quality of the civil service was upgraded as procedures of appointment and promotion were thoroughly revised. Tax and tariff collection was improved and standardized. A separate judicial system was created, so that courts were no longer controlled by bureaucrats or local landlords; trial by jury was introduced. New powers were granted to local governments. The government encouraged economic development, and the standardization of commercial laws and taxes was a positive step in its own right. In other

11. Denis Mack Smith, *Italy, a Modern History* (Ann Arbor, 1959), 1–62.

words, the revolutions of 1848 opened the way to substantial modernization in the Habsburg lands. The nationalities problem was not resolved, and the new civil service, being largely German, actually exacerbated the situation. The grievances of the urban masses were not met. But the middle class and the peasantry gained considerably. Businessmen could prosper. Professional people could look forward to more certain and useful careers in the state service.[12]

Changes in Prussia were almost as important. Unlike Austria, Prussia did emerge with a modified political structure. The parliament, however limited its powers and however skewed the voting system from which it derived, proved to be a significant factor in Prussian politics, capable of modifying, if not fundamentally changing, official policies. It was, by the end of the 1850s, an outlet for genuine political diversity. But other changes were probably more significant. The abolition of manorialism, coupled with a limited amount of land distribution, contented the peasantry, without, however, weakening the economic power of the landlords. Restoration of the guild system similarly won many artisans to the active support of the regime, though again the reform was in many ways superficial since the advance of industrialization continued at a rising pace. Some artisans won increased security, some peasants gained new freedom of action, while symbolic changes wedded still larger numbers of each group to a fundamental conservatism that endured well into the twentieth century. The middle classes in Prussia gained more substantially. The Prussian government now began to support industrialization, whereas before many of its policies, particularly in fiscal matters, had been negative. It sponsored industrial investment banks and played a significant roll in the economic upsurge of the quarter-century following the revolution. The bureaucracy was reformed as well. A large number of new positions were created, particularly in the judicial branch, which absorbed most of the young apprentices. The powers of junior officials were increased; local judges, for example, gained new rights. Promotion procedures were standardized, so that favorit-

12. A. J. P. Taylor, *The Hapsburg Monarchy, 1809–1918* (New York, 1965), 80–100.

ism was reduced. Within a short time an essentially modern civil service emerged, efficient, standardized, if a bit lower in status than its counterpart a few generations before. If bureaucrats could no longer ape the aristocracy, at least the stultification that had helped produce the revolution was removed. With its new economic policies and civil service procedures, Prussia was also open to further modernization.[13]

In both Austria and Prussia, the results of the revolutions helped create a situation in which economic modernization, with some attendant alterations in social structure, could take place without full political modernization. Bureaucrats changed, but the basic ruling class, deriving largely from the aristocracy, did not. The middle class prospered but did not win really liberal political institutions. The policy of wooing the older elements of the lower classes to support of the conservative state furthered this anomaly. Liberals in Austria and Prussia had failed to win lower-class support in 1848 and in fact they never were to win it; the lessons artisans and peasants learned from the revolutions played an important role in this failure. It would be an oversimplification to trace all the anomalies of the modernization process in Central Europe to the revolutions of 1848, in part because the revolutions themselves simply reflected preexisting trends. But the results of the revolution, both the achievements and the failures, undeniably played a formative role.[14]

The revolutions' impact on attitudes is extremely hard to assess. Everywhere they had provided at least a year of free, indeed frenzied political debate. A variety of opinions on economic, social, and political issues circulated widely. How much was learned, how deeply the lessons sank in, has not been adequately determined. On the one hand, the quiescence of the 1850s should not be taken as a sign that none of the newer doctrines had won durable support, though some people were undoubtedly so disappointed with the revolutions' results they turned away from

13. See E. N. and P. R. Anderson, *Political Institutions and Social Changes in Continental Europe in the Nineteenth Century* (Berkeley, 1967), 166 ff.; and John Gillis, *The Prussian Bureaucracy in Crisis, 1840–1860* (Stanford, 1971), 145 ff.

14. Theodore Hamerow, *Restoration, Revolution, Reaction* (Princeton, 1958), 197 ff.

politics permanently. Repression plus the exhaustion that inevitably follows a period of intense protest produced an apathetic mood, but a commitment to one or more of the revolutions' political ideologies could well survive this mood and play a role subsequently. On the other hand, it is erroneous to draw straight lines between the revolutions and developments that occurred in the 1860s and 1870s. By 1875, Germany and Italy had unified; Hungary had won substantial autonomy; a democratic republic was being installed in France; and Marxist socialism was gaining ground in several areas. Were these inevitable results of new political thinking set in motion by the revolutions? The question can be still more broadly phrased: How great an effect did the revolutions have in the politicization, the conversion to modern political interests and values, of the peoples of Western and Central Europe?

In France the revolution undoubtedly furthered a durable commitment to republicanism among the urban working classes and, in some regions, the peasantry.[15] This commitment was fundamental to the revival of republicanism at the end of the 1850s and to the ultimate formation of the Third Republic. It meant that a substantial minority of the lower classes in France wanted an active share in the political process. They wanted a meaningful vote for representatives who would have the power to defend their interests. They wanted an attack on the forces that opposed a modern political system, notably the Catholic Church.

A comparable conversion to an active political interest does not seem to have occurred in Italy or Central Europe among the lower classes. In Germany and Austria, as we have seen, several key groups won concessions from the conservative state without participating directly in politics; this was true particularly of the peasantry. Larger numbers of urban artisans and workers doubtless retained an active interest in democracy and related political goals, but the interest was not dominant in these classes and had little impact on subsequent political changes.

15. Charles Tilly, "The Changing Place of Collective Violence" in M. Richter, ed., *Essays in Theory and History* (Cambridge, Mass., 1970), 159–164; Roger Price, *Second French Republic* (Ithaca, 1972), 283 ff.

The revolutions undoubtedly spread a commitment to socialism, particularly among artisans. Austria and Italy were not greatly affected, in part because their economic development lagged. In France the greatest initial beneficiaries of a heightened desire for social justice were the Proudhonian socialists, whose organizations—particularly the producer cooperatives—enlisted wide support, until all such activities were firmly suppressed in 1852.

More generally the democrat-socialist agitators spread a new conception of social justice. The articulate workers of Marseilles, so docile before 1848, did not return to their apathy once repression struck down their organizations during 1852. And when the labor movement revived in the latter part of the 1860s Marseilles workers were in the vanguard. This was an unusually clear illustration of the revolution's enduring influence, but many other French workers and artisans were comparably affected.[16] In Germany some of the socialist leaders who emerged in the revolution continued their work subsequently. This is true of course of Marx, though the revolutions did not produce a durable grass-roots Marxist movement. Very small units of the Communist League remained into the early 1850s—fifty people in Kassel, fifteen in Darmstadt, probably between 500 and 1000 in the whole country, and the League was finally destroyed in 1852. What was important here was obviously not numbers, but a leadership cadre that would re-emerge when the repression lightened. Ferdinand Lassalle, ultimately a major leader of the revived socialist movement in the 1860s, had been active in the socialist efforts of the revolutionary and postrevolutionary years. From the Berlin Labor Congress of August 1848 emerged the Labor Brotherhood, which set up twenty-six district committees with a national central committee. This group also survived the revolution, although it finally yielded to repression. Again, this provided potential leaders for later labor movements and it gave a vital orientation for German labor. Although moderate

16. William Sewell, "La Classe ouvrière de Marseille sous la Seconde République," *Mouvement social* (1971), 27–66; George Rudé, *The Crowd in History* (New York, 1964); Edouard Dolléans and Gerard Dehove, *Histoire du travail en France* (Paris, 1953), 293 ff.

and undogmatic, the Brotherhood firmly condemned demands for revival of the guilds and helped wed the German labor movement to an industrial economy.[17]

For both France and Germany we are left with the question of what happened to the bulk of the supporters of labor and socialist movements after the 1848–52 period. We know that leaders survived. We know that certain ideological commitments survived with them, to reappear in better times. The Proudhonist legacy, for example, reappeared in French labor activities in the 1860s. But how many ordinary workers retained their own commitment during the period when no organizations remained? How many German workers continued to talk politics over their beer? A few clubs continued a clandestine existence; one in Hamburg is known, and there were reports of informal associations in the industrial area around Dusseldorf. A movement toward purely economic unions and activity definitely persisted. The strike rate rose in France during the 1850s, although it remained low; the focus was on strictly economic demands. In Germany unions and especially mutual aid groups multiplied. A tradition of activism thus continued. It affected journeymen more than factory workers and it did not directly enlist more than a small minority.

Among French workers the revolution added demands for social justice to the long revolutionary tradition. Hatred of the wealthy classes undoubtedly increased among some workers everywhere. But others learned that revolution is futile, even dangerous. This line of thinking probably was more important in Germany than in France, given the absence of previous revolutionary experience; it could color the nature even of a mature socialist movement, and some historians have seen links between the ultimate timidity of German socialism and the disappointments of 1848. But obviously we do not know exactly what was learned and retained by the mass of workers. There is no simple continuum between the revolutions of 1848 and the ultimate rise of socialism. At the least, various important socialist traditions were born or furthered in the revolutions, leaders pro-

17. Richard Reichard, *Crippled from Birth: German Social Democracy 1844–1870* (Ames, Iowa, 1969), 99–119.

duced, and a nucleus of support formed. Moreover, the revolutions, by increasing middle-class fears of social unrest, enhanced the general class consciousness of European society. This, at least in the long run, assured the development of new combat organizations on the part of the working classes.

The revolution of 1848 probably furthered nationalist sentiment in Italy. Victory had seemed so close that there was no reason to be completely discouraged, and the transformation of Piedmont furthered nationalist hopes. Soon after the revolution the Italian National Society was formed under the leadership of Manin.[18] It worked actively for unification and kept nationalist enthusiasm alive throughout northern and central Italy. Furthermore, the debate about the nature of Italian unification was now greatly simplified. Confederation was seen to be impossible. Manin and most nationalist leaders urged a pragmatic approach that would accept Piedmont as the sponsor of Italian unity and would subsume liberal or radical goals to the greater nationalist purpose. Outside Italy the question of nationalism is more complex, and even in Italy there is no sign that nationalist ideas spread below the middle classes. Interest in German nationalism was at a low ebb during the 1850s.[19] Even in the 1860s, with the successful example of Italy, an active commitment to nationalism was uncommon even in the middle classes. The revolutions clearly did not kill the nationalist idea. Like socialism it may silently have smoldered in many minds and hearts. But here again, the extent to which the revolutions permanently changed the political commitments of large numbers of people remains unclear.

The revolutions demonstrated the power of several new political ideologies to move men, at least temporarily. They converted some people to a new level of political commitment. They pointed the way to a manipulation of the new ideologies by other people who wanted to win popular support. They played a role in the clearly complex and protracted process of developing a

18. See Raymond Grew, *A Sterner Plan for Italian Unity: The Italian National Society in the Risorgimento* (Princeton, 1963).
19. See Theodore Hamerow, *The Social Foundations of German Unification, 1858–1871* (2v., Princeton, 1969–72).

modern political personality. Despite all the interpretive uncertainties involved, this may have been the revolutions' most significant legacy.

CONCLUSION: THE END OF REVOLUTIONS

The risings of 1848 proved to be a spectacular climax to the age of revolution in Western and Central Europe. After more than sixty years of recurrent revolt, revolution in the classic sense dropped out of the experience of much of the European continent. Only defeat in war would bring an occasional echo of the revolutionary experience.

The reasons for this historic change were varied. Improved transportation, particularly the completion of the railroad network, brought an end to famines. Bad harvests in one area could be met by importing food quickly from other regions; and with agricultural improvements bad harvests themselves became less likely. So the traditional kind of economic crisis, an essential precondition to revolution, ended save in the east and far south of Europe. The artisan class lost its distinctive character after 1850, as more and more crafts were mechanized. The journeymen who remained increasingly regarded themselves as workers and stopped trying to resurrect the artisanal past; thus another ingredient of revolutions was lost.

But the risings of 1848 themselves helped bring a halt to further revolutionary outbreaks. Conservatives, who continued to dominate most governments, learned that some concessions to the demands for change were necessary and reasonably painless. We have seen how they moved, even during the revolutions themselves, to conciliate groups such as the peasantry. Other concessions followed, particularly toward liberals and nationalists. The old-style conservatism of the Metternichian variety pretty well disappeared, except again in the east and south. At the same time conservatives tightened their defenses. Police forces were greatly expanded and were given better training in riot control. This, plus improvements in weaponry, made barricade fighting an increasingly risky venture.

The middle classes explicitly renounced revolution as a

method. They had gained enough from the revolutions of 1848 to reduce their sense of grievance and, above all, they had discovered that revolutions were far too risky to their own position. So the political movements that depended on middle-class support changed their tactics. Nationalists like Manin in Italy turned from revolution to diplomatic maneuver. Even in Hungary, moderate nationalists like Deák gained control of the movement. Liberals, though they might challenge existing governments, held back from a full confrontation. This was obviously true in Prussia during the early 1860s, where in a bitter constitutional conflict the liberals refrained from advocating any extra-legal agitation.[1] French republicans sometimes flirted a bit with agitation, but they too stayed mainly within the limits of the law.[2] And in most countries radicalism as a political force faded in importance. The working class, when politically articulate, turned increasingly to socialism, while the middle class found radicalism too dangerous. Particularly in Italy and in Central Europe the bulk of the middle class stuck to a moderate liberalism.

The revolutions of 1848 also killed off romanticism as a political movement.[3] Old romantics like Lamartine were embittered by their failure. Their generation soon died out, and it was not replaced. Younger intellectuals who had participated in the revolutions, like Wagner in Saxony or Baudelaire in France, turned away from politics in disgust. They passed aspects of the romantic heritage on in art, where stylistic experimentation grew increasingly bold. But the kind of enthusiastic idealism that played such a major role in 1848 was not to return to intellectual life. There were intellectual revolutionaries aplenty in the second half of the nineteenth century, but they were mostly calculating men who weighed their chances carefully and they did not benefit from an enthusiasm that gripped intellectuals generally.

In sum, the social class that had provided leadership to all the major revolutions withdrew from the arena. The intellectual

1. E. N. Anderson, *The Social and Political Conflict in Prussia* (New York, 1954).
2. Theodore Zeldin, *The Political System of Napoleon III* (New York, 1958).
3. George Mosse, *The Culture of Western Europe* (Chicago, 1961), 53–58 and *passim*.

mood capable of generating the spirit that could convert ideology to revolutionary action was gone. With a more flexible conservatism, great changes were possible in Central and Western Europe still. Advancing industrialization in fact made change inevitable. But revolution was no longer the vehicle for change, and some of the most cherished ideals of the revolutionaries of 1848 were never completely realized as a result.

The lower classes did not produce the kind of intense political interest that would substitute for middle-class demands. Granted the vote within a generation, they did not take to the streets to insist on further access to political power. Nor did they find the means to counter the increasingly strong repressive apparatus of the state. Their leaders, even when avowed revolutionaries, would more often than not advise them against a direct contest with the forces of the government.[4]

In fact, the revolutions of 1848, combined with more fundamental social changes that were beginning to produce a modern working class, helped teach the lower classes to use different methods in their protest. Not only revolutions but also riots declined. For almost two decades the aftermath of 1848, with its repression and disappointment, combined with relative economic prosperity to keep protest of any sort to a minimum. When the lower classes stirred again, around 1870, they normally worked through political channels, particularly socialist parties, and through strikes and demonstrations.[5] The organizational experience many of their leaders had gained in 1848 played an important role in this transformation of the methods of protest. The exposure to progressive ideologies helped teach workers to change their goals. Most obviously in France, many workers were learning to ask for more within the industrial system, rather than fighting the system itself. Those who still could not accept industrialization, declining in numbers, largely ceased active protest. Rural unrest dwindled to almost nothing, for example, until

4. Peter N. Stearns, *Revolutionary Syndicalism and French Labor: A Cause without Rebels* (New Brunswick, 1971), 73–102.
5. George Rudé, *The Crowd in History* (New York, 1964), *passim;* Charles Tilly, "Collective Violence in European Perspective," in Hugh Davis Graham and Ted Gurr, eds., *Violence in America* (New York, 1969), 4–44.

rural workers assimilated the new protest goals.[6] These were historic changes in the European experience; the revolutions of 1848 played a direct role not only in ending an era of European history but in opening a new one in which the methods, goals, and basic social alignments involved in protest were decisively altered.

The ending of revolutions reduced the drama of social conflict in Western and Central Europe. But revolutions had produced scant benefits for the urban masses that participated in them, often at great sacrifice. Freed from the goad of the worst misery, taught by their experiences in 1848, the working classes stopped fighting a futile battle against industrialization and gradually elaborated the concrete political and economic demands that had begun to emerge in the 1848 revolutions themselves. Each reader must judge whether the methods of protest subsequently developed have been more or less successful than those which produced the wave of revolutions. Each must judge, also, whether conditions may induce a return to the classic revolutionary method in the future. It is clear that the revolutions of 1848 encouraged a reorientation of expectations—or some might argue, a tragic narrowing of hopes—on the part of various classes in Europe. This conditioned the history of Europe for more than a century.

6. Charles Tilly, "The Changing Place of Collective Violence," in Melvin Richter, ed., *Essays in Theory and History* (Cambridge, Mass., 1970), 137–164; Gordon Wright, *Rural Revolution in France* (Stanford, 1964).

Bibliography

1. General

Several accounts can be used to supplement the present study. Priscilla Robertson, *Revolutions of 1848: A Social History* (Princeton, 1952) is usefully anecdotal and generally sound. A recent treatment of the whole period, with several chapters on 1848, is William L. Langer, *Political and Social Upheaval 1832–1952* (New York, 1959). Jacques Godechot, *Les Révolutions de 1848* (Paris, 1971) is the most detailed general survey. Arnold Whitridge, *Men in Crisis: The Revolutions of 1848* (New York, 1949) approaches the subject through the biographies of the leaders.

An interpretive framework is offered in R. R. Palmer, *The Age of the Democratic Revolution* (2v., Princeton, 1959–64). On Central Europe, Lewis Namier, *The Revolution of the Intellectuals* (New York, 1946). See also Eric Hobsbawm, *The Age of Revolution: Europe from 1789 to 1848* (New York, 1969) and Louis Bergerson and others, eds., *Das Zeitalter der europäischen Revolution, 1780–1849* (Frankfurt, 1969). There are a number of good interpretive essays: Francois Fetjö, ed., *The Opening of an Era: 1848, An Historical Symposium* (New York, 1966); Peter Amann, "The Changing Outlines of 1848," *The American Historical Review* (1963), 938–952; John Gillis, "Political Decay and the European Revolutions, 1789–1848," *World Politics* (1970), 340–373; Hans Kohn, "The End of 1848," *Current History* (1949), 276–283; Hans Rothfels, "1848: One Hundred Years After," *Journal of Modern History* (1948), 291–319.

A periodical, *Révolutions de 1848*, is of immense value, stressing the French experience.

For background see David Landes, *The Unbound Prometheus: Technological Change and Industrial Development in*

Western Europe from 1750 to the Present (Cambridge, 1969); Peter N. Stearns, *European Society in Upheaval: Social History since 1800* (New York, 1967); E. L. Woodward, *Three Studies in European Conservatism: Metternich, Guizot, and the Catholic Church in the Nineteenth Century* (New York, 1963). Also useful are several national histories: Paul A. Gagnon, *France since 1789* (New York, 1964); Alfred Cobban, *A History of Modern France* (II, London, 1966); K. S. Pinson, *Modern Germany* (New York, 1966); D. Mack Smith, *Italy from Napoleon to Mussolini* (Ann Arbor, 1959); and A. J. P. Taylor, *The Hapsburg Monarchy, 1809–1918* (New York, 1965).

2. Bibliography

There are a number of useful bibliographies, through which a wide variety of specialized work can be traced. For France, Peter Amann, "Writings on the Second French Republic," *Journal of Modern History* (1962), 409–429, is a good recent survey. See also Jacques Droz, *L'Epoque contemporaine: I, Restaurations et révolutions 1815–1871* (Paris, 1953) and Robert Schnerb, "1848," *L'Information historique* (1949–50). For Germany, Helmut Bleiber, "Literatur zur Geschichte der Revolution von 1848/49," *Zeitschrift für Geschichtswissenschaft* (1960) and Theodore Hamerow, "History and the German Revolution of 1848," *American Historical Review* (1954), 27–44.

3. Memoirs and Eyewitness Accounts

The revolutions produced a rich contemporary literature, including memoirs by participants and accounts by lesser-known observers, several of whom were English or American. The following list includes materials that are particularly well known, interesting, and/or accessible. Many offer valuable insights into various aspects of the revolution and provide an excellent basis for further study.

FRANCE: *Leading memoirs:* Louis Blanc, *1848: Historical Revelations* (London, 1958) is an important account. Auguste Blanqui, "Pages ignorées. Blanqui et les barricades de juin 1848," *La Pensée* (1948), 9–14; Marc Caussidière, *Mémoires de M. Caussidière, ex-préfet de police et représentant du peuple* (2v., Paris,

1949). Lucien Delahodde, *History of the Secret Societies and of the Republican Party of France from 1830 to 1848* (Philadelphia, 1856) attributes too much to plots, but provides a great deal of information. Vicomte de Falloux, *Mémoires d'un royaliste* (2v., Paris, 1888). Alphonse de Lamartine, *History of the French Revolution of 1848* (Boston, 1849) is a bitter but revealing statement. C. H. P. Normandy, *A Year of Revolution. From a Journal Kept in Paris in 1848* (London, 1857) is one of the best observer recollections. P. J. Proudhon, *Les Confessions d'un révolutionnaire, pour servir à l'histoire de la révolution de février* (Paris, 1851) and George Sand, *Souvenirs de 1848* (Paris, 1882) are obviously important. Nassau Senior, *Journals Kept in France and Italy from 1848 to 1852* (London, 1871) is an intelligent survey by the English economist. Of all the memoirs, Alexis de Tocqueville, *The Recollections of Alexis de Tocqueville* (London, 1896) is most frequently cited.

Eyewitness accounts: Paul Boutellier, *La Révolution française de 1848 vue par les Hongrois* (Paris, 1949); Heinrich Heine, *French Affairs, Letters from Paris* (2v., London, 1893); Justin Godort, ed., *Le Journal d'un bourgeois de Lyon* (Paris, 1924); D. G. Mitchell, *The Battle Summer: Being Transcripts from Personal Observations in Paris during the Year 1848* (New York, 1850); Quentin-Bauchart, *Etudes et souvenirs sur la deuxième république et le second empire* (2v., Paris, 1901–2); Richard Rush, *Occasional Productions . . . Including a Glance at the Court and Government of Louis Philippe and the French Revolution of 1848, while the Author Resided as Minister from the United States at Paris* (Philadelphia, 1860); Albert Vandam, *An Englishman in Paris* (New York, 1892).

GERMANY: *Memoirs:* Ludwig Bergstrasser, ed., *Das Frankfurter Parlament in Briefen und Tagebüchern* (Frankfurt, 1929); Stephan Born, *Erinnerungen eines Achtundvierzigers* (Leipzig, 1898) is an excellent statement by the socialist leader. Frances Bunsen, *A Memoir of Baron Bunsen* (2v., London, 1868). There are interesting letters by the Prussian king in Frederick William IV, *Briefwechsel zwischen König Friedrich Wilhelm IV und dem Reichsverweser Erzherzog Johann von Oesterreich* (Frankfurt, 1924) and Frederick William IV (Erich Brandenburg, ed.), *Brief-*

wechsel mit Ludolf Camphausen (Berlin, 1906). For memoirs by leading conservatives, Leopold von Gerlach, *Denkwürdigkeiten* (2v., Berlin, 1891); and Josef von Radowitz, *Nachgelassene Briefe: Aufzeichnungen zur Geschichte der Jahre 1848–1853* (Berlin, 1922). Carl Schurz, *Reminiscences* (New York, 1907) provides a wealth of information on student views and activities. Richard Wagner, *My Life* (2v., New York, 1911).

Eyewitness accounts and contemporary histories: Paul Boerner, *Erinnerungen eines Revolutionärs: Skizzen aus dem Jahre 1848* (2v., Berlin, 1920); Adolphe de Circourt, *Souvenirs d'une mission à Berlin en 1848* (Paris, 1908); A. J. Donelson, "The American Minister in Berlin on the Revolution of March, 1848," *American Historical Review* (1918), 355–373; Friedrich Engels, *Germany: Revolution and Counter-revolution* (New York, 1933); Rudolf Gneist, *Berliner Zustände: Politische Skizzen aus der Zeit vom 18. März 1848 bis 18. März 1849* (Berlin, 1849); Amalie Struve, *Erinnerungen aus den badischen Freiheitskämpfen* (Hamburg, 1850); Gustav Struve, *Geschichte der drei Volkserhebungen in Baden* (Bern, 1849). See also two useful source collections: Tim Klein, *1848, der Vorkampf deutscher Einheit* (Leipzig, 1914); J. G. Legge, *Rhyme and Revolution in German History, Life Literature and Character, 1813–1850* (London, 1918).

AUSTRIA: Austria is less abundantly served by contemporary comments, but there are some useful memoirs: Berthold Averback, *A Narrative of Events in Vienna from Latour to Windischgrätz* (London, 1849); Franz von Hartig, *Genesis: or Details of the Late Austrian Revolution, by an Officer of State* (London, 1853); Joseph von Hübner, *Une Année de ma vie* (Paris, 1891); Hans Kudlich, *Rückblicke und Erinnerungen* (Vienna, 1873); Adolf Pichler, *Aus den März-und-Oktobertagen zu Wien* (Innsbruck, 1850); Franz von Pillersdorf, *Austria in 1848 and 1849* (London, 1850); William Stiles, *Austria in 1848–49* (2v., New York, 1852).

HUNGARY: *Contemporary accounts:* Wilhelmine von Beck, *Personal Adventures during the Late War of Independence in Hungary* (London, 1850); Charles Brace, *Hungary in 1851* (New York, 1852); Arthur Gorgei, *My Life and Acts in Hungary in the*

Years 1848–1849 (2v., London, 1852) discusses Gorgei's military campaigns; Daniel Iranyi and Charles Chassin, *Histoire politique de la révolution de Hongrie, 1847–1849* (Paris, 1859); George Klapka, *Memoirs of the War of Independence in Hungary* (London, 1850). Ludwig (Louis) Kossuth, *Die Katastrophe in Ungarn* (Leipzig, 1849) is an apologia by the revolutionary leader. Charles Pridham, *Kossuth and Magyar Land; or, Personal Adventures during the War in Hungary* (London, 1851).

ITALY: *Contemporary accounts:* Massimo d'Azeglio, *Austrian Assassinations in Lombardy* (London, 1848) is a polemical piece; see also Massimo d'Azeglio, *L'Italie de 1847 à 1865: correspondence politique* (Paris, 1867). Carlo Cattaneo, *L'Insurrection de Milan en 1848 e le Considerazioni sul 1848,* C. Spallanzon, ed., (Turin, 1949) is an important memoir. Emilio Dandolo, *The Italian Volunteers and the Lombard Rifle Brigade* (London, 1951); Giuseppe Garibaldi, *Memoirs* (New York, 1931); Carlo Gemmellaro, *Cenni storici di la rivoluzione siciliana l'anno 1848* (Catania, 1951). M. B. Honan, *The Personal Adventures of "Our Own Correspondent" in Italy* (New York, 1852) gives an American journalist's view. Ferdinand de Lesseps, *Ma Mission à Rome* (Paris, 1849) and *Recollections of Forty Years* (London, 1887) deal with the French expedition against Rome. Material from other leaders include Daniele Manin, *Documents et pièces authentiques laissés par Daniele Manin* (2v., Paris, 1860); Giuseppe Mazzini, *Life and Writings* (6v., London, 1891); Marco Minghetti, *Miei ricordi* (3v., Turin, 1889); Margaret Fuller Ossoli, *Memoirs* (Boston, 1852) written by an American feminist, is unusually interesting; W. M. Ott, *Military Events in Italy, 1848–1849* (London, 1851); Silvio Pellico, *My Ten Years' Imprisonment* (London, 1886) is a moving statement on political repression; Joseph Radetzky, *Briefe an seine Tochter Friederike, 1847–1857* (Vienna, 1898) is quite revealing on the Austrian leader; Arthur Whyte, *The Early Life and Letters of Cavour, 1810–1848* (Oxford, 1925) provides some interesting information.

4. Biographies

FRANCE: Mary Allen, "P. J. Proudhon in the Revolution of 1848," *Journal of Modern History* (1952) is a useful account. On

Blanqui, Alan Spitzer, *The Revolutionary Theories of Louis Auguste Blanqui* is excellent; a more recent biography, Samuel Bernstein, *Auguste Blanqui* (London, 1971) is thorough but rather conventional. On Ledru-Rollin, Robert Schnerb, *Ledru-Rollin* (Paris, 1948) is the best work in French; in English, Alvin Calman, *Ledru-Rollin and the Second French Republic* (New York, 1922) is good. Lamartine can be followed through H. Remsen Whitehouse, *The Life of Lamartine* (2v., Boston, 1918). Georges Duveau, *Raspail* (Paris, 1948) is excellent, as is Leo Loubère, *Louis Blanc: His Life and His Contribution to the Rise of French Jacobin Socialism* (Evanston, 1961). Finally, Edward Gargan, *Alexis de Tocqueville: the Critical Years, 1848–1851* (Washington, 1955) provides a useful analysis.

ITALY: Two classic biographies, unusually readable, are by G. M. Trevelyan: *Garibaldi's Defense of the Roman Republic* (London, 1907) and *Manin and the Venetian Revolution of 1848* (London, 1923). See also, on Garibaldi, Paul Frischauer, *Garibaldi, The Man and the Nation* (London, 1935) and D. Mack Smith, *Garibaldi* (New York, 1956). On Mazzini, Stringfellow Barr, *Mazzini, Portrait of an Exile* (New York, 1935) and Gaetano Salveimini, *Mazzini: A Study of His Thought and Its Effect on 19th Century Political Theory* (London, 1956). E. E. Y. Hales, *Pio Nono* (New York, 1954) is an intelligently sympathetic treatment of the pope.

CENTRAL EUROPE: There is considerably less relevant biographical material on Germany and the Habsburg Monarchy. On Kossuth, Otto Zarek, *Kossuth* (London, 1937) is heavily biased in favor of the revolutionary. R. Charmatz, *Adolf Fischhof* (Stuttgart, 1910) is competent. Wilhelm Friedensburg, *Stephan Born und die Organisationsbestrebungen der Berliner Arbeiterschaft* (Leipzig, 1923) is first-rate, going well beyond pure biography. Friedrich Meinecke, *Radowitz und die deutsche Revolution* (Berlin, 1913) is illuminating. See also E. H. Carr, *Michael Bakunin* (London, 1937) which is an excellent study of the anarchist leader.

5. France

Karl Marx, *The Class Struggles in France, 1848–1850* (New York 1924) and *The Eighteenth Brumaire of Louis Napoleon* (London, 1852) offer major interpretations.

Background. Useful surveys of economic and social history include Arthur Dunham, *The Industrial Revolution in France* (New York, 1955) and Georges Dupeux, *La Société française, 1789–1960* (Paris, 1964). On the lower classes, Louis Chevalier, *Laboring Classes and Dangerous Classes* (New York, 1973) is provocative though undoubtedly exaggerated. Adeline Daumard, *La Bourgeoisie parisienne de 1815 à 1848* (Paris, 1963) is the best available study of the middle classes, and it is extremely good. On political background, Sherman Kent, *Electoral Procedure under Louis Philippe* (New Haven, 1937) is useful, while René Rémond, *The Right Wing in France from 1815 to De Gaulle* (Philadelphia 1966) is particularly good in sorting out strands of conservatism in the period. On intellectual background, D. G. Charlton, *Secular Religions in France 1815–1870* (London, 1963) and Pierre Quentin Bauchart, *La Crise sociale de 1848* (Paris, 1920).

The revolution. The best survey account is Georges Duveau, *1848: The Making of a Revolution* (New York, 1966); see also Louis Girard, *La Deuxième République* (Paris, 1968). Roger Price, *The French Second Republic: A Social History* (Ithaca, 1972) is a solid job, particularly useful for developments in 1849–51; it incorporates much recent work. Rémi Gossez, *Les Ouvriers de Paris* (Paris, 1966) deals with the crowds. Donald McKay, *The National Workshops* (Cambridge, Mass., 1965) is a thorough monograph. See also Charles Schmidt, *Les Journées de juin 1848* (Paris, 1926).

Agitation in the provinces. Much interesting work is now going forward on this topic. See Albert Soboul, "La Question paysanne en 1848," *La Pensée* (Nos. 18–20, 1948). Three recent and provocative essays are Leo Loubère, "The Emergence of the Extreme Left in Lower Languedoc, 1848–1851: Social and Economic Factors in Politics," *American Historical Review* (1968), 1019–1051; William Sewell, "La Classe ouvrière de Marseille sous la Seconde République; Structure sociale et comportement politique," *Mouvement social* (1971), 27–66; Charles Tilly, "The Changing Place of Collective Violence," in Melvin Richter, ed., *Essays in Theory and History* (Cambridge, Mass., 1971), 139–164.

6. Germany

The best single study is Jacques Droz, *Les Révolutions allemandes de 1848* (Paris, 1957). Veit Valentin, *Geschichte der deutschen Revolution 1848–49* (2v., Berlin, 1930–31) [abridged in English as *1848: Chapters of German History* (London, 1940)] offers a liberal interpretation. Louis Namier, *1848: The Revolution of the Intellectuals* (New York 1964) looks primarily to ideological factors, dealing with the Habsburg lands as well as Germany. The most thorough German survey is Rudolf Stadelmann, *Soziale und politische Geschichte der Revolution von 1848* (Munich, 1848); see also his interpretive "Das Jahr 1848 und die deutsche Geschichte," *Deutsche Rundschau* (1948). On the radical phase of the revolution, C. W. Dohlinger, *The German Revolution of 1849* (New York, 1903); see also W. A. Ellis, *1849* (London, 1892) on Saxony.

On the Frankfurt parliament, the best general account is Frank Eyck, *The Frankfurt Parliament* (New York, 1968). See also Ulrich Allers, *The Concept of Empire in German Romanticism and Its Influence on the National Assembly at Frankfort* (Washington, 1948) and Roy Pascal, "The Frankfurt Parliament, 1848, and the Drang nach Osten," *Journal of Modern History* (1946), 138–152.

Specialized studies. On the forces of order, two books are particularly important: Gordon Craig, *The Politics of the Prussian Army* (New York, 1955) and John Gillis, *The Prussian Bureaucracy in Crisis, 1840–1860* (Stanford, 1971). See also Manfred Kliem, "Die Rolle der feudaljunkerlichen Reaktion in der Revolution von 1848–49," *Zeitschrift für Geschichtswissenschaft* (1969), 561–582, which is a thoughtful Marxist statement. On students and the middle classes: Arthur May, "Austrian and German Universities in 1848," *Journal of Central European Affairs* (1949), 18–22; Priscilla Robertson, "Students on the Barricades:

Germany and Austria 1848," *Political Science Quarterly* (1969), 367–379; and Edward Shorter, "Middle-Class Anxiety in the German Revolution of 1848," *Journal of Social History* (1969), 189–215.

There is considerable work on lower-class agitation. Theodore S. Hamerow, *Restoration, Revolution, Reaction: Economics and Politics in Germany, 1815–1871* (Princeton, 1958) deals mainly with artisans and peasants, and is the most useful single work in English on the German revolution. A slightly different view on the artisans is Paul Noyes, *Organization and Revolution: Working-Class Associations in the German Revolution* (Princeton, 1966). On peasants, Günther Franz, "Die agrarische Bewegung im Jahre 1848," *Hessisches Jahrbuch für Landesgeschichte* (1959). On more general working-class and radical agitation, Karl Obermann, *Die deutschen Arbeiter in der Revolution von 1848* (Berlin, 1953) is particularly useful; see also Max Quarck, *Die erste deutsche Arbeiterbewegung* (Leipzig, 1924) and Lenore O'Boyle, "The Democratic Left in Germany, 1848," *Journal of Modern History* (1961), 374–383. An important interpretation of German liberalism, which bears significantly on 1848, is Leonard Kreiger, *The German Idea of Freedom* (Boston, 1957).

Two unusual approaches to the revolution are W. A. Coupe, "The German Cartoon and the Revolution of 1848," *Comparative Studies in Society and History* (1967) and K. Spalding, "The Idiom of a Revolution: Berlin, 1848," *Modern Language Review* (1949), 60–74.

Marx and the German revolution: The best single survey is Oscar Hammen, *The Red 48ers: Karl Marx and Friedrich Engels* (New York, 1969); see also Auguste Cornu, *Karl Marx et la Révolution de 1848* (Paris, 1948). For source material, Karl Marx and Friedrich Engels, *Correspondence, 1846–1895* (New York, 1934). On more specialized subjects, particularly Marx's organizational efforts: B. Nicolaevsky, "Toward a History of the Communist League, 1847–1852," *International Review of Social History* (1956); Karl Obermann, "Zum Anteil des deutschen Proletariats und des Bundes der Kommunisten an der Vorbereitung der Revolution von 1848," *Zeitschrift für Geschichtswissenschaft*

(1968); Karl Obermann, "Über den Anteil von Marx und Engels am der politischen Bewegung und Vorbereitung der Revolution von 1848," *Zeitschrift für Geschichtswissenschaft* (1959).

7. *Italy*

General: There is nothing really satisfactory in English on the Italian revolution as a whole; some of the best work is biographical (see above). G. F. H. Berkeley, *Italy in the Making* (3v., Cambridge, 1932–40) is reasonably thorough. Kent Greenfield, *Economics and Liberalism in the Risorgimento: A Study of Nationalism in Lombardy* (Baltimore, 1965) is excellent for economic and political background. A. W. Salomone, "The Liberal Experiment and the Italian Revolution of 1848," *Journal of Central European Affairs* (1949) offers a sound interpretation. On Piedmont, Ferdinand Boyer, *La Seconde République, Charles-Albert, et l'Italie du Nord en 1848* (Paris, 1967). On southern Italy, Federico Curato, *La Rivoluzione siciliana del 1848–1849* (Milan, 1940) and E. Dicarlo and B. Falzone, eds., *Atti del congresso di studi storici sul '48 siciliano* (Palermo, 1950). On Rome, Domenico Desmarco, *Una Rivoluzione sociale: La repubblica romana del 1849* (Naples, 1944) and Luigi Rodelli, *La Repubblica romana del 1849* (Pisa, 1955) are both excellent; see also R. M. Johnston, *The Roman Theocracy and the Republic, 1846–1849* (London, 1901). On Milan, Antonio Monti, *Il 1848 e le cinque giornate di Milano* (Milan, 1948). For military history a thorough survey is Pietro Pieri, *Storia militare del Risorgimento* (Turin, 1962). See also Howard Smyth, "Piedmont and Prussia: The Influence of the Campaigns of 1848–1849 on the Constitutional Development of Italy," *American Historical Review* (1950), 479–502.

Social analysis: On students, Benato Marmiroli, "Studenti toscani allo guerra del 1848," *Rassegna storica del Risorgimento* (1953), 238–252. On the lower classes there is considerable controversy: Paul Guichonnet, "Quelques aspects de la question ouvrière en Savoie à la veille de 1848," *Rassegna storica del Risorgimento* (1955), 305–319; Gino Luzzatto, "Aspects sociaux de la révolution de 1848 en Italie," *Revue socialiste* (1948), 80–86; Guido Quazza, "Le Forze economico-sociali e la preparazione del

1848 nel Lombardo-Veneto," *Critica sociala* (1949); and Franco Valsecchi, "Le Classi popolari e il Risorgimento," *Cultura e scuola* (1965), 82–93.

8. Austria

The most useful account in English is R. John Rath, *The Viennese Revolution of 1848* (Austin, 1957). For social background, Jerome Blum, *Noble Landowners and Agriculture in Austria, 1815–1848* (Baltimore, 1948); for intellectual background, Eduard Winter, *Romantismus, Restauration, und Frühliberalismus im österreichischen Vormärz* (Vienna, 1968). On the nationalities question, Robert Kann, *The Multinational Empire: Nationalism and Reform in the Hapsburg Monarchy* (New York, 1950); see also Geistlanyi, *Das Nationalitätenproblem auf dem Reichstag zu Kremsier* (Vienna, 1920). The most thorough overall survey is Rudolf Kiszling and others, *Die Revolution im Kaisertum Oesterreich, 1848–1849* (2v., Vienna, 1948–52). On more specialized topics, Ludwig Brügel, *Geschichte der Oesterreichischen Sozialdemokratie* (Vienna, 1922) deals with the impact of the revolution on the course of Austrian socialism. On the police, Hermann Oberhummer, *Die Wienerpolizei im Revolutionsjahr 1848* (Vienna, 1928). Liberal aspects of the revolution are taken up, in various ways, in: Minna Falk, "Alexander Bach and the Leseverein in the Viennese Revolution of 1848," *Journal of Central European Affairs* (1948), 139–159; R. R. Lutz, "Fathers and Sons in the Vienna Revolution of 1848," *Journal of Central European Affairs* (1962), 161–173; and R. John Rath, "Public Opinion during the Viennese Revolution of 1848," *Journal of Central European Affairs* (1948), 160–180.

9. Hungary and Bohemia

Paul Bödy, *Joseph Eötvös and the Modernization of Hungary* (Philadelphia, 1972) deals with moderate opposition in Hungary. On diplomatic aspects, Charles Sproxton, *Palmerston and the Hungarian Revolution* (Cambridge, 1919). On the South Slavs, Juraj Krnjevic, "The Croats in 1848," *Slavonic and East European Review* (1948), 106–114, and Gunther Rothenberg, "Jelačić, the Croatian Military Border, and the Intervention against Hungary in 1848," *Austrian History Yearbook* (1965), 45–67.

The Czech revolution receives thorough coverage in Stanley Z. Pech, *The Czech Revolution of 1848* (Chapel Hill, 1969). See also Helfert, *Der Prager Juni-Aufstand 1848* (Leipzig, 1897) for a narrative account. I. I. Udalzow, *Aufzeichnungen über die Geschichte des nationalen und politischen Kampfes in Böhmen im Jahre 1848* (Berlin, 1953) is an excellent Marxist study. An important aspect of the nationalist current is studied in S. B. Kimball, *Czech Nationalism: A Study of the National Theatre Movement, 1845–83* (Urbana, 1964).

10. Eastern Europe

On Poland the major work is R. Hepke, *Die polnische Erhebung und die deutsche Gegenbewegung in Posen im Frühling 1848* (Posen, 1948). See also Henry Batowski, "The Poles and Their Fellow Slavs in 1848," *Slavonic and East European Review* (1949), 404–412, and C. E. Black, "Poznan and Europe in 1848," *Journal of Central European Affairs* (1948), 191–206.

On stirring among Ukrainians, Martha Bohachevsky-Chomiak, *The Spring of a Nation: The Ukrainians in Eastern Galicia in 1848* (Philadelphia, 1967).

On Romania the most general survey is C. C. Bodea, *The Roumanians' Struggle for Unification, 1834–1849* (Bucharest, 1970), but it is rather partisan. More balanced, if more limited in scope, is Keith Hitchins, *The Rumanian National Movement in Transylvania 1780–1849* (Cambridge, Mass., 1969).

On nationalism, Dan Berindei, "Les Révolutionnaires roumains de 1848 et l'idée d'unité," *Revue Roumaine d'Histoire* (1968) and two articles by C. C. Bodea, "Moment de la lutte révolutionnaire pour l'unité nationale roumaine entre 1835–1848," *Revue Roumaine d'Histoire* (1966) and "Le Problème de l'unité nationale roumaine, 1845–1848," *Revue Roumaine d'Histoire* (1965). On the impact of the revolution, Carpathinus, "1848 and Roumanian Unification," *Slavonic and East European Review* (1948), 390–419. On the vital peasant question, A. Oţetea, "La Révolution de 1848 et les paysans roumains," *Revue d' histoire comparée* (1948), 19–34.

Index